Transforming Ethnographic Knowledge

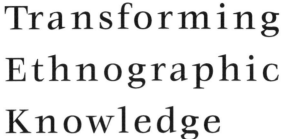

Transforming Ethnographic Knowledge

Edited by

REBECCA HARDIN

and

KAMARI MAXINE CLARKE

The University of Wisconsin Press

Publication of this volume has been made possible, in part, through support from the **University of Michigan School of Environment and Natural Resources.**

The University of Wisconsin Press
1930 Monroe Street, 3rd Floor
Madison, Wisconsin 53711-2059
uwpress.wisc.edu

3 Henrietta Street
London WCE 8LU, England
eurospanbookstore.com

Printed in the United States of America

Library of Congress Cataloging-in-Publication Data

Transforming ethnographic knowledge / edited by Rebecca Hardin and Kamari Maxine Clarke.
p.   cm.
Includes bibliographical references and index.
ISBN 978-0-299-24874-1 (pbk.: alk. paper)
ISBN 978-0-299-24873-4 (e-book)
1. Ethnology.   2. Applied anthropology.
I. Hardin, Rebecca.   II. Clarke, Kamari Maxine, 1966–
GN316.T87   2012
301 — dc23
2011052830

Contents

CONTENTS

Foreword

JENNIFER STAPLE

I developed an interest in anthropology because of the discipline's broad applicability to my interests in medicine and cross-cultural health practices. Like Rebecca Hardin, whose entrée into anthropology was through development and environment, and Kamari Clarke, whose entrée was through traditional religious movements and legal anthropology, I found a space for ethnography in the development of strategies in public health through medical anthropology. As a student at Yale University, I took courses ranging from Hardin's Classics in Ethnography to contemporary approaches in anthropology. I grappled with the changing conceptions of "the field" and the evolving forms of research in a wide range of contexts. Writing a research paper on Zora Neale Hurston, I explored how, between the mid-nineteenth century and the mid-twentieth century, anthropology was constantly reinvented and refined, expanded, and contested.

Such an exploration into a vibrant and changing field prompted me to organize the lectures that constitute the core of this edited volume. During the series of presentations and discussions, I learned a great deal about how anthropological practice has changed and adapted with evolving global connectivity. The question of how ethnography contributes to and captures global change is one that I address briefly here in terms of my own experiences in the field of global health.

Traditional Fieldwork

In 2002, I pursued ethnographic fieldwork for my undergraduate senior thesis in the Kalaupapa, Hawaii, community of patients with leprosy, to record their accounts of the stigma and isolation associated with their experience with the disease. When I climbed down the steepest sea cliff in the world to reach the community and stood at the shore where patients had been exiled, I was saddened by the history of the settlement, yet inspired and touched by the patients' poignant stories. My interviews with the patients provided introspective accounts of their life experiences. As of 2002, the community comprised fewer than thirty patients who were afflicted with leprosy and sent into isolation during the 1940s and 1950s. Through the advancement of modern medicine and antibiotic development, the remaining residents were free of this disease, which was heretofore incurable. They became permitted to leave the peninsula, but voluntarily chose to remain.

Building on interviews with survivors as well as historical archival materials, my research documented the establishment and transformation of the Kalaupapa Leprosy Settlement from its inception in 1865 to its present state as a national park. The Kalaupapa Settlement was first established by the colonial Hawaiian state based on a theory of moral contagion that reduced sufferers to degraded patients who were responsible for their own afflictions and in need of physical isolation for the protection of the wider community. The total population of leprosy patients between 1865 and 1969 was eight thousand, while an additional eight thousand leprosy "suspects" were isolated for two years on the peninsula. Many leprosy patients married and had children, but the children were forbidden to live in Kalaupapa and instead were sent away to live with relatives. The Kokuas (assistants) were the husbands and wives of the patients who voluntarily accompanied them. With new leprosy patients continuously being added to Kalaupapa, many patients dying due to their illness, and children being removed, a kinship system based on pedigree and genealogy was absent.

My conversations with the patients indicated that against the political and social context of leprosy and the Hawaiian state policies, the Kalaupapa patients developed a cultural scaffold within which to comprehend and survive their exile. Activism became central to the framework, social organization, and identity of the Kalaupapa community. The movement began in 1866 when a small group of thirty-five patients organized the Church of the Healing Spring. Activism became pervasive with the arrival of Father Joseph de Veuster Damien, who proffered hope to the patients who were most in despair. After his death, Father Damien became a heroic, mythic figure through exaggerated biographies, and his legendary status simultaneously became a personal symbol to the Kalaupapa patients during the twentieth century. In the mid- to late-twentieth century, he was reappropriated and refunctionalized as a sign of an activist leprosy patient and someone who could transform society. During this period, his legacy inspired the activism that resulted in the freedom of the patients from the quarantine in 1969 and the subsequent preservation of Kalaupapa as a national park.

During my field experience, I brought with me the wisdom shared by the speakers whose lectures are printed in this volume. I often contemplated their words about the ethnographic experience: the feelings of imposition when first arriving in a community, the intimacies of the conversations with individuals, and the regretful departure when the inspiring fieldwork experience concludes. I also came to realize that an ethnographic or anthropological approach to life is not something that begins and ends when one enters the field, but rather is a way of thinking about and being in the world. As my essay about Kalaupapa matured into a prize-winning paper for the Society of Medical Anthropology, and then into a publication, I was also considering what elements of my research experience and anthropological education could shape my hopes to develop new health care initiatives.

Beyond the Traditional Ethnographic Experience

At the same time that the traditional ethnographic experience continues, anthropology is undergoing unprecedented change, both in terms of its topics and its techniques. One of my last anthropology courses as an undergraduate was an independent study with anthropologist Barney Bate on the history and cultural variations of a particular technological innovation: eyeglasses. As had Rebecca Hardin, he encouraged me to use the diversity of anthropology as a field and the depth of its methods of inquiry to hone in on my interests in particular types of innovations and interactions. I realized the richness of anthropological theory for understanding human change, in a different way than through my field project in Hawaii.

Not just a topic of anthropological study, technology is transforming fieldwork as well. The global social space of the Internet is the new ethnographic field experience, connecting us in new ways and creating an increasingly ubiquitous space for people to work. Global connectivity, being able to communicate with and learn from people continents away, is a concept never envisioned by anthropology's past leaders. How can one unravel the ethnographic experience without seeing a face or hearing a voice? How can one become a participant in the community rather than simply an outside observer?

In my efforts to build a nonprofit global health delivery organization, Unite For Sight, I knew that anthropology would be central to my work. I am daily seeing the power and potential of this new ethnographic field space. The Internet is a collaborative, intimate space that enables the formation of new communities, despite the traditional boundaries of time and space. Through the Internet and telecommunication, I listen, discuss, and communicate daily with local healthcare professionals in communities throughout the world. In addition to the comprehensive eye care provided by the local eye doctors to patients living in poverty, there are also local community members who are trained by the local eye doctors to serve as community eye health workers. They disseminate knowledge and help to reduce barriers to care for thousands in their own village, town, or city. This participant observation is exactly the type of anthropological practice discussed by Mary Catherine Bateson in this volume: participant observation is "not just something that happens in the field, but something that is potentially pervasive in life and that is hugely helpful."

The Internet creates a place for people to work together as participant observers in more than one community at a time. It can never replace more traditional field experiences, but it certainly expands the anthropological experience and offers a new set of encounters or locations, if you will, for field study. As Unite For Sight rapidly expanded and drew on the energies of medical professionals, researchers, volunteers, and community leaders alike, I applied anthropology's lessons about social change, health care, and human interaction. The papers in this volume present a series of views on anthropology's past and on its position and prevalence in contemporary life. By contributing to this book of lectures, I hope, as do the editors, that future students will become as enthralled as I have by the transformations in ethnography that we create by engaging with its methods and perspectives.

Preface

In a book such as this one there are so many influences to acknowledge that it is impossible to mention them all. For most of us, our mentors and teachers—those whose footprints have indelibly shaped the field of anthropology—are to be credited for the development of a discipline that grows increasingly crucial for today's changing world. Here we are also indebted to our students. They reveal to us the particulars of key trends, including the proliferating practices that constitute ethnography, and the rise in interdisciplinary borrowing of ethnography's techniques.

Jennifer Staple was an undergraduate in the Yale anthropology department at the time of this project's first stirrings. She founded the Yale Anthropology Society as a student group for the exchange of ideas about anthropology, its relationships to other fields, and its future as a set of methods and questions. As a student in Rebecca Hardin's Classics in Ethnography seminar, she had begun investigating some of the central concerns in this volume by questioning canonical notions about what constituted "classic" monographs and ethnography. Under her leadership, the Yale Undergraduate Student Union organized a distinguished lecture series for undergraduate students to learn about the challenges and changes in ethnographic work through the experiences of renowned leaders in the field. Without Jennifer Staple's original vision, her daring invitations to prominent anthropologists to address undergraduate audiences, and her careful transcriptions of their talks, much of this book could not have existed. Jennifer reflects on how ethnography has enriched her own work in the short foreword that precedes this preface.

At roughly the same time as Jennifer was organizing her series, Kamari Clarke organized a two-year lecture series at Yale on multisited and transnational ethnography, with a particular emphasis on critical transformations in ethnography. Together, these series contributed to a period when students and faculty alike were offered a wide range of perspectives on the history and practice of ethnography and the role of such knowledge in addressing major global problems. The Yale University Provost Funds, the Yale anthropology department, the Yale University

Student Union, and the Edward and Dorothy Kempf Fund, administered by the Yale Center for International and Area Studies (YCIAS), now the Macmillan Center for International and Area Studies, all contributed generously to those intellectual processes.

Most chapters of this book originated as lectures in one of these two series. Others were written later, also in the crucible of the Yale campus, and in the context of conversations between students and teachers, theoreticians and practitioners. The combination of perspectives captures foundational contradictions as well as new directions in ethnographic work. Essays in part 1 by Mary Catherine Bateson, Sidney Mintz, and George E. Marcus are conversational and autobiographical in tone. Each one precedes transcripts of actual dialogue between these scholars and the students and faculty they addressed during the original presentations. They explore the personal and professional meanings of how ethnographic research is taught, conducted, experienced, and used. The essays in part 2, also intimate and impassioned in tone, are authored by J. Lorand Matory and Marcia C. Inhorn, and they represent distinct applications of ethnographic studies attuned to mobility and diasporic issues. The essays in part 3, by Csilla Kalocsai, Melissa Remis, and ourselves, pick up on Inhorn's interest in emerging sectors or markets for knowledge, technology, services, and intervention worldwide. They reflect ethnographic work that attends to educational, political, and environmental challenges. The authors in parts 2 and 3 write from interfaces with fields such as law, environment, business, and global health. They portray ethnographic projects as processes entangled with others: social change and continuity, conflict resolution and prevention, wildlife conservation and economic development, biomedical intervention and public health policy, and professional training, to name a few.

Many of this book's questions illustrate the value of anthropological methods while also highlighting the diverse ways in which anthropology has been or should be put to use. We owe a debt of gratitude to members of Yale's cultural anthropology faculty—Eric Worby, Barney Bate, Bill Kelly, Helen Siu, Joe Errington, Enrique Mayer, John Szwed—and particular graduate students at the time—Ahmed Afzal, Csilla Kalocsai, Joseph Hill, Lucia Cantero, Abby Dumes, Omolade Adunbi, Sheriden Booker, Lydia Breckon, and Robert Clark—whose participation in the two Yale series led us to the themes taken up here. We are grateful to the anthropologists who responded favorably to our initial invitations, and equally grateful to those authors, such as Kalocsai and Inhorn, who later agreed to contribute essays amplifying and extending those themes.

Particular thanks are due to Brackette Williams for her engagement during the early, conceptual stage of this volume on questions concerning "the doing of ethnography" and its contributions to understanding social diversity. Carolyn

Martin Shaw, Ann Kingsolver, Lieba Fairer, and Ariana Hernandez-Reguant have consistently raised critical questions for our rethinking the role of ethnography in fieldwork, and we are grateful for those conversations. This text has also benefited enormously from the thoughtful comments and contributions of Webb Keane, Nadine Naber, Sean Brotherton, Jafari Allen, Siba Grovogui, Julia Paley, Andrew Shryock, and Miriam Ticktin. It would not have come together were it not for the hard work of Aixa Alemán-Díaz, Sarah Cwiek, Yair Leventhal, and Jesse Worker. Also, thank you to Tina Palivos, Jennifer Lee Johnson, and Renee Henry for editing and formatting the manuscript. Our editor, Gwen Walker, has shown patience and persistence in her pursuit of excellence for this project. Thanks also to four anonymous reviewers for the University of Wisconsin Press, who pushed us to clarify our aims and terms, thereby making the topic relevant to a broad readership. Many thanks to J. Naomi Linzer Indexing Services for creating the index.

Finally, we thank the non-anthropologists who have inquired searchingly about the methods and approaches that can be termed *ethnography*. It is a privilege and a curious responsibility to represent—even partially—one's "discipline," especially with respect to a field so inherently diverse as anthropology. This volume represents an array of perspectives, from more critical and philosophical to more applied and practically ambitious, from more humanities oriented to more scientifically inclined. In discussing our own differing approaches, we have appreciated anew the generous intellectual contours of anthropology as a field. We try to honor in this volume the wide range of ways one can do good ethnography; we also try to show ethnography as a singular approach to the study of human affairs, both for how it works at the level of lived experiences and for how it inquires into what such work means, and to whom.

We seek to contribute a clearer picture of social/cultural anthropology—its contradictions and its contributions—to those who are contemplating the role of ethnographic work in their own lives, be they undergraduates, academic anthropologists, practicing anthropologists, or non-anthropologists. The latter category includes our respective families. Kamari thanks her family for their endurance through the process—especially Viola and Linton Clarke, Ronald Crooks, but also Joseph Clarke-Crooks and Talia Blaire Clarke-Crooks—born into ongoing discussions about the radical transformation of ethnographic enterprise. Rebecca thanks Arun Agrawal for suggesting that she draw these lectures into a manuscript. She also thanks Naina Maria Agrawal for bringing into personal focus the project's potential significance to future readers, as well as for bringing work on this manuscript into better balance with life beyond the written page.

Transforming Ethnographic Knowledge

Introduction

REBECCA HARDIN and

KAMARI MAXINE CLARKE

> The special-ness of "what anthropologists do," their holistic, hu-
> manistic, mostly qualitative, strongly artisanal approach to social
> research, is (so we have taught ourselves to argue) the heart of the
> matter. Nigeria may not be a tribe, nor Italy an island; but a craft
> learnt among tribes or developed on islands can yet uncover dimen-
> sions of being that are hidden from such stricter and better organized
> types as economists, historians, exegetes, and political theorists.
>
> CLIFFORD GEERTZ, *Available Light: Anthropological Reflections*
> *on Philosophical Topics*

Few of us working in anthropology today conceive of our sites
and themes of study as the "islands" and "tribes" that Geertz
refers to above. Rather, we work in international courtrooms, in nature reserves,
in hospitals, in corporate boardrooms, even in fields of military conflict. Whereas
anthropologists were once more concerned with small-scale localized phenomena,
today we are engaged in a range of expansive domains that connect localized and
international spheres, revealing the deep histories of their formative connections to
one another. In so doing, many of us appear increasingly strict and well organized
about our methods and research designs, relative to Geertz's claims above. Yet we
remain a particular breed of scholar, set apart from many trends in social or natural
science that characterize other disciplines.

This volume explores what it means to do ethnography of the contemporary,
and how that relates to self-identification as an anthropologist in academic and
wider worlds. The word *ethnography* combines two significations of abstraction.

One suggests the classificatory logics inherent in many human ways of organizing social worlds, and particularly those devised during Western expansion in the latter half of the nineteenth century (*ethnic*; *ethnonyms*; *ethnology*; *ethnocentric*). The other suggests the production of images and texts used to describe different cultural practices across the globe (*graphic*; *iconography*; *monograph*). While it may thus seem anachronistic, the term is in wider use today, and in a wider range of sectors, than ever before. At the same time, it remains at the core of anthropology's coherence as a social science tradition.

Referring to a very basic practice of describing and interpreting social worlds, the practice of ethnography links anthropologists of various schools, within the subfield of sociocultural anthropology, which is distinct from the discipline's other fields of archaeology, linguistic anthropology, and biological or physical anthropology. These schools include European "social anthropology," American "cultural anthropology," and emerging anthropologies such as "Siberian anthropology" or "Andeanist anthropology" (Ribeiro and Escobar 2006), which explore native anthropology from the perspectives of those who live there, as well as a range of transnational practices of applied and more theoretically oriented work. This range of "anthropologies" is dizzying, yet it is central to most anthropologists' understandings of the complex field of which they are a part.

We consider ethnographic knowledge produced within more or less formally recognized schools, while also inquiring into the contemporary expansion in ethnographic knowledge production that involves both the anthropological specialist as well as the nonspecialist ethnographer working in a range of domains—sports events, medical clinics, environmental disaster sites, and classrooms, to name just a few. This book delves into a central paradox: despite its complexity, *ethnography* itself retains some core definitions and contradictions that have come to constitute a specific and widely shared approach to the study of human social life. As many authors in the volume argue, ethnography is more than a particular topic or type of field site. It can (some would say *should*) involve a deeply personal process of sustained inquiry into meaning, belonging, and difference in our world.

Almost all would agree, however, that the scope of ethnography has changed significantly over the past three decades. So too have its purposes, uses, and techniques, as well as its consequences. Questions proliferate about what constitutes ethnography in this increasingly globalized and interconnected world, what its essential elements and uses now are. Such issues are at the heart of this book, articulated by different generations of American ethnographers, covering a range of regions and areas of specialization. Not only a tool for transforming the world in urgently needed ways, as Jennifer Staple's foreword to this book and her example with Unite For Sight suggest so clearly, ethnography is also a set of practices that can transform anthropologists themselves, in both immediate and more enduring ways, as Mary Catherine Bateson eloquently explains here. How can something so complex become such a convenient "toolkit" for making money, or making war, or making the world a better place?

The book reflects our substantial engagement with intellectual communities both in anthropology departments and in professional school settings.[1] The essays herein are directed not only to anthropologists but also to students and professionals outside the discipline who work with its distinctive intellectual and methodological legacies of fieldwork, participant observation, dialogue, and attention to life or work histories. These legacies, we argue, are crucial elements for constructing and protecting critical terrain in these times—even, we hope, for extending such terrain to those (within and outside the discipline) whose work will not look like anything anthropology has yet seen, yet whose accomplishments can reflect and respect the irreducibility of ethnographic experience.

Ethnography for Whom?

In the years since we convened the actual conversations at the core of this volume, we have met one another in workshops on international legal scholarship and anthropology, or at Wenner-Gren seminars on ethnography and corporate responsibility or engaged ethnographic practice. Increasingly we have been sought out by students in medical schools, law schools, and public health programs that seek to "incorporate ethnography" during an internship or clinical or research experience. Progressively more applicants come to our doctoral programs after significant work in environmental conservation, international development, or humanitarian-aid experience "in the field," seeking to make sense of those experiences through anthropological training. Students such as Jennifer Staple, as undergraduates, have shown us that anthropological frameworks and ethnographic field methods can be rigorously and innovatively embraced in the interest of building new local or transnational programs and institutions.

Some of these ethnographic options have emerged from broad changes in the world. The local and transnational terrain within which we work has required more and more mobility (Sassen 1996; Gupta and Ferguson 1997); former colonial regimes have shifted to new, increasingly mobile regimes of wealth and work. This evolution has created new cultural and institutional alliances, forcing ethnographers to rethink the field—where it is, how to identify and map it, and how to reconstitute its history. Other changes, though, have been neither as sweeping nor as transformative as some might claim, or wish. Deep economic disparities still characterize the world, configuring communities along variously defined and shifting axes such as north–south, urban–rural, masculine–feminine, and, at a growing rate, healthy–ill. The fundamental problems of poverty continue to plague developing economies disproportionately, creating forms of struggle that are historically rooted while being thoroughly modern (Williams 1991). Colonial institutions that gave rise to ethnographic explorations (Feuchtwang 1973) cannot be relegated, as anachronisms, to some previous era. Despite efforts to alter or abolish them—whether through critical reflexivity or ardent political engagement—many are transmuted into new domains of exploration and exploitation. The complex matrix of sites within formal economic systems fosters informal economies, as well as new, increasingly collaborative forms of ethnographic description across national and disciplinary distinctions (MacGaffey and Bazenguissa-Ganga 2000).[2]

This volume explores the shifting terrain on which anthropologists—as professionals, and intellectuals, and people—stand at present, practicing their craft. Our authors are all engaged in ethnographic inquiries that also interrogate definitions of the anthropological "field": how that field intersects with other sectors, industries, and sites of rapid social change, and how the future of anthropology is being shaped by those intersections.

We ask several key questions in this volume about what ethnographers study as well as where, how, and for whom ethnographers today carry out their work. First, in this age of new intellectual incursions into intimate, everyday life through formal behavioral studies as well as marketing or political polls, just which objects and relationships are deemed appropriate for ethnographic investigation? Ethnography increasingly explores not only the politics of sexual practice (Rubin 1984, 2011) but also the erotic aspects and aesthetics of fieldwork itself (Taylor 1998). Moreover, the intimacies that delimit and also constitute how we understand humanity have also included cyborgs or other species (Haraway 1991, 2003), pathogens (Lindenbaum 2001), bills and treaties (Dezalay and Garth 1996, 2002; K. M. Clarke 2009) and even entire landscapes or non-human actors (Raffles 2002, 2011). Ethnography is also increasingly linked to the arts and to practices of consumer culture—texts and films for markets beyond academia.[3]

As anthropologists investigate new conventions for ethnographic expression writing styles proliferate, appropriating the conventions of autobiography (Taylor 1998; Freedman and Frey 2003), fiction writing (Shostak 1981; Behar 1993), and engaging the methods and characteristics of investigative journalism (Klinenberg 2002, 2007; Ehrenreich 2001; Cramer and McDevitt 2004). At the same time, ethnographers are engaging the production of public culture, media images, and journalistic narratives in complex ways (Shryock 2004). Thus, the way an "ethnographic monograph" (most often still a single-authored book) uses ethnography these days is far more varied than at any time in the history of the field.

Increasingly, ethnographers "poach" on disciplinary and empirical territories previously reserved for other fields. As we consider where ethnographers locate themselves, we are concerned as much with the geophysical as with the social and structural location. Anthropologists have always been inserted within multiple communities of knowledge production, and at the turn of the twentieth century, the "fathers" of early American, British, and French anthropology mediated the divides between elites within structures of empires and those only just within or beyond its reach. In more recent decades, anthropologists have increasingly worked in corporations or nongovernmental organizations, on the one hand, and in village settings and dusty archives on the other. How does our mobility across such sites reconfigure the old distinctions between "applied" and "basic" research? And what does that tell us about the contemporary moment?

We consider the following fields as having readily adopted ethnographic methods: business practices with growing focus on corporate social responsibility; environmental management with its concern for "community-based conservation"; various medical regimes along with the therapeutic and ethical practices that constitute them; and finally conflict prevention and mediation, through militarized practices but also through justice systems and their legal and ethical frameworks. Ethnographic work in these varied arenas, as in more "traditional" academic veins, still calls for fine-grained approaches to highly localized studies. However, it also calls for attention to such domains within rapidly shifting global spheres.

This collection looks back at ethnographic legacies and forward to the challenges of living life as an ethnographer in an increasingly diverse terrain. The changes we describe, though not necessarily new, are gaining what one might term "critical mass" vis-à-vis the core of a discipline—and a method—that has long resisted any single definition. We sketch possible ways that ethnography is moving forward under conditions of politicized and market-driven dynamics of value for ethnographic (and other forms of) knowledge (Brenneis 2004). To this end, the present volume offers the voices of both seasoned and emerging anthropologists who write about their ethnographic work and how they have seen it used and taught. We hope thereby to highlight some of the key tensions and debates among those who share a strong commitment to ethnographic endeavors. The perspectives represented here reflect deep personal commitment and intellectual creativity that make them more than an "approach" or "tool kit" for application to social challenges.

What Is Ethnography, and What Is It Becoming?

> An ethnographer is an anthropologist who attempts—at least in part of his or her professional work—to record and describe the culturally significant behavior of a particular society.
>
> HAROLD C. CONKLIN, "Ethnography"

Ethnographers were once trained primarily in field methods that emphasized linguistic and logistical competence within rural or extremely impoverished urban field settings (Frake 1964, 1980). Much has changed. Today, ethnographers debate the virtues of online translation programs for our field notes and publications. Major logistical questions about communication within and from the field include "What is the Internet connectivity like?" and "Can I dress elegantly enough to inspire confidence from my upper-level corporate interviewees?"

Of course, the problems of termites and of computer terminals can be encountered in a single site where forces of nature and technological and social change combine to shape our investigations (see Handler 2006). As those who came of age within anthropology through the 1980s and 1990s can attest, for several decades there has been a felicitous profusion of approaches and definitions—indeed, philosophies—of what fieldwork is, what ethnography does, and what distinguishes it from "the doing" of everyday life. For example, since the 1980s one major change in sociocultural anthropology has been an increased focus on global flows of populations, ideas, goods, and resources and on the transformations that such massive movements provoke among the populations involved (Trouillot 2003, 1).

Here, we home in on the essential questions: "What is ethnography?" and "What is it becoming in this age of rapid transnational reconfigurations?" The former question was one that prompted George W. Stocking Jr.'s History of Anthropology series with the University of Wisconsin Press, and his 1983 book *Observers Observed* became one crucial reference from the reflexive years in American sociocultural anthropology. The late 1980s and 1990s were marked by critical reconsideration of how ethnography's practitioners conducted and construct it, and how those whom it takes as its research subjects perceive it. If that moment is now over, how can we characterize the present moment in the practice of ethnographic work? In response to this question, we felt it crucial not only to survey the newer uses being made of ethnography but also to reflect on its past uses.

Many of the contributors herein direct our attention to the anthropological traditions left us by previous generations of scholars. Sidney Mintz, for instance, would have us reconsider the legacy of Franz Boas—a researcher and teacher deeply involved in several key transitions within the field of anthropology; Mary Catherine Bateson points us toward the legacies of both Margaret Mead (who had studied with Boas) and Gregory Bateson. But alongside those legacies are other intellectual and foundational trajectories that took shape out of the British and French anthropological traditions, respectively, or out of feminist and postcolonial scholarship, or even the growing urban and transnational anthropology that emerged following the Cold War, the post-1989 restructuring, and poststructural adjustment in African and Latin American countries.

In following Boas's trajectory, contributors in the first third of the volume are interested in the development of an anthropological specialization that spanned empirical fields of knowledge from various museum-based preoccupations to a field-based and fully social-scientific discipline. It grew from a white-male-dominated society of anthropologists to a more diverse community of anthropological inquiry. Presiding in some senses over these shifts in participation and conceptualizations, many consider Boas to be the father of a distinct American school of anthropology, whose emphasis on the culture concept was unique in his time.

Boas, as Mintz notes in his essay, was also remarkable for deploying the concept in politically unpredictable and visionary ways. One of his most crucial contributions to ethnography is his insistence that the study of culture involves constantly relating context to content, as against the social determinism and classificatory impulses that preceded his approach.[4] For example, Mintz reminds us, Boas spoke as a Jewish scholar both to and about African Americans during the late 1930s, offering a clear vision of them as descendents of complex African civilizations rather than as uncivilized and racially inferior (see Mintz and Price 1992).

Bateson's parents, Margaret Mead and Gregory Bateson, also stand out particularly in the pantheon of past anthropologists, both for the historical moment of their work and for the remarkable intellectual and personal charisma with which they popularized ethnographic studies. Their meeting in Papua New Guinea is legendary, for several reasons—not only were they to become intellectual celebrities, but they also represented a confluence of hitherto largely distinct anthropological ideas that have continued to inform a kind of "genealogy" of thought and action for contemporary students.

Gregory Bateson had been trained at St. John's College at Cambridge and engaged critically with the notions of social structure (1958), following the British anthropologist Alfred Radcliffe-Brown, the latter following the legacy of sociologist Émile Durkheim, who was interested in systems and how they changed. Later, Radcliffe-Brown became fascinated by function as it explained and resolved tensions within and across cultural systems, following the British-trained anthropologist

Bronisław Malinowski. Mead, on the other hand, critically engaged with Boasian intuitive approaches to culture, as stemming from individual emotional and intellectual experiences, arranged in cultural patterns that reflect and reveal personalities. Both thinkers, of course, were concerned with a range of ideas and their consequences for the interpretation of cultures.[5] They considered, during their lamplit evenings in the field, the recently published work of Boas's student Ruth Benedict, *Patterns of Culture* (1934), creating through their conversations a new combination of British and American anthropological approaches of that time.

As Mary Catherine Bateson's introspective and somewhat philosophical contribution to this volume attests, her parents lived their ideals deeply at the level of personhood and family. What special sensitivities or abilities has she experienced as a result of having been raised, as it were, "anthropologically"? Complementing our concern with the ends to which ethnography is put, she describes the means by which we can participate in, and observe, and make sense of our own lives and the lives of those around us. She also interrogates the power relations inherent in ethnography's key method of participant observation, from the unique perspective of one whose childhood was exhaustively observed by those most important participants: her parents.

During the original lecture on which Bateson's chapter here is based, a student asked: "Isn't it somewhat dangerous to think of oneself as a participant observer who is somehow distant from (or even defended against) participation in life?" In response, Bateson reflected on the situated nature of knowledge, reminding us that the intellectual is not necessarily "disconnected" from the real, the emotional, the popular, or the political. She affirmed aloud, as she has in her writing, the role that observation can play in constructions of self and of projects, "how much the capacity to combine new roles to create an innovative and integrated whole might depend on exposure to another culture, . . . the idea that one could study culture, one's own or that of others, truly attending to it rather than using the stance of an observer as a way to dominate" (M. C. Bateson 1989, 63–64).

George Marcus stands with Bateson and others such as Michael Fischer and James Clifford as an intellectual leader in reconsidering those inequities and ironies of cultural anthropology's history (Marcus and Fischer 1986; Clifford 1988). Such work elaborated new theoretical dimensions to the contributions we mentioned above by Stocking and suggested the use of ethnography to critically engage the ethnographer's own social context, its conceptual and practical norms and assumptions. Further, such work pointed to the politics of power and the relevance of context in the writing of ethnography, reminding us that the making of social worlds is also haunted by former, often inexorable relationships to imperial expansion and colonial control.

Other anthropologists have challenged these enduring legacies. David Schneider (Schneider and Gough 1961; Schneider 1968, 1984) questioned the very conceptualization of kinship, and his students followed by denaturalizing notions of the heterosexual family. Michel-Rolph Trouillot (1995) and Brackette Williams (1991) recast the politics of history, memory, and identity and, along with a range of scholars, turned modernism on its head by demonstrating that the very basis upon which modernism produced racial distinction involved the fundamental inclusion of race at its core. But the paths toward acknowledging and addressing those issues are not always commonly defined within anthropological communities. In response to a student audience at his talk that seemed as concerned about these issues as those who attended Bateson's talk, Mintz suggested that the successive strides made by anthropologists such as Boas and his students toward understanding social distinctions and dismantling the inequities within a given society based upon such distinctions have been overlooked in recent decades. Instead we have engaged in constructive (and deconstructive) critical articulation of anthropology's roles in imperialism (Diamond 1974), colonialisms (Asad 1973), and exoticisms (e.g., Fabian 1983) of more pervasive and enduring varieties. We return to the questions of linked internal and international asymmetries briefly in our conclusion; for now we signal them as they have shaped our editorial process and our ethnographic practice.

Kamari Clarke (2004) and Clarke and Deborah Thomas (2006) have demonstrated that notions of human difference have sparked constructions of race and blackness, in particular, which reveal how cultural diversity is not disappearing but is changing in complex ways. J. Lorand Matory's chapter in this volume cautions that while ethnography should counter discourses and policies that belie—and indeed may belittle—the complexity of social relations, the continued and varied production of cultural difference to varying degrees also requires our attention as an important arena of study. In keeping with his book on the Afro-Brazilian Candomblé, *Black Atlantic Religion*, Matory argues that ethnography's emphasis on local cultural practices in the contemporary present has ignored the history of these societies, in particular their mobility within transnational circuits as both pioneers and prisoners who created new forms of citizenship even as they suffered great oppression (2005, 3). He reflects on his discovery of African diasporic influences in his own life and work and summarizes some of the intellectual and intercultural importance of such insights for contemporary ethnographic work. As Matory observes, "The translocal, transnational, and trans-Atlantic slave trade and its consequences have, however, been a major blind spot in the genesis of the currently fashionable anthropology models of cultural history. The parallel study of African-American and Native American 'acculturation' by Melville Herskovits, Robert Redfield, and others long ago fell by the wayside in American anthropology"

(2005, 4). Similarly, Clarke's (2004) earlier work asserts that the geopolitics of race and culture are connected to various specific sites and require not just conceptual or theoretical recognition but also spatial and historical mappings. At the center of her inquiry are the ways that social imaginaries intertwine to produce transnationally complex notions of place and belonging.

On the one hand, contacts across cultures are so common that they can appear deceptively banal and feed popular notions (and fears) of universalism, integration, and individualism. On the other hand, as Matory notes in the present volume, although specific cultural identities change and their relationship to sites is contingent, they are still bounded in a range of ways. During the past three decades, cultural studies, the history of science, and the sociology of knowledge have all illuminated genealogies of authorial knowledge and the consequences of ethnographic interventions. In the wake of those developments in intellectual life, and with the advancement of the life sciences, among other key transformations, ethnography is at a crossroads (Taussig 2003; see also Augé and Colleyn 2006). Today, more routinely and effectively than ever before, we interrogate ethnography as a knowledge practice and examine the power relations implicit in the circumstances of its production.

Doing Ethnography: Conscience, Context, and Content

No matter how attentive anthropologists try to be to history, transnational relations, and mobility, they cannot control the way their work is received and interpreted—the uses made of it. Herein lies one of the central anxieties shared by the authors in this collection; we conceive of knowledge itself as relational and dynamic. It is empirically rich, yet open to intangible features that deeply structure human lives. It is fascinated to the point of obsession with various forms of alterity, or otherness, yet transformative of the self and hence fodder for a great deal of reflexive analysis. Its rough impulses and precise methods alike are designed to foster deep involvement in others' lives, even some sense of parity or belonging in those lives. Yet we see the clear consequences, often unintended, that can stem from its expression. We seek to immerse ourselves in the contexts and circumstances of others, in order to gain more subtle and clear understandings of their perspectives and practices. We wonder about the limits of our knowledge and worry that its circulation could have negative impacts on those with whom we interacted to produce it.

In sum, to talk about ethnography is to discuss relations of inequality, desire, responsibility, and contradiction. However, given that anthropologists are still engaged in justifying the centrality of locally detailed ethnography to their discipline, and even in debating the legitimacy of the discipline itself, ethnography's exact definition and its relationship to the history of colonial power and its contemporary permutations remain unresolved. What stands is the status of good ethnography that emerges from highly textured and long-term interactions across shifting social divides, in multiple spaces and sites subjected to careful interpretive analysis without reducing them to an "archive" nor necessarily distilling elements of them into datasets that enable broader comparisons with other human groups, geographical sites, or time frames. We write at a time when much insight has accrued about the relationship of anthropology to other disciplines and research traditions (Cohn 1987; Clifford and Marcus 1986; Bourdieu 1990; Di Leonardo 1991). And yet, some of the more fundamental, ontological, and intellectual implications of conducting ethnographic work remain shrouded in mystery, venerated but also at times overrated.

Ethnography in its fullest form is in many ways exasperating to those who seek to place knowledge in explicit relationships to policy or politics, through reproducible, generalize-able, coherent, and yet dynamic social science methods, as George E. Marcus describes in his contribution to this volume. His essay, like that of Bateson or Mintz, is personal in tone. Yet it marks a transition from reflections on the past and present toward issues about the future of the field and the training of its practitioners. Analyzing contemporary markets for expert knowledge, and the way they shape ethnographic work, Marcus argues that much of the way anthropology is taught in universities requires updating and rethinking in order to move ethnography into the twenty-first century.

A terse story by Jorge Luis Borges entitled "the ethnographer," often cited as a *réplique* to the arrogance of expert knowledge in academic institutions in general, serves poignantly to capture this pathos-laden and profound quality of earnest ethnographic engagement. The story's protagonist, doctoral student Fred Murdock, commences field research among a Native North American community where he is eventually accepted, trusted, and taught many of the secrets and details of their lives. Thus enlightened, on even the subconscious levels that enable him to "dream of buffalo" when the moon is full, he returns to his university campus. Ultimately unable and unwilling to convey that knowledge through a completed dissertation, Murdock ends his days as a librarian in dusty collections, still dreaming when the moon is full, but never becoming Dr. Murdock.

Let us bracket the troubling convenience in this narrative of purportedly mystical Native American culture as a foil to expert knowledge production, realizing that knowledge forms of various kinds are mutually constitutive, even if formal scientific knowledge can be insidiously linked to some forms of domination. We can still acknowledge that Murdock's dilemma, as described by Borges, resonates with many anthropologists, and also with those from other fields who have found collaboration with us to be vexing. An ethnographic monograph is an idiosyncratic output based on highly personal investments in sustained inquiry into others' ideas and ways of being in the world. Even when compellingly written, it is almost always haunted by the information that it cannot or does not convey. Ethnographers are prone to paroxysms of conscience as they attempt to reconcile the complexity of their experiential learning trajectory with the demands for detailed knowledge that scientific and other sectors demand.

That said, in naming the mute ethnographer "Murdock," and showing us the consequences of his refusing the necessary reduction of experience for analysis, Borges has captured one of the central tensions within anthropology, not just between it and other social scientific or scientific fields. George Murdock, former chair of Yale's anthropology department, identified himself not narrowly as an ethnographer, nor only as an anthropologist, but as a social scientist interested in using statistical methods and fostering anthropology's interface with other fields. His systems of coding for field data were in part aimed at making anthropological contributions to the crosscutting analysis of complex changes in the world. He wrote prolifically and intelligently about cultures he had never visited. Further, he played a range of roles within the profession of anthropology, the contemplation of which can produce cognitive dissonance: apparently an informer against some of his colleagues under McCarthyism, he later chaired the American Anthropological Association's Committee on Scientific Freedom. We return to his legacy with respect to anthropological engagement in and with warfare later in this introduction. For now, we wish to think a bit further about the nature of ethnographic knowledge. For surely there are ways forward for our field that move beyond these curiously popular poles of silence, on the one hand, and fraught service to the security state, on the other?

Those who have been practicing ethnographers over the course of a long career are uniquely placed to comment on how it takes intertwined notions of human differences and power relations as key concerns, without abandoning an interest in what can be said to constitute humanity as something held in common across those differences. During his discussion with students at Yale—a return visit to the campus where he too had spent decades of his early career and indeed overlapped with Murdock—Sidney Mintz mentioned that *Worker in the Cane* (1960), the life history of his friend and informant in Puerto Rico, was the hardest book to write of his whole career. Why? As he put it: "I felt so responsible for getting that representation right; and so nervous about whether I was doing it the right way." To a reader, the book flows naturally; it simply, and without a lot of textual and analytical fanfare, combines a variety of narrative perspectives and strategies to make one man's life seem accessible to those who have never known him. Mintz's book had been, for the critics of its time, an example of *overly* intimate study, one that makes all too obvious the affection and connection between Mintz and his "informant" and thus lacked the important feature of scientific objectivity. More recently, critics have not found it reflexive *enough* about the relationship between the two men, and particularly the differential in power that Mintz as ethnographer and his informant as a colonized subject constrained to wage slavery must have experienced.

As Mintz himself noted wryly in response to questions from the students at his lecture, it is not the book that changed but rather the concerns of anthropology that have changed in the intervening forty years. Through this work Mintz came to be seen not only as an ethnographic portrait artist but also, himself, as an "ethnographic portrait" of anthropology's past. Even as he commemorates a key informant and friend, he becomes himself a kind of intellectual icon whose attention to work and work history both feeds on and feeds into related fields. Ethnographic writing is always an experimental combination of elements and roles—the novelist, the traveler, the writer, the naturalist—drawing on and contributing to narrative conventions in other fields.

Mary Catherine Bateson's work has exemplified the capacity to "cross over" from one era of anthropological concerns to another. She published the book *Composing a Life* in 1989, at a time when gender was only beginning to be considered carefully within the practice of anthropology.[6] In step with, or perhaps even ahead of her time, Bateson daringly described the divided energies of a woman as lover, mother, and individual, intellectual self. She used such description to build a model for creative productivity in the face of multiple and shifting roles amid changing economic and social forces in the United States and other postindustrial countries. It is a model for which she need make no extended case. Indeed, she has subsequently completed another project about aging. For the 1989 book, she marshals ample evidence from her own life and her success as a participant observer among her colleagues and friends: "Perhaps Kierkegaard was wrong when he said 'purity is to will one thing.' Perhaps the issue is not a fixed knowledge of the good, the single focus that millennia of monotheism have made us idealize, but rather a kind of attention that is open, not focused on a single point. Instead of concentration on a transcendent ideal, sustained attention to diversity and interdependence may offer a different clarity of vision, one that is sensitive to ecological complexity, to the multiple rather than the singular" (M. C. Bateson 1989, 166).

Over the course of her career Bateson has applied her intellect to issues as diverse as Arabic language and poetic form; HIV-AIDS; links among homemaking, self-expression, and stewardship of the environment; the give and take within marriages; even the complementary and complex energies that make a workplace function well. Her work has moved from personal practices and personalities to broader agendas and reflections on the imperfections and possible perfectibility of the society in which she lives, where "adjusting to discontinuity is not an idiosyncratic problem of my own but the emerging problem of our era" (1989, 14).

Her points about complexity raise related ones about how we envision ethnography, less as a project of translation or interpretation than as a way of questioning and describing the world around us. Can we discuss the endeavor of ethnography such that there is no need for the illusion of objectivity, nor for an illusion of some subjectivity so self-aware as to absolve itself of any responsibility for the difficulties inherent in the politics of representation? Can we conjure ethnography as a set of practices situated staunchly in some messy middle ground, where accounts are rendered up with all their imperfections, as tokens of encounters within shifting, sometimes surprising, and often remarkably exploitative systems?

Mintz's humorous and highly accessible contribution to this volume constitutes a series of disarmingly candid accounts of such work. Cloaked in the person of "Franz the ethnographer," he recounts the frustrating, neurosis-producing nature of ethnographic fieldwork, as it weathers changes in the world and increasing competition from outside the confines of formal anthropological training. He thus reminds us, too, of the differences between ethnographers and those who come to resemble them—travelers, TV reporters, and novelists—cautioning us that fieldwork is much more than "telling stories." Ethnographic texts are, of course, suffused with the details of lives poured into them, but they are also framed in ways that pose important questions and suggest rich and cross-culturally meaningful interpretations of those details. They are, at their best, intensely alive, open to multiple interpretations, and able to survive the test of time.

New Uses of Ethnography

The work of ethnography as an effort to enter others' worlds or frames of reference is distinct from studying the behaviors of consumers in checkout lines to assist supermarket chains in their organization of merchandise. By drawing such distinctions, we do not seek to reinforce the boundaries of applied and basic research, of scholarly versus socially engaged intellectual labor. On the contrary, we would like to emphasize what connects our work with that of colleagues in schools of law, education, public policy, or public health who also rely on ethnography for some component of their research. But in talking with seasoned anthropologists, we also note that ethnography, as a way of thinking and living, does contrast with more descriptive or prescriptive work, such as travel writing, consulting reports, medical or intelligence briefs—of which the world is currently experiencing a dizzying glut. Such works often take difference as a deliciously marketable commodity, a politically inscrutable (and often essentialized) category, or a problem to be resolved through the elaboration of universal norms and standards of human social and institutional practice.

Ethnography, by contrast, provides the possibility for ethnographers to challenge or resist the attitudes typical of these other approaches. But the ethnographic approach should not be equated with intellectual detachment. On the contrary, this volume urges ethnographers to take seriously the call of engaged anthropology as a means by which to critique the application of intellectual knowledge. This more engaged anthropology (like other applied forms of cultural anthropology) means different things to different people with different interests. In a variety of fields, from legal and medical professions to ecological management to military spheres, ethnographic work is finding or claiming new relevance—with both intended and unintended consequences.

CORPORATE SECTORS AND BUSINESS PRACTICES

The business world increasingly shapes and is studied by anthropologists, but it also makes use of anthropological insights. Since the 1970s, applied anthropology has been contributing to research on the marketing and consumption of products; today these strains of anthropological work are under new scrutiny, and their practitioners are writing more reflexively about their relationships to the core of the discipline (Sunderland and Denny 2007), even as they travel across sectors from high-tech product design, where terms such as "situational fluency" gloss professionals' abilities to read cultural and interpersonal cues skillfully in business settings. At Cornell University's Johnson School of Business, scholar and sustainability guru Stuart Hart, who developed with C. K. Prahalad the "bottom of the pyramid" approach to seeing poor people as part of crucial "emerging markets," encourages students to engage in "rapid ethnography" to formulate business plans or marketing strategies. Ethnography also has obvious relevance to the assessment of risks in emerging markets and new basic business practices in the context of global change and market volatility (Millen 2000).

Harvard Business School's Tom Davenport posted a short piece in his blog *The Next Big Thing* titled "The Rise of Corporate Anthropology" (Davenport 2007). It makes for entertaining reading, inasmuch as he exhorts business leaders to consider the value of anthropological research despite its slow and deliberate pace—so out of synch with the fast tempo of the corporate world. Beyond the actual employment of anthropologists in corporate settings, recent strains of successful corporate leadership and management paradigms emphasize flexibility. In this respect they echo Bateson's points from the preceding section. Many managers now talk about departing from the "great leader" and "strong hierarchy" models of days gone by and instead valuing multitasking, mentorship skills, and the nurturing of human developmental capacities as crucial to economically competitive performance (Collins 2001).[7] Such approaches are creating myriad new uses for ethnographic methods in information flow, monitoring, and evaluation or improvement of operations (Aguilera 1996). Both Csilla Kalocsai's and George Marcus's chapters in this book speak to the idea of markets for anthropological expertise.

Such changes within corporate entities are occurring within increasingly charged social fields regarding the role of transnational corporations in contemporary social and environmental problems. While much of the broader literature tends either toward stringent criticism of corporate actors (Bakan 2004) or toward ambitious visions about their positive accomplishments (Berman and Webb 2003; O'Rourke 2004), some middle ground is emerging. The concepts of corporate culture and institutional culture offer new examples of relevance for ethnographic work as it relates materiality to meaning, and context to content (Ashforth and Mael 1989; G. G. Gordon 1991). Ronen Shamir (2004), writing on the concept of corporate social responsibility (CSR), notes, "CSR is first and foremost a field that consists of a multitude of social actors . . . saturated with experts of various sorts and with an array of nonprofit organizations that benefit from, are drawn into, or advocate the idea of CSR" (641). As such, there are significant opportunities for "studying up" and documenting the practices and perspectives of corporate actors from ethnographic locations more and less embedded within corporate spheres. As Anna Tsing's 2009 publication on supply chains illustrates, to study the corporate is to take interest in a rapidly moving target. Capitalism constantly fosters new social forms of supply and labor. These can be different for the industrial transformation of resources than for the consumption of them in their natural form, as with wild-caught foods. Moreover, identity itself can become a resource in such systems, making ethnographic knowledge of particular value.

Rebecca Hardin, with colleagues Damani Partridge (University of Michigan) and Marina Welker (Cornell University), organized "Corporate Lives: New Perspectives on the Corporate Social Form," a seminar jointly sponsored by Wenner-Gren and the School of Advanced Research in August 2008 and published as a special issue of *Current Anthropology* in 2011. At that event anthropologists and "corporate intellectuals" came together to discuss the corporation as a social form. The project was based on the idea that the corporate—never truly distinct from social life and cultural production—has created specific practices such as branding, or benchmarking, or accounting, that increasingly characterize other arenas of production, such as arts or politics. Corporate social forms are appropriated by actors whose corporate status is more identity based, rather than business based, but who are increasingly savvy capitalists (such as the Seminole Nation; see Cattelino 2005). Corporate forms are increasingly involved in governance, as in Michael Bloomberg's approach as mayor of New York, or proliferating public-private partnerships in resource management and conservation.

In the present volume, Csilla Kalocsai's essay offers an ethnographic perspective on corporate management in an era of transnational corporate dominance and crisis in order to unpack the complicated interconnections of knowledge and influence, as well as to engage effectively the contexts within which contemporary global capitalism is taking shape. Kalocsai shows how transnational corporations utilize various forms of business expertise to retool corporate managers into cosmopolitan, entrepreneurial selves in postsocialist Hungary. She thus traces relational and historical connections through the assemblages of global business knowledge not only to reveal radically reconfigured sites of knowledge production and circulation but also to show how particular vernacular forms of meaning are being rearticulated alongside and in relation to hegemonic, universalizing forms. Kalocsai follows the story of an international business school in Budapest and highlights the vernacular forms and actors of socialist corporate knowledge that remain important in launching and (re)constructing the new global apparatus of corporate business education in Hungary. She explores socialist entrepreneurial ethics, anchored in Hungary's first and second economies of the 1970s and 1980s, and considers how they have provided a ground upon which new neoliberal ethics could take root and hybridize. She then looks at how the new, albeit hybrid, structures and technologies of training young professionals in order to produce "new," more appropriate kinds of "selves." This example highlights the ways that ethnography used in corporate worlds can shed light on the changes in governance, cultural production, and daily life.

In sum, in the context of the growth and spread of transnational corporate practices, many business communities are making use of anthropological approaches. Not the least of those appropriating corporate practices and identities are nongovernmental organizations, or NGOs, which constitute a vast range of nonstate actors with mandates in development, humanitarian aid, religious activities, artistic arenas, and beyond. We limit ourselves in this volume to a closer look at those working at the interface of environmental conservation and development.

ADAPTATION, CONSERVATION, AND
ENVIRONMENTAL JUSTICE

It would be a mistake to characterize environmental arenas as ones into which anthropology is expanding, for they were instrumental in the emergence of behavioral and field studies as a core set of approaches and methods across anthropological subfields. Historically, insights about the diversity of humans and of the natural world were intertwined and derived in large part from a richly documented history of imperial and colonial scientific practices of natural historical studies that led to evolutionist and taxonomic impulses in early human sciences. Anthropology as we now know it, however, emerged in many respects from a break with such legacies. During the 1937 Asiatic Primate Expedition to Thailand (in an area now part of Vietnam) to study wild gibbons, noted primatologist Sherwood Washburn joined forces with film enthusiast Clarence Ray Carpenter. Carpenter was intrigued by the power of film both for capturing interactions as data and for conveying scientific knowledge as results. It was a watershed; together they established some of the first primate research sites in which the animals were observed and recorded, rather than being shot, dissected, and preserved for museum collections.

Washburn retained a behavioral agenda while studying baboons during his work in East Africa in the 1950s. Himself primarily a physical anthropologist, Washburn was a "bridge builder . . . of the modern synthesis of evolution in the 1940s and 1950s," who "saw issues and problems, not disciplinary boundaries" (Zihlman 2000, 61). Later studies by Washburn and his physical anthropology students informed the study of human evolution, situating humans and their closest relatives in nature and making predictions about environmental consequences for early hominid social behavior (DeVore 1965). Washburn's work diverged from classificatory impulses in early anthropology; he refuted the racialized typologies of his early education and advocated more dynamic approaches and holistic concepts for the study of human (and animal) evolution and behavioral change (Washburn 1951). Further, in relation to the emphasis of this volume, we note that his intellectual contributions emphasized links to sociocultural anthropology that emerged from fieldwork in collaborative interdisciplinary teams.

Washburn's adaptationist approach resonated with the early twentieth-century human cultural ecology of his anthropological colleagues. Julian Steward, during his time at the University of Michigan in the 1930s, developed an approach and method known as cultural ecology. It articulated with work after the 1950s by another University of Michigan scholar, Leslie White, who wrestled mightily with

Boasian legacies, and re-engaged ideas about evolution from the natural sciences, arguing for the unique power of technology to shape human societal changes. During the 1960s and 1970s, powerful work was published in which human and nonhumans were seen as parts of whole systems, borrowing from cybernetics but also still linking to emerging concepts from the young science of field ecology and back to notions of evolution and adaptation (Rappaport 1984; Bennett 1976).

All of these streams of early environmental anthropology have since been aptly criticized as somewhat synchronic and prone to considering human ecology as a closed system with its own internal regulation mechanisms, rather than a more dynamic set of flows and feedbacks that relate to historical changes, political economies, and other forces (Peet and Watts 1996, 4). Contemporary works in environmental anthropology have elaborated cultural anthropology's interface with sociology, political science, and geography. They move away from concerns with bounded systems, evolution, and debates about environmental determinism versus constraint that characterized the ecological anthropology of the 1950s to 1970s (see Orlove 1980; Kottak 1999). More recent approaches analyze changing local ecological practice within larger local and regional economies through colonization, migration, state formation, and global trade (Peterson 1978; Leacock and Lee 1982; Solway and Lee 1990; Kent 1996; Brosius 1997). Emerging work, including that by Orlove, takes climate change processes and human responses to them as a new topic for ethnographic work.

These pendulum swings within sociocultural streams of environmental anthropology have their corollaries in biological or physical anthropology. For instance, although the development of sociobiology in the 1970s (E. O. Wilson 1975) urged primatologists to integrate evolutionary theory into behavioral explanations, most physical anthropologists rejected overly reductionist genetic explanations (Richard and Schulman 1982), emphasizing the roles of the environment and development in shaping behavior. Broader, very public debates and tensions over sociobiology, like those about the notion of evolution in studies of human ecology, reflected a growing polarization within scholarly communities. In some cases such debates, akin to more recent ones about the human genome project or the relevance of microbiological and chemical techniques to anthropological inquiries into human diversity, health, and paleoecology, produced deep institutional schisms in anthropology departments where physical and cultural anthropologists ceased to be housed in a single department. In others they strengthened anthropology as a field where apparently opposed approaches can coexist and receive critical attention within a single intellectual community and institutional home (Sahlins 1976). Such tensions within anthropology call to mind Geertz's assertion (2000, 90) of the four-field approach to anthropology as an ideology that has "held together an uncentered discipline of disparate visions, ill-connected researches, and improbable allies: a triumph, and a genuine one, of life over logic."[8]

Politicized tensions regarding the boundaries between natural and social science, or more biological and more cultural concerns, are not, however, limited to the academic institutions where anthropologists study. They abound, as well, in the professional and ecological sites where anthropologists and others work. Recent debates in the literature on environmental conservation have seen public intellectuals accuse international NGOs with environmental mandates of "going corporate" and losing sight of previous partnerships with indigenous peoples the world over (Doh and Teegen 2003). J. Peter Brosius (1999), in musings on the dual activist and analytical imperatives of new "environmental anthropologies," notes that an emerging complex of environmental management practices, with increasingly standardized methods and logics, does require that anthropologists act as advocates for indigenous peoples.

In their essay in this volume, Rebecca Hardin and Melissa Remis turn the ethnographic gaze on the interactions that characterize research in contexts of rapid environmental change. Their chapter describes the varying social roles researchers play in interacting with Central Africans and the transnational actors shaping forest use and monitoring in the Central African Republic (CAR). It suggests the hierarchies of gender and formal knowledge that can be reinforced or redressed through particular field-based practices such as training and collaboration across differently valued forms of expertise including animal tracking for data collection versus data entry and analysis. These hierarchies extend well beyond particular conservation sites, which makes anthropologists crucial mediators of resources, training, and mobility for forest residents. It raises a whole series of roles that anthropologists can inhabit but often attempt to transcend: broker, advocate, expert, evaluator, activist, and educator. All of these are useful in what we might characterize as control chains of surveillance, assessment, monitoring, and enforcement. These accompany the supply chains described by Tsing (2009), who writes of mushrooms traded in chains that reach from the forests of the Pacific Northwest into multiple markets worldwide.

Scholars writing in the tradition of environmental justice make such roles explicit, considering under what circumstances communities can forge effective alliances with experts or scientists. Barbara Allen's (2003) ethnography of Louisiana petrochemical corridors, where residents take up the question of pollution, illustrates how such alliances help keep industrial abuses in check. Melissa Checker's book *Polluted Promises* (2005) is another in this tradition. We can only suggest and hope that more such works will soon emerge in contexts beyond the United States, and in ways that deploy recent anthropological reflexivity, multisited methods, and emphasis on the transnational, to link postcolonial sites abroad with the industrial and postindustrial ones in North America. It is largely from these postcolonial contexts that environmental justice has arisen as a field that combines quantitative and qualitative work in novel ways. The boundaries between rural and urban, industrial and agrarian, and domestic and international are increasingly blurred by the consequential reach of phenomena such as global climate change (Crate and Nuttall 2009), the flows and afterlives of contaminants (Fortun 2001), or criminalized commodities such as exotic animals, which can bear pathogens and also be ciphers for anxiety about other forms of illegal trade—drugs or human trafficking, for instance.

New complexes of accountability, philanthropy, environmental assessment, and local governance emerge from decentralized governance practices as those mesh with transparency initiatives, in certification schemes that are at once ecological and social in their criteria (Hardin 2011). If these new practices sometimes steamroll previously diverse local ways of engaging with natural environments, they are also articulating local demands and providing various skills to local development and conservation "entrepreneurs" who seek access to increasing international flows of knowledge, skills, and financial support to biodiverse areas (for reflections on these ironies, see Hardin and Remis in the present volume). Tania Murray Li (2002) suggests that such strategic essentialisms are justified in cases where environmental change is proceeding rapidly and is accompanied by the increasing precariousness of rural livelihoods and political disenfranchisement of entire groups. She thus attempts to reduce the divide between scholarly analyses and more socially engaged work on such issues.

For new work to adequately address and reflect such issues, as they influence particular cultural and ecological contexts, more dialogue with those working in legal and medical anthropology will be essential (Baer 2008). Indeed a compellingly blurred boundary is that of crisis itself, as both a punctual phenomenon and a more protracted characteristic of our environmental and social era. Many anthropologists, however, are already engaged in elaborating such standardized practices. They merrily carry out the work of "capacity building" and "rapid appraisal" among "focus groups." Increasingly they are also engaged in what some are calling "disaster culture" whereby response to environmental extremes is increasingly intertwined with humanitarian relief work and with longer-term development and environmental planning processes (Baer and Singer 2009; Button 2010).

MEDICINE, HUMANITARIANISM, AND BIOPOLITICS

Severe circumstances such as storms, drought, or flood, combined with ongoing concern over deforestation, carbon sequestration, and containment of toxins, all foster the convergence of previously distinct legal, financial, and technical regimes: humanitarian aid, environmentally based advocacy, and basic development work seem increasingly interrelated, for example. New interventions for the healing and rebuilding of both individual bodies and communities in the wake of genocide, flood, drought, epidemic, or tidal waves (to name only a few such events) have far-reaching consequences (Young 1995; Farmer 2003). Indeed, the production of this volume was gradual and challenging as we tried to accommodate authors whose contributions were not completed in time, due to their commitments in the administration of institutions and programs as diverse as universities and crisis relief campaigns responding to the unimaginable suffering of Haitians after the earthquake that struck their country in early 2010.

Some scholars within anthropology are studying the history of humanitarianism (R. Wilson 2008). Many new works are attentive to the role of narrative in healing processes (Mattingly and Garro 2000) and to the new forms of social movement that spring from medicalized definitions of community (Staple 2004). Others consider the unintended political consequences of humanitarian intervention, as it contributes to particular forms of access to knowledge and care, and even to citizenship (Nguyen 2004; Ticktin 2006). In her foreword to this volume, Jennifer Staple describes continued engagement with anthropologists to build the organization Unite For Sight. She describes their roles in her own understanding of the challenges inherent in the largely volunteer forces providing basic health care among poor communities where various forms of social inequality and prejudice almost always constrain access and acceptance of biomedical services.

Many of these interactions are not captured in published literature and require a metaethnographic eye for how the field is evolving. For instance, Jim Yong Kim delivered a keynote speech at a recent Unite For Sight meeting that not only touted the clinical efficacy of treatments for multi-drug-resistant tuberculosis in poor communities but also targeted a structural bias in the institutional culture of global medicine that envisions poor patients as less treatable for complicated, chronic conditions. When we attended Unite For Sight meetings at Yale University in 2007 and 2010, we found many panels with undercurrents of continued bias by medical care providers against rural and urban poor populations as superstitious, skeptical of science and technology, and unable to maintain complex medical regiments. Yet many other panels featured structurally sensitive "applied" ethnographic practice in medical fields and reported on organizational and social dialogue with clinicians and their patients that constitute important positive, if imperfect counterweights to what Craig Calhoun (2004) has called the "emergency imaginary," as it enables incursions by state and other nonlocal actors into the spatial and social arrangements of rural populations. These incursions can be salutary, but also challenging regarding the sovereignty of groups and individuals.

Not just biopolitical changes that alter how people experience state and other institutions' control over or surveillance of their bodies but also biotechnological change that alters our ability to perceive, manipulate, or even create life forms beckons to ethnographers, who help make sense and meaning of such new frontiers in human economies of knowledge. As we develop gene therapies for many biological ailments and reckon with our capacity to clone human life, the boundaries of the biological and of human control over nonhuman worlds become redefined. Emerging frontiers of ethnographic knowledge include biosecurity, epigenetics, and related interfaces of capital, governance, and scientific process. Medical debates abound over the different cultural conceptions of life (Deacon 1997; Agamben 1998), death (Lock 2002; Mbembe 2003), the body (Scheper-Hughes and Wacquant 2002), race (Gilroy 2004; Fullwiley 2006), and fertility (Ginsburg and Rapp 1995; Inhorn and van Balen 2002).

Even as these dilemmas are catalyzing crosscutting work, the history of medicine is converging with the study of politics and history to flesh out a community of medical anthropologists who are not only documenting but theorizing such innovations and interactions (Hyde 2009). Further, the ways that individual actors use or refuse new medical technologies are being studied in ways that combine the study of gender, culture, and medicine (Birenbaum-Carmeli and Inhorn 2009). Marcia Inhorn's essay in this volume is concerned not only about dynamics of access to basic medical care and sanitation but also about the ways in which new technologies for enhancing human productive and reproductive lives are being defined, diffused, and driven by cultural desire and trends in social or actual human mobility. She reports on research on the global phenomenon of "reproductive tourism," with infertile couples crisscrossing the globe in pursuit of twenty-first-century, high-tech conception. At the same time, scholars are interrogating the cultural encounters through which botanical and ecological knowledge continues to become pharmaceutical knowledge, with its growing complement of legal and institutional tools for defining intellectual property (Hayden 2003; Osseo-Assare 2005).

These debates become bound up with the endeavor of ethnography in new ways, as medical and psychological applications of ethnography range from the training of medical practitioners in cultural sensitivity to trauma and stress (Good 1994) to the ethnography of social practice within both hospitals and laboratories

(Rabinow 1999). They are, of course, also relevant to the growing practice of managing trauma, both medical and emotional, from intractable conflicts described below as fronts where both exposure to direct violence and vulnerability to disease and stress-related immune system impairment can be seen, without inordinate exaggeration, as reaching epidemic proportions.

Ethnography and the Security State

An increasingly predominant use made of ethnography in the United States (though by no means "new" in the field of anthropology) is that by the military and intelligence communities. In the wake of the events at the World Trade Center on September 11, 2001, anthropologists are offering clearer understandings of the ideas and the realities of "terror" (Price 2002; Atran 2003; Gusterson 2003). With attention to the past, they are also exploring the Cold War roots of containing, controlling, and deploying anthropologists (Wax 2003; Price 2004). Christopher Varhola (2004) notes that as the boundaries between waging war and peacekeeping become less and less distinct, the skills and knowledge required are also changing and make cultural knowledge more important. Robert H. Scales Jr. (2004, 6) goes even further, reducing diplomacy to a sort of software that can be loaded into each soldier and arguing: "Every young soldier should receive cultural and language instruction, not to make every soldier a linguist but to make every soldier a diplomat with enough sensitivity and linguistic skills to understand and converse with the indigenous citizen on the street. . . . To assist in the acculturation process, the Department of Defense should be required to build databases that contain the religious and cultural norms for world populations—to identify the interests of the major parties, the cultural taboos—so soldiers can download the information quickly and use it profitably in the field."[9]

Perhaps Scales is aware that his suggestion of a database echoes the origins of the Human Relations Area Files, or HRAF. That collection was founded using Murdock's coding system in 1949, and during the year that we editors spent teaching together at Yale University it was still housed there, in a curiously gothic house a few blocks from campus, on a hill overlooking an affluent neighborhood. The HRAF included information generated for strategic purposes during World War II, but under the leadership of Marvin and Carol Ember it has been partially digitized and rendered more relevant to a range of pedagogical and research-related uses.[10]

Its origins, however, support David Price's (2002) suggestion of a cyclical (or at least recurring) aspect of ethnographic knowledge, as it is valued strategically during times of particular geopolitical transition. In addition, it speaks to the frontiers of knowledge that combine ethnographic insights, or some elements of them, with other knowledge forms—such as survey methods and even mathematical modeling—to develop complex analyses of global change (see, e.g., Downey and Dumit 1997; Boslough et al. 2004). There are also, of course, more intimately tactical deployments of ethnography in wartime, for which the political stakes are hotly contested (see Gill 2004; Rhode 2007).

Writing as Montgomery McFate (2005b), one Yale-trained anthropologist laments the fate of the HRAF files. She notes that the files were originally "established by the Carnegie Foundation, the Office of Naval Research, and the Rockefeller Foundation" to provide "information on Japanese-occupied former German territories of Micronesia. Although the database was maintained for decades after the war with Army, Navy, Air Force, and Central Intelligence Agency funds, U.S. Government agencies seeking 'an anthropological-level of knowledge' have sadly now forgotten its existence" (47). McFate has been a contentious figure in recent debates on blog and journal pages, where anthropologists are expressing concern about how and whether ethnography should engage security, intelligence, and counterinsurgency in contemporary wartime contexts. She participates almost performatively, but not without irony, in a web of ever-changing corporate firms, information flows, and assumed identities that, by their very functioning, pose particular challenges to the notion of sustained ethnographic engagement, as both a self and a scholar.[11]

Yet within Washington circles, as well as in her publications, McFate has consistently argued that ethnography is key to military uses in contemporary conflict situations primarily because of its capacity to limit casualties. In a piece called "Anthropology and Counterinsurgency" she goes so far as to suggest that the postmodern legacies we have so briefly reviewed here contribute to what is today a nearly wholesale rejection by anthropologists of any engagement with strategic or military interventions. But though much of poststructuralist and postmodern theoretical insight emerged in reaction against the abuses of science as racialized power in the massive-scale conflicts of World War II, they took shape and developed against a backdrop McFate herself summarizes as a shift in the postnuclear era in the meanings and modalities of war; away from large-scale global conflict toward "small wars" (2005a) and manipulative, politically complex, and increasingly covert operations.

Responses to her position that differ with her historical analysis of anthropology's legacies on these issues and spell out negative consequences of anthropological engagement in war and related forms of conflict have been formulated by individuals (Sluka 2010) and by groups of scholars, such as those who gathered at a 2008 workshop at the University of Chicago on "Anthropology and Global Counterinsurgency." At the same time, as the sense of political possibility in the United States shifted with the November 2008 presidential elections, anthropologists reassessed the stakes involved in collaboration with the U.S. government,[12] or what Lesley Gill (2004) has called "the security state."

Whatever the specific political landscape, the political economic forces that structure much scholarly work are encouraging collaboration beyond the academy, as participants considered in a March 2008 workshop, at the City University of New York, on "the diffusion of ethnography: new ideas of corporate collaboration." The latter linked the challenges of military anthropology with those of business anthropology, including a thicket of difficult issues about intellectual property, ethical obligations to employers versus informants, domains of research that are distinctly emphasized by either academic or corporate researchers, and so on.

Meanwhile, highly funded initiatives for the graduate training of scholars willing to serve on conflict fronts are being rolled out at rates that only raise the stakes in such pointed debates (Gusterson and Price 2005) and have resulted in pointed calls from various corners of the scientific and social-scientific community for the United States to reconsider the relationship between research and security or military operations. The processes of global integration and intensification of translocal connections that we take as our backdrop for the changing uses of ethnography have themselves conditioned the ethical and practical contexts within which anthropologists reflect on their work, and what uses should or could be made of it.

Such tensions surrounding anthropological engagement, whether with commercial, environmental, military, or legal sectors, are at the heart of our own effort to describe the ethnographic practices of today, just as they embody the contradictions of anthropology's legacies. Kamari Maxine Clarke's chapter for this volume contemplates the enormity of exposure to various forms of violence in sub-Saharan Africa, tracing the history of legal and institutional frameworks that govern flows of aid, both military and civilian, into that world region. Clarke offers a lucid, insightful discussion of the way anthropologists might think about precedents and personal issues involved in working beyond the walls of academe on some of the most pressing, oppressive issues confronting humanity today.

Further, she delves into the history of ethical debates within our field on such matters. The lamplit evenings alluded to previously between Gregory Bateson and Margaret Mead occurred in the wake of Bateson's operational work in the Office of Strategic Services (which preceded both the Central Intelligence Agency and U.S. Army Special Forces) in Asia. Much of Ruth Benedict's oeuvre resulted from a Department of Defense contract to do "remote ethnography" on our Axis adversaries during World War II, and Mead was also involved in research and publication on the home front to advance the war effort (McFate 2005a). That war was different from World War I in crucial respects due to the massive and methodical elimination of particular civilian populations; this harnessed notions of moral indignation about the violation of fundamental human rights to a national war effort and its relationship to Nazi Germany. It is partly thus that even students of the ardent pacifist Franz Boas came to participate and to develop an attendant reflexivity.

The American Anthropological Association (AAA) sanctioned Boas for his condemnation of anthropologists who contributed to the World War I effort. Debates over the past decade within the AAA about ethics in the field have revolved around the work of Napoleon Chagnon in the Amazon, and whether he and his colleagues might, wittingly or unwittingly, have exposed Amazonian forest dwellers to a strain of measles for which they had no resistance, thereby contributing to their decimation by disease. After having commissioned a detailed report on the wrongdoings of Chagnon and his team, AAA members voted by a relatively narrow margin to decommission the report, revealing the ambivalence in contemporary anthropologists' concern about our impacts on the communities, institutions, and traditions within which we work. In such times, the notion of a true "ivory tower" becomes especially seductive, even as it appears constantly to be receding before our eyes—or never to have truly existed.

Living Contemporary Ethnographic Challenges

Personally I do not find that any acrobatics are necessary to speak sometimes as an anthropologist within the anthropological field, sometimes as an anthropologist within other fields, such as those of politics and administration, and at most times not as an anthropologist at all. Misunderstandings and self-deception can alike be avoided by making clear not only in what capacity one is speaking but also in what field.

E. F. EVANS-PRITCHARD, "Applied Anthropology"

The critique of anthropology should not stop at its understanding of so-called "others," but should help show how, in any given instance, even "we" (however defined) are not who we think we are. It should insist on sustaining the project of anthropology as an epistemological critique of received categories, of their givens, and accept that this project involves the anthropologist in commonplace strategies of (partial and situated) estrangement and self-estrangement, objectification and self-objectification.

WEBB KEANE, "Self-Interpretation, Agency, and the Objects of Anthropology: Reflections on a Genealogy"

Sitting around a rustic dining table on a Michigan winter night with Webb Keane, Stuart Kirsch, Gillian Feeley-Harnik, and Anna Tsing, Hardin commented on the spicy Thai food. The conversation turned to the changes in one's own tastes and gestures that can occur during ethnographic research. Can one become a different person in the field, with different likes and dislikes? Someone had asked the question half-jokingly. A colleague in linguistics, also at the table, spurred us on: "What do you mean? You are in a different context, but you are still the same self." We bracketed any discussion of the social theories of multiple selves and spoke simply about our own experiences as sensory selves. How is it, Tsing wondered aloud, that the durian fruits offered to her in Indonesia could seem to smell putrid at first, but within weeks they would elicit a response of craving and satisfaction at their flavor and odor? How could one's body language suddenly become—whether unconsciously or self-consciously—more humble, the incline of one's head slightly shifted in relation to one's gait when in the market-place? What embodied, experiential, emotional, communicative, ontological trans-formations occur in us as we move across geographical and cultural boundaries, and what imprints do such changes leave in our minds, bodies, and ways of speaking, sitting, sleeping . . . teaching?

Today, the theoretical tools of reflexivity help ethnographers make sense of such questions, with respect not only to power relations but also to the ontological fragmentation and transformation that can occur in immersion experiences, high-lighting the fragile notion of a unitary self. Immersion experiences have come to include those of the virtual world, ever extending with Internet increasingly avail-able on laptop computers and handheld instruments such as smartphones. Such notions, ever new, of the world that we come to understand as "the real" can both enrich and potentially impoverish our work. As with debates about war, or un-witting impacts of our presence on the communities where we work, a concern about violence suffuses our musings. This can be true whether we wonder about avatars or actual communities whose experiences with violence and connections with each other are mediated by new technologies (see, e.g., Axel's [2001] discussion of Sikh websites or Boellstorff's [2008] ethnography of the online world "Second Life").

Today also, rather than worry (or in addition to worrying) about boundaries of geographical discovery, difference, and erotic desire, we wonder at the extent to which they connect with particular forms of violence that appear to be embedded in our ways of being variously modern: mass murder; alienation and abuse, both of humans and animals; environmental damage on scales difficult to imagine and accurately track. Michael Taussig's *Shamanism, Colonialism, and the Wild Man* (1986) coins the concept of a thoroughly transnational "culture of terror," theorized with regard to both the politics of representation and the political economies of precolonial, colonial, and postcolonial contexts.

We are witnessing a mix of new fears, such as those mentioned here, and old complexes for the making of war and military technology (see Gusterson 2004). These become increasingly enmeshed with growing networks for service provision, communication, and biomedical, faith-based, or development-sector interventions across national lines. These intertwined arenas each entail close attention to and transformation of "institutional cultures" within U.S. organizations. For the Department of Defense such internal transformations, conceived in cultural terms, are a crucial condition for the improvement of joint operations with forces from other nations and traditions. In the corporate world the same could be said with respect to success in joint ventures; in the environmental management field, for decentralized, community-based monitoring of natural resource use on the one hand, and ever-vaster and more expertly managed networks of protected areas on the other; in the biomedical world, for the tracking and treatment of disease with newly developed drugs in ways that themselves become constitutive of epidemiological outcomes (Petryna, Lakoff, and Kleinman 2006). In the present volume, we are less curious about whether ethnography might enhance any of these processes (clearly, it has already been called upon to do so) than about the depth of involvement in them that may be a precondition for—or preclude—the anthropologist's critical engagement and experiential journey toward the production and transmission of knowledge.

Also important to those represented in this volume are the incremental adjustments to the anthropological craft that we have fashioned from the work of our predecessors and interlocutors. Despite transnational and institutional shifts in the "objects" and modalities of study (Firth 1981), ethnography today is not unlike the ethnography of Boas's time: conducted against a backdrop of previously unprecedented global integration and tensions, it involves the constant relating of context to content (of intimacy to estrangement). What can and should be ethnography's place—or places, as Evans-Pritchard and Keane (several anthropological generations apart in their observations) remind us—in this proliferation of pathways across human cultures?

There can be no single "next step" for a field so intimately engaged, in fact, with many contemporary frontiers of knowledge production. We find ourselves writing in the hope that steps "into the field" be taken into an increasing number of contexts by ethnographers from increasingly diverse backgrounds (Burawoy 2000; Burawoy et al. 1991). Acknowledging as we have here how many different versions of anthropology's history are valid, and how important it is to refresh our memories about conflicts at every turn in our field's past, it nonetheless seems appropriate to hope that steps into new fields be taken less and less in the footsteps of our more troublesome nineteenth-century antecedents (Herbert 1991; Trouillot 2003). Rather, we should struggle to reclaim the most powerful and positive contributions made by our predecessors (Mintz, present volume), for they are instructive pedagogical legacies of the modernity of knowledge today. Further, we should work to ensure that such steps reflect more of a comparative perspective (Gingrich and Fox 2002), as well as new combinations of anthropology's own subfields and inventive interstices between or across those fields (Hardin and Remis, present volume); that they embrace new global sites for the production of contemporary and future anthropological thought (Ribeiro and Escobar 2006); and that people be trained to take them both within and beyond the confines of the academy (M. C. Bateson, and Marcus, present volume). All of these things are crucial to the future of ethnography and emerge from its unique heritage.

The sustained study of relationships among humans will continue to be vital to the elaboration of human connections, and of human relationships to worlds beyond those conventionally defined as human. Overly restrictive notions of a common anthropological legacy could fetter expansive new ethnographic practices. This is because we are working in a climate of rapidly restructured conditions of sociopolitical action (Appadurai 2002) and human labor—both within the academy and without. Crucial changes include the rise in what Marilyn Strathern (2000) calls "audit" related logics and practices, the rise in scope and power of particular review processes regarding human subjects work, and the constraining effects of recent legislation in the interest of national security (Cole 2003).[13] Under such circumstances, consideration of the challenges and constitutive contradictions of the field's past can shed crucial light on contemporary "appropriations" and expansions of ethnography, both as a set of methods and as conceptual toolkits regarding culture, power, meaning, and practice.

We consider here only a few of these axes of appropriation: corporate social practice, environmental management, medical practices across cultural contexts, legal scholarship, and the new "cultures" of war. Each of these examples shows us how ethnographers are internalizing new conventions in and criteria for their work, even as that work is affecting complex processes of change. However, there are many more arenas in which ethnography is securing its place, such as in studies of sustainable development, emerging modes of travel and tourism, education (Demerath 2009), or the media (see Ginsburg, Abu-Lughod, and Larkin 2002; Shryock 2004, 50). Many who hold highly specific intellectual debate dear feel somewhat embattled by what might be termed an ongoing and intensifying "banalization" of ethnography. It is true that the lexicon that anthropology offers, at its most specialized, is crucial to critical thinking and rethinking relationships of power, knowledge, and meaning. Yet, to over-isolate separate streams or axes of anthropological work from one another—emphasizing the distinctions between applied and basic work, between more cultural and political phenomena, or between theoretical and ethnographic writing—risks rendering less visible the relationships among new valences for concepts of "culture" and the ways in which power relations, political economic situations, and popular meanings are coming into realignment. It also risks rendering anthropological pasts even less relevant to undergraduate and graduate students of anthropology, as well as to others who are, for widely ranging reasons, increasingly involved in crafting anthropology's future. The conversations and experiments captured here convey a continued (and continually contested) notion of ethnography as a lived intellectual practice of engagement with power—even that of dominant anthropological narratives themselves.

NOTES

1. Rebecca Hardin teaches in the School of Natural Resources and Environment and the Department of Anthropology at the University of Michigan. She previously occupied a joint appointment in the Department of Anthropology and the School of Environment at McGill University in Montréal, Canada, and her dissertation committee comprised faculty from Yale's School of Forestry and Environmental Studies as well as Yale's Department of Anthropology and Department of History. While on research leave from McGill and Michigan, she has been a fellow in the Harvard Academy for International and Area Studies and has taken courses in Harvard's Department of Visual and Environmental Studies. Kamari Clarke teaches in the Department of Anthropology at Yale University. She has studied law at the Yale Law School and holds a courtesy appointment there. While on sabbatical leave during 2005-6 at York University in Toronto, Canada, she spent her time both in the Department of Anthropology and in libraries at Osgoode Hall Law School.

2. Notes from the fourteenth annual meeting of the International Congress of Anthropological and Ethnological Sciences (Williamsburg, VA, July 26–August 1, 1998) suggest that the new "global anthropology" can emerge from a network of semi-independent "local anthropologies" that were formerly "divided-and-ruled" by the "metropolitan anthropology"; see IGNCA (1998). The Project for a World Anthropology/ies Network (WAN), as one example of such initiatives, includes scholars from the United States (Chapel Hill), Brazil (Brasília), the United Kingdom (Manchester), and Colombia (Bogotá).

3. An example is the work of Ruth Behar (1993), much of which has been included in fiction anthologies, produced for the stage, and incorporated into her own film work.

4. For a well-researched journalistic account of Boas's legacy, see Pierpont (2004).

5. Bateson, for instance, wrote of both *ethos* (the affective–emotional emphases of a culture) and *eidos* (the cognitive processes of a culture) as subdivisions of Benedict's "configuration" (G. Bateson 1958, 32).

6. Appearing two years before Michaela di Leonardo's *Gender at the Crossroads of Knowledge* (1991), and nearly ten years before Mariniello and Bové's *Gendered Agents* (1998), the book gained a wide readership beyond the field of anthropology. There had been earlier works on gender in anthropology, of course (Reiter 1975; Martin Shaw 1980; Bell 1983; Moore 1988).

7. Martin G. Carver, CEO of the Fortune 500 company Bandag, Inc., mentioned to Rebecca Hardin his reading of Collins and its impact on his "deep change" campaign within his company. See Bandag (2004).

8. On the four-field approach, see Segal and Yanagisako 2005.

9. Scales elaborates: Soldiers who spend time overseas immersed in foreign cultures—particularly those most likely to become engaged in conflicts of strategic importance to the United States—should be rewarded for their efforts. At the heart of a cultural-centric approach to future war should be a cadre of global scouts, well educated, with a penchant for languages and a comfort with strange and distant places. These soldiers should be given time to absorb a single culture and to establish trust with those willing to trust them (2004, 3).

10. For further information on the HRAF see http://www.yale.edu/hraf/.

11. McFate's apparent multiple identities emerged from entanglements with those of her former husband's family; see Ridgeway, Schulman, and Corn 2008.

12. Thanks to James Brooks for his insights on this mutability, in the wake of a summer 2008 workshop on military anthropology at the School of Advanced Research in Santa Fe, New Mexico.

13. For an interesting overall look at academic life, see the "auto-ethnography" by Anne Meneley and Donna J. Young (2005); for a collection of reflections on changing practices regarding human subjects research, see the special issue of *American Ethnologist*, February 2007.

Part 1

Living and Teaching Ethnography

Participant Observation as a Way of Living

MARY CATHERINE BATESON

This talk was given to an interesting mixed group: students from various fields, including a number of anthropology majors; some faculty; and at least one family accompanied by their daughter who was considering coming to Yale. Although in its written form it is most likely to be read by anthropologists, I would like readers to imagine that it was directed to that family because it deals with the larger question of what anthropology contributes to education today, not so much in terms of information but in terms of preparation for lifelong learning. Interestingly, the visiting parents were journalists and commented from that background on the issue of objectivity.

When I was at college in the 1950s, students who weren't really sure what they wanted to do but wanted a major that would enrich their understanding of life, whatever they might encounter, chose English as their major. English was the prototypical major for those who were undecided but wanted to be educated and wanted to grow through their studies. Literature stimulated the imagination and exposed students to many different kinds of experience, especially after the effort to go beyond the traditional canon and actually include the experiences of women and people of color. Inevitably, some of those students became English professors, and some of them became writers or editors, but many others went on to do very different things. In the 1960s sociology became an important major, with anthropology growing on its coattails; following that, however, there was an upsurge in vocational or prevocational emphases such as economics in choosing majors.

Before talking about the context for choosing a major today, I want to comment on the vocational and prevocational emphasis, which is still very much with us, even where there is a strong liberal arts tradition. I see the emphasis on choosing majors for practical reasons as connected with changed methods of financing undergraduate education, since a very large proportion of graduates have been receiving substantial student loans that they have to worry about beginning to pay off. The students who marched and protested in the 1960s had neither the benefit nor the burden of modern financial aid packages. We are living in a society where debt of all sorts is both a convenient way of life and a major form of social control, though not so crude as the old debt servitude of the "company store." Debt promotes short-term thinking—for students, an emphasis on the first job—but the choice of a major should be informed by a whole life ahead. Changes in life expectancy combine with accelerating cultural and technological change and globalization to demand lifelong learning and a higher and more sustained level of flexibility and tolerance for ambiguity than ever before.

I think one can argue that in the world in which we live today, anthropology is a prime undergraduate major, not necessarily as preprofessional training but as a preparation for living in a complex, interconnected, multicultural world. Some anthropology majors will indeed become professional anthropologists, and of course a good department has to have the capacity to train professional anthropologists. But we need to resist the temptation to see our teaching primarily as a way to reproduce ourselves. I think we need to be reminded repeatedly of what our discipline has to offer to students who go on to other professions, some of which do not even have names yet.

By presenting information about very diverse human groups, past and present, anthropology offers an opportunity to expand one's sense of what it is to be human and therefore offers a certain kind of flexibility and adaptability, stretching the imagination, even more than literature. I like to think that exposure to the patterns of another culture offers the capacity for thinking "outside the box" of familiar assumptions. The "payoff" for that kind of breadth comes in adaptability five, ten, maybe forty years after graduation. Part of the analogy to a literature major is that encountering another culture is like exposure to a work of art, integrated, eloquent, and surprising, except that the masterpieces of living we encounter in anthropology are usually outside the Western canon.

The methodology of anthropology is at least as important here as the subject matter. Participant observation is often regarded as the primary method of anthropology, and as one of the range of methods of sociology. I want to make the case today that a consideration of what we mean by participant observation is illuminating for thinking about living and acting in a time of rapid social change, such as is going on all around us and all around the world. I hope that the things I say today about participant observation will be useful in thinking about what we do as anthropologists and also as skills to be transferred from professional activity to the rest of life.

I am going to start with a story about a pre-anthropologist: a story about me when I was about eight, growing up with parents both of whom were anthropologists of some distinction, Margaret Mead and Gregory Bateson. My mother took me to visit some friends who had a little boy, whom we'll call Bobby. Already at that age, I had learned that people often said, "I know you'll get along because he's just your age." Age, however, is not enough to automatically create friendship. (I have been following the variations on that theme all my life. When you live in a multicultural world, dealing with huge gaps of difference, it is important to remember that *similarity* is no guarantee of compatibility. When we were living in Iran, people used to invite us to dinner and then say, "We invited the Jones family; you will like them because they're Americans too." Oh dear. In the Philippines, however, people used to invite us with other Americans precisely because they knew we would not agree. Usually what they wanted was for me to have an argument about the Vietnam War that they'd enjoy immensely.)

My mother had something different in mind. "Bobby is your age," she said, "but his parents are kind of worried about him because he is having trouble getting along with the children at school, and I wonder how you will make out."

Bobby was definitely a problem. He was very difficult to play with, alternating between withdrawal and attack. Several hours later we left, and in the cab my mother asked, "Well, how did you make out with Bobby? What did you think of him?" I said, "Let's go home so I can dictate something about Bobby. I want to do that so if any other child ever has to play with a child like him, they'll know what to expect."

(I should explain; another tangent. You hear a lot nowadays about how important it is to read aloud to children and how it makes them readers. In the same way, taking dictation helps children of six or seven or eight become skillful writers, because it gives them the opportunity to observe the transition of their thoughts onto a page, at a time when—even if they've learned to write a bit—the mechanics of writing take so much attention that what they write is limited and frustrating. So dictation is a very useful thing for children to experience. I tended to treat my mother like a secretary, pacing up and down, and telling her where to put in parentheses.)

This is the earliest memory I can put my finger on of what it meant for me to have grown up in a household where the combination of participation and observation was the norm. In this particular case, the fact that my mother had essentially set the stage—that is, she had given me the idea that afterward she would ask about Bobby—launched me into an experience with this very difficult child that was satisfying rather than painful. With a conscious effort to observe and understand, I reframed an experience that would otherwise have been frustrating and uncomfortable. This effort could then be shared with others.

This is why I think anthropology is such a great thing to study: one learns to observe and participate at the same time. This is not just something that happens in the field, but something that is potentially pervasive in life and that is hugely helpful. You would not think it would be, but imagine yourself in a horrendous committee meeting. Even though people are behaving outrageously, you know you need to keep your temper and limit yourself to an occasional comment. So you sit back and take notes (not necessarily on paper); you not only observe but you also look for patterns in the general outrageousness and in your own reaction. Perhaps you notice a particular rhythm to the conversation, or undercurrents and alliances between particular people (often expressed in posture). Something that would be very boring or irritating suddenly becomes fascinating.

I recommend this approach when you are waiting for a bus, sitting in a committee meeting, or attending a dull dinner party—or, for that matter, a fascinating dinner party—as long as you don't forget to be present to other people, catch your bus, second a motion, or flirt with your neighbor. In other words, this is not a withdrawal or an escape but an additional, enhancing layer of experience, one that is a particular relief when the immediate experience itself is unsatisfactory, boring, or difficult, but is always enriching. Interestingly, although observation can reduce your discomfort in an unpleasant situation, it may increase your pleasure in a pleasant one.

Nevertheless, the concept of participant observation is a difficult one that elicits some resistance and ambivalence. When I wrote a memoir of my parents, I described my mother's approach to my birth and early childhood. She was approaching forty when I was born, which was late for an American woman at that time to have her first child, but she had been studying child rearing in other cultures for years. If you include adolescence in childhood, virtually all of her fieldwork before World War II focused on questions of when and how one becomes a member of a particular culture: When does a Thai become a Thai? When does an Iroquois become an Iroquois? And how? How does a human newborn learn not only to *behave like* a member of his or her culture but also to feel the emotions appropriate to a member of his or her culture and to respond to other people according to the patterns of that culture?

If you look at Margaret Mead's work, which I have been doing rather intensively because of her centennial in 2001, you see that her primary focus was on enculturation. The focus on women and sex roles (they did not use the word *gender* in those days the way we do now) was in a sense secondary to the focus on childhood. She tried to understand men and women as parents, as models, and as embodying certain traits valued by the culture. Gender was a question that came at her in many ways, since she grew up in a firmly feminist household, but I believe her interest arose from her interest in children. So naturally, when she had a real live baby of her own, she saw this as an opportunity to learn, observing the parent-child relationship even as she participated in it. At the same time, she saw this as an opportunity to apply some of what she had learned about child rearing around the world. In my memoir I described her note taking and the photographic lights set up ready in every room of the house, in case my parents spotted something in the course of their ongoing observation that they wanted to document. (I don't think that the observation did me any harm, but it may have been my good fortune that World War II intervened before I became quite as well documented as I might otherwise have been.)

When my memoir came out, it got a reaction that I had totally failed to anticipate. A lot of people read the passages about Margaret's use of child rearing techniques that she had learned from studying preliterate peoples—for example, breast-feeding, which educated, middle-class American women did not do in those days—and were scandalized. They were even more scandalized to realize that she was taking notes. She was not doing these things on the advice of the books, the doctors, or the experts, for at that time American doctors and experts were recommending bottle-feeding of formula on a strict schedule. It's hard to believe that today. In fact, I was the first breast-fed self-demand baby Benjamin Spock ever saw. I have to say here that I am incredibly grateful to have had a mother who had looked at enough different mothers and children around the world to understand the importance of breast-feeding. I wasn't taking notes, but she was. She thought that there were better choices, and it was surely an advantage to have someone really intelligent, with a lot of comparative knowledge, making the choices.

What amazed me was how many reviewers thought this was terrible. They thought that here was this poor baby being treated like a laboratory rat, and they were appalled. I believe that it is essential to understand that reaction, both for professional anthropologists and for anyone who wants the benefits of participant observation in living. After all, all parents observe the development of their children, moderating their behavior at least to some degree as a result of what they learn, for no number of books can prepare one for a particular infant who is different from day to day. You have to keep relearning the behavior of an infant, and parents try out new approaches, not because it would be interesting to experiment, but because they hope such approaches will work.

A *Newsweek* reviewer was particularly vehement, so I wrote to *Newsweek* and asked why anyone would believe that "love requires fuzzy-mindedness." It was the fact that she was *thinking* that was offensive, because she should have just been feeling—that would have been love. There is a widespread view that there is something antithetical between thought and emotion, and of course there is the old chestnut that mothers have an "instinct" that tells them how to care for a child. In fact, human parents have to learn how to care for children and do so differently in different places. William Blake once said that "a tear is an intellectual thing" and so is a laugh or a sigh. Emotion is in a real sense a form of cognition, and it is something that we can bring to consciousness and examine and think about.

When I talk about participant observation as a way of living, I am talking about participant observation as something we can do as parents, as lovers, and as patriots, in all the situations where we feel deeply and try to act sincerely. Indeed, I am talking about the possibility of being a participant observer in one's own illness and dying. Consider Robert Murphy's 1990 book *The Body Silent*, a study by an anthropologist of experiencing a degenerative disease that eventually led to his paralysis and death. He studied his own bodily process and emotional responses, the responses of people around him, and the social effects of disability. I feel sure that the decision to be a participant observer in his own dying helped to make even what was most awful something that he could accept and claim. Dying is serious business, and worth paying attention to. Writing about it was a contribution to the lives of others who may encounter the same kinds of suffering.

I tell the story of the *Newsweek* article because it is important to be aware that we have blocks or inhibitions to this way of being. Thinking too much is seen as cold, manipulative, and potentially destructive of authentic human relationships, but thinking made the difference for Murphy between being a helpless victim and someone engaged in a worthwhile task. What makes thinking repellent is our association of thought with objectivity and impersonality. Objectivity is a part of scientific ideology that suggests that observers can be accurate and scientific only if they have no emotional response or involvement, but I do not believe that complete objectivity is necessary or possible. I also believe that the illusion of objectivity is a form of self-deception that produces bad science.

Participant observation came to be regarded as the central methodology of anthropology in the context of the classic ethnographic situation, an anthropologist living in a village on an atoll or in an isolated mountain valley. The fact is that if you go and do that, living alone for a long period in an unfamiliar place, it is very hard to hang on to the notion of yourself as an objective observer. You cannot leave your emotions at home. You are not sitting behind a pane of glass or a one-way mirror; you are not dissecting dead amphibians or juggling bloodless statistics. And generally you cannot go home at the end of the day and vent the emotions you have been feeling to a compatriot to whom they will make sense. Malinowski's diary was an embarrassment to many anthropologists because it revealed the fact that he felt loneliness and lust, as well as some distaste for the people he was studying—of course he did, for they were not the people for whom he was homesick.

Being a participant is sometimes explained as though it means only that the ethnographer is present and visible to the people he or she is studying, but it is always more. Though anthropologists have generally tried to make their participation as neutral as possible and tried to avoid influencing the behavior of the people around them, realistically, one cannot avoid influencing other people. Every question asked and every choice of whom to ask has an effect on the community. Maintaining an artificial distance also has an effect, making people dislike your company and inhibiting conversation. Inevitably you are an engaged participant, with likes and dislikes and the human desire to contribute in some way—even if only by providing comic relief. Inaction is an action. You are like someone studying plants growing, either watering them or not watering them, with consequences either way.

Anthropologists make a serious effort to suspend judgment in their research about customs and behaviors they do not fully understand, but this does not mean they do not have emotional reactions. I think that the illusion of objectivity dies relatively early for most anthropologists, but we have only recently begun to face that fact with a wave of introspective writing. You can sit in the field and be homesick and irritated and try to deny it and pretend it is not so. Or you can take your own reactions as part of the field work. To the extent that anthropologists or sociologists feel that they can conduct their research with no feedback between themselves and the people they are studying—no interaction and no subjective response that then affects the interaction—I believe it is an illusion. People struggle with objectivity in all sorts of contexts: journalists, judges, classroom teachers. One of the things that anthropology reminds us of is that we view everything through the lens of past learning and experience.

Clinicians sometimes speak of *disciplined subjectivity*, and this is my preferred way of addressing the objectivity issue. In recent years, anthropologists have elaborated a related stance in terms of *reflexivity* and self-observation. You cannot disregard your emotions or your responses to the people around you, but you can do your best to examine those responses, look at yourself as a participant, and learn from your own subjective experience. I still have a preference for the clinical term because I think sometimes reflexivity becomes so interesting that ethnographers give up on trying to learn about anything except their own emotions.

Anthropologists today no longer study what they once erroneously idealized as small, isolated, homogeneous, stable, and unchanging groups. No society is really homogeneous. Any society that you look at has some change and conflict. There have always been some outside influences, and at the moment these are

43

increasing, everywhere on the planet. Today, even on an isolated atoll, there are some people who know what anthropologists do and have a vague idea why. We still go into the field thousands of miles from home, but the people we study now at least have transistor radios and may well have computers and television; often they know a lot about human diversity and the customs in other places. At least a few of them are probably going to read any book that gets written about them. Even though they are geographically isolated, they have an awareness of their own culture as something that one can think about and study. It is not just the air that they breathe.

Furthermore, people are in the process of change everywhere. It used to be that ethnographers were sufficiently weird and exotic in some places so they did not get asked many questions. Today, you may think that you are going to get answers to your questions, but in many places in the world you find yourself being intensively interviewed, both out of curiosity and also as a source of comparative information. The people you hope to study are likely to think that you can provide information that will help in their next step of societal change, including access to resources. The illusion that you can avoid being an agent of change becomes a great deal harder as people ask more and more complicated questions than we were asked in the past, whether about disease prevention or how to start a school. The notion of participation and awareness of the responsibilities of the participant, and the need for an ethics related to that participation, have become much stronger. And in fact we are steadily rethinking the ethical issues around both action and inaction, not just professionally but at a societal level: Is there ever such a thing as an innocent bystander? When is active participation a right (for the disabled for instance)? When is it an obligation?

Now I want to take us back to our own society. I want to make the connection between participant observation as a model that we might borrow from the social sciences and lifelong learning. Notice that the observing ethnographer is an *adult who is learning* about another way of life. And the local people who interview the ethnographer about the American school system are also learning how to deal with change and how to be part of an interconnected world in various ways. Although it is important to defend the rights of indigenous peoples to preserve and defend their customs and ways of life, we also have an obligation to tell them what they want to know about the wider world. It should be their choice. And in most cases, they will want to engage to at least some degree. The ethnographer and the native are therefore both learning in their encounter, which is more nearly mutual than it was in the early years.

As a society, we have adopted lifelong learning as a mantra. PBS tells us to "stay curious." I have my own personal version, which I adopted a good while before CNN's motto, "you are what you know." I have been saying for quite a few years, "you are not what you know; you are what you are willing to learn." I think we sometimes forget how weird this emphasis on new learning in adulthood is. In most societies through human history, by the time people are old enough to bear children, they are pretty much competent in their cultures. There are probably kinds of specialized knowledge they don't have, but they probably do have more skills than they use. Very often people are not only competent in the skills of their sex, but they know about the other sex as well, and they have had the chance to observe a range of specialists. We are told that Eskimo women do not know how to build a snow house because of the division of labor. In fact, they do know how to build one in an emergency, but they just do not normally do so.

It is no wonder that with many years of refining that basic knowledge and supplementing it with the detail of specific events, most societies are in one way or another gerontocracies. Old people have authority so often because they really do know more than younger people, and often in old age both men and women are revered for their wisdom. But in our society it is not necessarily true that the old know more than the young. There are so many changes going on that it is hard to look up to someone who has not continued to learn, not necessarily by going to school or some other institution, but through experience and openness to new information, new ideas, even new ethical standards. As for being competent in one's own culture, we are all competent in parts of our culture, but there are huge areas that we do not know how to navigate, and new ones keep popping up; we have to live with the experience of incompetence and keep learning as we go along. When I was an undergraduate at Radcliffe, the president of Harvard used to welcome the graduates to "the company of educated men." We educated you, he seemed to imply; we did the job; it is complete. I am not sure that there is such a thing as an educated man or woman today in the sense that the job is complete.

In a very real sense, we are no longer the kind of society in which first you learn and then you do. It has never been quite like that, of course, but that has been a sort of ideal model: You go to school, you learn, you finish learning, and then you are an actor in the world. From being that kind of society, we have moved to a society where it is clear that nobody can claim to be an even moderately competent participant without learning steadily, remaining open even to the type of learning that represents really profound change. I would include psychotherapy in the range of learning here.

We are slowly realizing that much of what we do in schools dis-equips and dis-empowers children for learning after they leave. When they are in school, rather than suggesting to them that they should explore and find their own answers, it is all too often suggested that there is a fixed set of correct answers. What is slowly emerging, however, against all sorts of resistance from people who still have the old concept of education, is an increasing emphasis on learning by doing, because that is what people are going to have to do all their lives. If you replace the word *observer* with *learner*, broadening the modalities for taking in new ideas and information, you have *participant learner* as a description of all of us.

This represents a really complex change. Just as you cannot now think of learning as preceding participation, you cannot even think of participation and observation as running along in parallel, so closely are they intermingled. I have given you the example of a mother observing her child's development, and the example of me observing little Bobby, but we need further examples. For instance, you might be an applied anthropologist, going somewhere as part of a team that is concerned with the introduction of family planning in a community. If you have any sense at all, you know that you cannot go in as the outside expert, telling people how to run their family life. It just doesn't work. They will not accept what you say. You have to go, listen, look, and find out what they care about in family life and how decisions are made and who talks to whom about it, in order to learn how to couch your message. The process of learning is already a form of participation and already setting the tone for the actions you will take later. Even though the two continue to happen simultaneously, the processes are intermingled rather than being two separate streams flowing side by side.

In the reflexive model, I can be observing three things: I'm observing myself, and I'm observing the system I'm looking at, and I'm observing the larger metasystem in which both of those are linked. Is the participation conceptualized as part of the observation, or is the observation part of the participation? At what level of systemic organization am I aware of the pattern of what is going on? It gets very tricky. Of course we recognize the risk of people who think they are doing good without thinking about the nature of the system in which they are interfering. But this is insufficient. I would argue the need to understand the metasystem and the impossibility of doing that without *self*-awareness. Thus, agricultural extension workers need to understand the ways in which their own advice (and employment) is influenced by the economics of agriculture and the way farmers experience their choices, as well as the effect of adding various kinds of products and chemicals to the local ecosystem.

What does it mean when a school child, for instance, becomes an observer of the system represented by the school and the classroom? This is not something that teachers would necessarily want to encourage, and yet it creates the possibility of a very important type of consciousness as an alternative to alienation. At what point does a third grader (a child of the age at which I met Bobby), dealing with the stress of being in school, become able to say, "All right, I'm going to observe this system consciously and figure it out, and then I will be able to cope without having to buy in to all of it." Participant observation involves thinking at more than one logical level. This is something that we do more in college than in school, but not enough. Students are more likely to turn away from instructors and disciplines with which they disagree rather than observing and attempting to contextualize and relativize what they see and hear.

I was thinking the other day about such English stories for children as C. S. Lewis's book *The Lion, the Witch, and the Wardrobe*. There is a benevolent uncle in the story who periodically asks rhetorically in the presence of the children, "What *do* they teach these children in school?" He keeps giving them the message that school offers an oversimplified vision of a complicated world, and that when they are in school they should be critics of the school. I remember my father (who was English) saying approximately the same thing, which gave me license to question and be critical.

This seems to me to be the most important lesson to be gained from studying anthropology: awareness of the possibility of lifelong learning as both an observer and a participant. If you are in the army, you should be critics and observers of the structure of the military. When you are voting, you should be engaged and passionate but also analytical, not only about the candidates but also about the larger system in which you are one of many actors. In a sense, we should all be functioning all the time at multiple levels. And when those levels feel contradictory, we need to notice and think about the contradictions. Anthropology depends on doing this, legitimates it, and offers the opportunity to acquire it as a skill that will be more and more important as we move into an uncertain future.

Discussion Questions with
Mary Catherine Bateson

MARY CATHERINE BATESON: Professor Hardin's comments after the talk touched on the different legacies of Mead and Bateson and the circumstances of their connection to one another across training traditions in anthropology. Some of those points are summarized in the introduction to this volume; they stand as an invitation to compare my parents.

One of the advantages of moving away from simplistic notions of objectivity is the recognition that different observers will notice different things and participate in different ways. I think it is important not just to think in terms of separate theoretical streams in anthropology but also to understand that anthropologists have personalities and that the intellectual and emotional styles of fieldworkers will play out differently. It is interesting to me, looking at my parents, to notice the limits on their own self-knowledge. They had very different kinds of minds. They were both introspective and thoughtful, but they each had their particular blind spots. People see the world through lenses that develop over time, but the best corrective is to work as a member of a team, with complementary points of view. You try to discipline your subjectivity and to understand your own mental processes and observations, but there is only so much that you are going to succeed in seeing.

Gregory was exasperated by Margaret's interest in data, not numerical data, but in getting as many details and observations as possible. He was also exasperated by her activism and optimism because he, especially after the war, was profoundly pessimistic about virtually all actions. Although he was a participant, he did not think of himself as a participant most of the time. He met with patients as part of his research on psychiatry and on family communication, but he was reluctant to intervene to bring about change. Margaret, on the other hand, was in favor of social action and believed that things could be changed and improved. She was optimistic. He was terribly pessimistic.

Was this personality? National culture (English vs. American)? Intellectual tradition? Can we properly choose between them to say one was wrong and the other right? Or should we look at the work of these thinkers as complementary ways to see related phenomena, which is the way I tend to see it. I tend to be exasperated by theoretical debates because so often what the debaters are talking about are points of view that are actually supplementary to each other, not mutually exclusive.

Do I get exasperated at the excessive reflexivity that sometimes appears in anthropology? You bet. Partly because people act as if reflexivity were a brand-new idea, and I do not think that it is a new idea. I think that is one reason why I prefer the term *disciplined subjectivity*, which is an older phrase, for talking about it. Maybe if we realize that people need to think about themselves at least some of the time, we can get on with trying to produce some description going beyond that as well. Epistemologically, we know that, by definition, our descriptions are going to be incomplete and inaccurate and distorted, but they're still worth making and worth trying to improve.

ENRIQUE MAYER: I love the way you describe participation and observation as simultaneous. But I think that field notes are part of the observation process as well. You observe an event and plunge into the next one, but when do you dictate into your tape recorder? How does one gather the observations and organize them, right?

BATESON: I think that's the nub of the question, because if you think of yourself in life as learning along the way, there have to be times of stepping back and sorting out that learning. Everyone says experience is the best teacher. If experience is the best teacher, then most of us are lousy students because we don't take the step from experience to reflection, which may include recording, but I think it is even more key. The act of recording is often where the act of reflection takes place, but all too often it is skipped. This is one of the reasons why you should not be a 100 percent participant. You know, some people go home from the field without writing anything down and just have a few anecdotes.

I opened a book of mine called *Peripheral Visions* with a story that took place when I was present with my daughter at the sacrifice of a sheep on the Islamic Feast of Sacrifice. I included what she was seeing, what I was seeing, what it meant to the Iranian children, and what it meant to my daughter to see the Iranian children observing the sacrifice, so that she knew not to get upset about the sheep being killed in front of her. This happened in 1972, and for years I told the story as an interesting anecdote of my life in Iran. The truth is that I did not seriously reflect on it for more than ten years. Then at a certain point when I was thinking about the question of participant observation and reflexivity and multiple points of view, I suddenly realized that there were a dozen layers in that story, and I finally actually reflected on it. It took that long to go from an experience that might be amusing to tell about to actually reflecting on my experience, seriously getting the juice out of it. When you are in the field, you can set up a regular discipline of note taking or recording because you know you had better have some materials when you come back. But how do you keep the process of reflection on your observation going? That's where I think the conflict and strain actually come, as well as the illumination: thinking every day. How do you get on about the business of living? And what about when you're not in the field?

QUESTION FROM A PARENT OF A STUDENT: I found it fascinating as a journalist listening to you because of what my husband and I do for a living. Journalists have to strive to be totally honest and objective, and it's exactly the same sort of challenge.

(*Editor's note*: Here Mary Catherine Bateson smiled and nodded, noting that it was an "interesting comment." Afterward, she commented that she didn't want to get into a critique of journalism; however, Sid Mintz, in his talk and chapter in this volume, bravely ventures into that complicated set of issues, with humor and reflexivity about the similarities and differences between ethnographers and journalists.)

QUESTION FROM A STUDENT: I had never heard of participant observation before. Now that I have heard of it, and applied it to my own life, I realize that it has been in my consciousness since I was a small child. I realize that there is . . . not a tremendous amount of guilt, . . . but questioning whether there was a certain amount of two-facedness, or a desire to distance oneself from normal experiences, by having a hyper-experience. Hearing you talk about it, I wonder if there was something wrong with it. Because you are living two lives and interacting with people on one level, but criticizing and analyzing on another level. How do you explain to people that it is a way of living?

BATESON: First of all, I try to make people aware that this is a possibility, and it is enriching, and that we are inhibited about it. I think there are a lot of cultural components to that inhibition. Having read some of the psychoanalytic literature, I also think that over-intellectualizing can be a defense because you go around in circles. But I think that the more you can let yourself see and hear and reflect and think and look for patterns, really the richer and more compassionate a human being you can be. Compassion does involve knowledge; it involves a relationship of knowing, knowledge that connects rather than knowledge for the sake of control. How can that be a bad thing?

REBECCA HARDIN: You write about that in *Composing a Life*, which I like a lot on that front, because of the very personal register of that book. At the same time that it talks about anthropology, it says how much the capacity to create innovative and integrative roles depends on exposure to another culture. The idea that one could study one's own culture, truly attending to it, rather than using the stance of an observer to dominate is a really interesting distinction and a really hard one to get right, as work by George Marcus and colleagues made clear, in their formulation of "anthropology as cultural critique." One ends up thinking seriously about one's own personality and dealing with issues of loyalty and respect, I think . . .

Loveless
in the Boondocks

Anthropology at Bay

SIDNEY MINTZ

Though it is always possible to trump up a story retrospectively, I cannot confidently explain why I became an anthropologist. Now that I am at the end of my career, I think harder about how the choice was made when alternatives seemed to beckon. Thinking this way has obliged me to think as well about the profession I entered.

By many measures, anthropology is an odd line of work. As those among you who are anthropologists know, in the United States it is at least four different lines of work. And though they overlap importantly—more than is now generally acknowledged or even recognized—they really are different: physical anthropology, archaeology, linguistics, and cultural anthropology, or ethnology. This fourfold division is traceable to the early decades of anthropology as a profession in this country, at the start of the century just ended. Though there were North American anthropologists well before 1900, including at least one brilliant autodidact, Lewis Henry Morgan, the professionalization of anthropology as a discipline in the United States really began only after the Columbian Exposition of 1893.

Cultural anthropology found its raison d'être in a profound division that was widely seen to typify the world's peoples. This division had to do, it was thought, with the differences between what were called, on the one hand, *civilized* peoples and, on the other, *primitive* peoples. We need waste no energy taking pleasure in how much smarter *we* are now about those imagined differences than others were then. But such differences were not, in fact, altogether imaginary. The societies of the so-called primitive peoples were typically small, non-Western, highly localized, nonliterate, non-machine-in-technology, relatively unstratified, and both integrated and divided by ties of blood and kinship. Of course, those societies were many other things, too. But they were not Western, or big, or literate, or based on machines, or prodigal in consumption of fossil fuels, or urban, or anonymous in their social relations; and their economic systems were qualitatively different from our own.

That is not to say that they were altogether like each other, either; there is no need to reduce the so-called primitive world to a sample of one, any more than for capitalist society, which clearly takes on a different character in different cultures. Nor does this mean that the ethnographic portraits that we were given of these societies by our predecessors are complete or correct in every detail, or that the societies were frozen in time, unchanged and unchanging. Yet it can be argued that they were in important ways more like each other than like, say, U.S. society, or British society, or Japanese society of that time.

It was in studying these societies that our anthropology, anthropology as a profession, took shape—when people, mostly male, from the white Western capitalist world went somewhere else, to a somewhere else that was distinguished by being what the West was not. What anthropologists did when they got there was called fieldwork. Its practice was ethnography, the method of cultural anthropology, and it became highly prized. The British anthropologist C. G. Seligman was not merely joking when he said that "field research in anthropology is what the blood of the martyrs is to the Church" (Stocking 1996, 115). A romanticism with which anthropology has always been affected gave special, near-mystical power to the words *the field*. It was in so-called primitive societies that this first happened.

Ethnography addressed societies such as those for good reasons. It has been remarked that ethnographers were sometimes incorrigible romantics, sometimes servants of imperialism, and often egotistical; but none of those things really explains where they went. As Alfred Louis Kroeber was to write, anthropology specialized in studying "primitive" peoples because no other field took them seriously. But he also made clear that anthropology never intended to study *only* such people; it was a field worldwide in scope, interested in the most exotic in humankind, but also, as he put it, "equally [interested] in ourselves, here, now, at home" (Kroeber 1953, xiii).

Over time, what anthropology made understandable by means of ethnography was nothing less than a wholly different conception of humankind, shattering many Western preconceptions about the peoples who made up anthropology's subject matter. I cannot possibly stress sufficiently the importance of this achievement. But the fieldwork upon which the new views were based was usually humdrum and often tedious. It required resourcefulness and called for patient recording of everyday details. Only by the steady accumulation of such findings were the broadest and most profound meanings about our common humanity eventually realized.

Before such fieldwork was done, the world's vision of those so-called primitive societies was mostly contemptuous or fearful, based largely on myths, soldiers' stories, and the tall tales of traders and explorers. What ethnography uncovered was what daily life in those seemingly exotic societies was like. It turned out that the people in them worked intelligently and had to feed and clothe themselves; their food did not fall out of the trees into their laps. They had languages that were as complex as our own; their kinship groups were often more elaborate than our own; they had ideologies and religious systems, and like us, they kept themselves motivated through their distinctive philosophies. They were very different indeed from you and me in many ways; but they were just like us in many others. All this seems tiresomely familiar now. That is in grand measure thanks to the success of anthropology.

Anthropologists argued on the basis of their ethnographic findings that commercial instincts were in fact not instincts at all; that war was not inevitable; that monogamy was not "natural," any more than is polygamy, or any other such socially created form for setting up housekeeping; and that *human nature* is at best a slippery term, not to be used too nonchalantly. When Kroeber convincingly trashed Freud's speculations about the origins of the incest taboo, he did so using the results of ethnographic fieldwork. When Malinowski raised basic questions about Freud's Oedipus complex, he used his own fieldwork to do so. And anthropologists made what might be called philosophical observations, too, that were thought-provoking, at least for some. Perhaps humans should be valued not for what they have but for what they manage to do with what they have. The way *we* do things is our way, and the way we prefer, but it's not the *only* way, and not necessarily even an awfully good way, all of the time. Each human society is a kind of experiment, after all, and there have been thousands of such experiments. I think that it is difficult not to concede that each such experiment has some value just because it exists—because it is itself a human product, created over time by the ancestors of the people in it.

Such observations held a mirror up to ourselves, made us wonder—perhaps even instilled a bit of doubt in our assessment of the world—all of it much to the good, I believe. It made us recognize that each tiny society was itself a cultural product, possibly with an answer or two to a human problem that *we* had never thought of. The concept of culture, as anthropologists used it, developed largely out of such ethnographic learning. All human beings have culture; it's not a monopoly of those who have writing, or internal combustion machines, or Kleenex; and every social system and its values involve trade-offs. No society's perfect; each forgoes some things in order to have others. Cultures as constructed within analysts' brains are made up of patterns of behavior, but obviously not everybody in any such culture does things exactly the same way, and there are always some people who are deviant or eccentric or recalcitrant.

What the idea of culture provided, it still seems to me, was a useful way of thinking about our species and its social behavior; and anthropology had more to say than any other discipline about *how peoples on a group level are alike and how they differ*. It also had solid things to say about claims of differential racial intelligence; about the grounds for racial desegregation in the United States; and about religious and other rights for Native Americans. It was a source of ideas and of judgments affecting the way this country behaved and how it saw itself. During World War II, anthropologists like Benedict and Lesser, and ethnographers of the Pacific such as Oliver, did yeoman work for the armed forces, choosing sides because they thought our side was right—or anyway, righter than the other side. During the Vietnamese conflict, many anthropologists had insightful things to say about what was wrongheaded about that war, and their taking stands probably helped to end it—though probably not without cost to the profession. In looking carefully at daily life; in making a good case for public education; in defending the rights of groups who had no other defenders in academia and before the public, anthropology served the society of which it was a part.

And yet for several reasons many of those early achievements were called into question. First of all, societies of the sort ethnographers had first studied were changing radically and sometimes being destroyed. And when ethnographers persisted in such studies, they sometimes got into trouble.

Another reason that the status of ethnography declined was because critics decided its products were really literary and not scientific works. *Ethnographic authority*, as it came to be known, had to be stripped of its pretenses. In some ways this is obvious. As human beings studying other humans, anthropologists are denied the objectivity possible in a field such as physics or mathematics. Indeed, whether anthropology really can be a science is an ancient controversy, in some ways unanswerable. But many anthropologists were disoriented by the attacks on ethnography, which were engineered at first as attacks on ethnographers. Some practitioners are not quite sure where they should be going with what they do; others may not think it really much matters. In speaking of "anthropology at bay," it is to this uncertainty—*malaise*, even—that I mean to refer.

A third reason for self-doubt, perhaps, is that these days, particularly as more people travel to less conventional places, other vocations or professions or activities may increasingly be confused with the doing of anthropology. This source of doubt may be useful, though, if it enables me to specify more exactly what ethnographers do by comparing them with other visitors to far-off places. The list of look-alikes is long. But I take account here of only three kindred fields: tourism; a variety of journalism; and literature. Noting what such activities entail, in contrast to ethnography, may help us see its distinctive character more clearly. By *tourism* I mean what we all recognize as now more important than ever before: travel aimed at pleasure and at times enlightenment. The kind of journalism I have in mind arose particularly in relationship to television, and for that reason it carries with it the conviction that the meanings of spoken messages depend a lot upon their visual background. In contrast to that explanation, the writing of fiction is self-explanatory. Some tourists write fiction; now and then we learn to our apparent dismay that some journalists may write fiction, too. But I seek here to set these activities apart from each other.

I have a protagonist to represent each profession, and as luck would have it, all three have turned up in a lovely mountainous little nation to the south of the United States. It is not to be confused with Honduras or El Salvador, though. It's the sleepy little authoritarian republic of Mercenaria. By chance all have come to the same picturesque town, nestled in the smoky blue hills—the charming pueblo of San Juan de las Porquerías. The hills of San Juan are covered with those romantic shiny-leaved coffee bushes that have made Maxwell House, Folgers, and Starbucks so progressive and moneyed and rich and civic-minded and wealthy. And we—you and I—have fortunately landed there ourselves, just in time to catch our friends doing their respective things.

Behold, then, yon turquoise-and-silver-bedecked tourist, Ms. Yetta Samovar (with apologies to the late Max Shulman)—fresh from New York City's SoHo district, where she is gainfully employed, on her first trip south of the border. We come upon her as she sees her first wild parrot, swooping down screeching—the parrot, *not* Yetta—through the *flamboyán* trees! Yetta's daily trials, the birdlike beating of her heart, the experiences she is gathering in, the pictures her camera is seizing to carry off, the ethnic art—placemats, salad bowls, hangings, baskets, wallets, toothpicks, beer mats, scarves, rings, belts, *schmatas*, with which her bags are being filled—all are treasures with an important future. These material objects have to do with who Yetta is, what Yetta is becoming, and what Yetta can project herself as being, after her first trip to this darling, sunbathed, slightly fascistic country. All those folkloric materials are, in an intense and particular way, personal. Yetta is related to them forever: she dreamed of them, of having them, before she saw them; they will be part of her, even after she gives them away. They are she; and she—in even more ways than she can imagine—is they. She does not question them, spurn them, push them away, sneer at their lack of authenticity, in the manner of highly qualified, highly trained, highly snobbish anthropologists of a sort known to us all. She prizes them because she picked them, bargained for them, paid for them, accumulated them, has them. If they become presents, it will be she who gives them away. By giving these exotic objects from far away to someone who knows her, she becomes a larger and more exotic object herself.

Yetta's photography serves these same dimly perceived ends. Taking the picture is really *taking* it. Many unsuspecting friends and relatives are going to see the pictures, too; she and they will be different, after they have heard about the pictures while they are seeing the pictures. And so Yetta is in a continuous process of becoming, coming as she does from a country obsessed, even when sitting stuprous before TV screens, with a spirit of reform, self-improvement, and activity for its own sake. But let us leave Yetta for now, just as she discovers to her intense discomfiture that a bird as beautiful as that colorful and screeching parrot can *shit*— and do so in full flight. Poor Yetta has yet to find out that dry cleaning facilities in S. Juan de Porquerías do not match those in New York City.

But look, there is the well-known TV personality J.V. Neuborn. Who is he, you ask?—why, J.V. on horseback, yak, and camel, J.V. of the traveler's vest, the water bottle, the J.V. we *Yanquis* all know and love. He stands before the Cathedral of San Juan de Porquerías, awaiting a cue, while looking rather fiercely into the cameras. Scurrying natives, all engaged in the idiotic daily tasks in which scurrying natives are always engaged, serve, unawares, as an exotic background to J.V.'s famed knowledge. Actually, J.V. is not altogether comfortable here in Mercenaria, because local children, even though they still fear foreigners, do leap in the air in front of the cameras, waving and grimacing gaily, as J.V. explains to us this year's World Bank debt payment crisis in Mercenaria.

But J.V., even though of the same nationality as Yetta, perceives San Juan de Porquerías in a manner totally different from her. Exactly the way the experiences, objects, and feelings associated with the place are personal for Yetta, they are not personal for J.V. They do not have to do with who he is, or what he is, or with what he can project himself as becoming. Instead, whatever we notice about J.V. and his surroundings exists for him as we see him *in* it, as he alone delivers it to us. It is all background for what J.V. says, and that is how J.V. experiences it. J.V.'s view on Mercenaria's World Bank debt crisis is trite and superficial: there *is* a crisis, Mercenaria *must* ask for an extension, it's *serious*, *no one* knows what will happen (J.V.'s eyebrows furrow). But J.V.'s report would ring far more hollowly, were it not for the Cathedral and the scurrying natives, and J.V. knows it. If he had to deliver those lines in his living room with a sheet stretched behind him, the whole exercise might suddenly become ludicrous. In a figurative sense, J.V. has some difficulty distinguishing his vest from the Cathedral and the scurrying natives, because all of these things metamorphose into what he is, and what he will fight to the death to retain as his distinctive message, his package, his *self*.

56

Whereas we can watch Yetta becoming fuller of herself in San Juan, J.V. has for quite a long time now been very full indeed. This is striking because he is nearly always similarly inflated, no matter when we see him and listen to him, no matter where he is, and most importantly, no matter what he says. *He* certainly doesn't need any ethnographic authority. So while Yetta greedily soaks up Mercenaria, J.V. has a Gore-Tex defense against it—not just against Mercenaria, but against concrete daily reality everywhere, even at home. From J.V.'s perspective, New York City and San Juan de Porquerías really are the same, even if New York has better dry cleaning. Let J.V. notice just once where he is—let alone like it or dislike it—and what he thinks of as his own reportorial neutrality, *his* version of ethnographic authority, may be stripped from him forever.

But who is this, strolling reflectively down the cobblestone street in front of the cathedral and plaza, on his way from San Juan's best hotel to its only cybercafé for his morning coffee and daily reading of the *International Herald Tribune*? It's Ralph, Ralph Lugner. (Ralph also carries the local paper, *El Montón de Porquerías*, but actually he does not read Spanish.) Ralph will study the human condition, as he does each morning, from the gay open-air terrace of the café, figuratively immersing himself in the pullulating humanity that surges through the streets of San Juan. His somewhat rumpled white suit, the crushed fedora he wears, the expensive notebook he carries indolently under his arm together with his newspapers, all bespeak another more gracious age, as well as a smidgen of affectation. It is all lost on the busy folk of Porquerías, but who knows when the ghost of Augusto César Sandino, or even a live Tom Wolfe, might wander through the town, looking for a kindred spirit?

Yetta Samovar is a tourist; J.V. Neuborn a TV anchor; but Ralph Lugner is a *belle-lettriste*, a *littérateur*, a sojourner, a novelist, a feeling person, different from the rest of us, hewn from wood of a finer grain. Ralph has distinguished himself by an uncanny ability to inject into his books the very essence of life in a place like San Juan de Porquerías, and many other places like it, without ever learning a single word in any local language anywhere (except French). For Ralph, the data and experiences that his stay in Mercenaria have provided are different, yet again, from those of Yetta or J.V. Like Yetta, Ralph draws an intense personal yield from his experience in San Juan. But, of course, he recasts it as fantasy, in which form it becomes truer than fact, richly refracted by his considerable inventive gifts. Lots of people, on reading Ralph, say that he enables them to feel like the natives of whatever country he was imagining about at the time. They think it's absolutely uncanny how he can capture so well that *indigenous* feeling. And indeed it *is* uncanny; Ralph makes them feel like the natives, and more—he even helps them to think that they can tell what it feels like to *be* a native. It's sort of the way the old TV series *Mission Impossible* used to make viewers feel they could speak and understand Russian. With Ralph to help, those scurrying natives suddenly become as understandable as you or I—probably more so.

I cannot dwell for long on what the natives think of Ralph. The people at the hotel—waiters and so on—find it difficult to integrate his extremely affable manner with the fact that he is such a lousy tipper. Ralph, however, feels he has them psyched out just about perfectly. The people whom he observes from the coffee bar have no opinions of him at all, other than that he seems awfully silent, bleached looking, yet red faced. And those folks who have on one or another rare occasion been addressed by him in English—for example, the time he tried to buy an orange from a passing woman carrying about eighty pounds of them on her head—mostly just wish he'd go back where he came from. The bartender in the hotel does like Ralph, and Ralph thinks he likes *him*. Ralph tells him about baseball (though in fact he knows very little about baseball), has showed him how he makes a Martini, and tips him handsomely.

Et voilà our *dramatis personae*: a tourist, a TV anchorman, and a novelist. You can surely imagine them, despite the frailty of my powers of description. But what happens if to this motley array we add an ethnographer? With my question there enters the last and saddest of all the characters: Franz. I am sure that you know all about *this* character already—speaking Spanish poorly, carrying his ridiculous soiled canvas backpack and his stained and rumpled notebook, looking anxious, and having to go to the bathroom—it seems to him—just about all the time. Franz the ethnographer is interested in who picks coffee, how much they're paid, where the coffee gets washed, decorticated, and dried, who buys it from the growers, where it ends up, who finally drinks it, and what Starbucks and the consumers say about it.

Well, I tell you he's interested. But maybe it would be safer to say he *was* interested, or he is interested part of the time. Franz got money from a research foundation and also from some philanthropic capitalist who got him to San Juan in the first place. He feels kind of guilty about being so slow to find out any of the things he'd asserted in his application that he'd find out. He is also bored a lot of the time, partly because he's too cowardly to ask the right questions of the right people. And so he sort of does busy work, like copying his notes over, and sending e-mail messages to people he never wrote to much before, just to avoid asking those questions. And his teacher, who sold him on the screwy idea of coming to this weird place to study this dorky subject in the first place, is a terrible pain in the ass—and scary, too. Whenever Franz thinks someday he might have to explain to his teacher what he's actually been doing since he got to San Juan, he has to go to the bathroom again.

Franz suffers because to get answers, however imperfect, to any of the really exciting questions, he has to make something of a fool of himself—and he does. Do not underestimate the enormous importance of his willingness to do so. It is not shared by most tourists, TV anchors, or novelists known to me. Yet it is the rock upon which Franz's embryonic competence is built. Franz's spoken Spanish is poor at first; he knows little of local etiquette; and his eating habits differ considerably from those of the *porquereños*. No one really likes being a fool, and Franz lacks Yetta's insouciance because, he keeps telling himself, he's *supposed* to be an *expert*. Also like Yetta, though, he gets a terrific personal charge out of being in Mercenaria. But he's still not entirely sure what to make of it—of San Juan, of coffee, and most of all, of the people who are befriending him. They are baffling because he is discovering, somewhat to his surprise, that he really likes them, and they help him, even though he's pretty sure at times that they are laughing at him.

But Franz's difficulties are more serious than Yetta's, or J.V.'s, or Ralph's. That is because, unlike them, his work demands that he make a conscious, continuous effort to separate his feelings from his findings. Not like Yetta, who figuratively eats her findings and battens upon them. Not like J.V., who really has no findings, just a text he has to read without mispronouncing, while trying to remember to *look* a certain way. Not like Ralph, who profitably imagines all this stuff that then becomes his findings.

Franz's success will depend on what he himself really finds out; and he doesn't think he has found out anything yet. His Spanish is getting better, but it seems to him it is hardly improving at all. As often happens to people in such situations, he is underestimating himself. And who would not, using Malinowski and his own crazy teacher back home as his models? It is likely that in what Franz has read of theirs, both of them exaggerated shamelessly. And Franz worries, because he knows that some of what he will have to handle in the future is going to be even harder to deal with, and that some of the dilemmas he will face will prove unavoidable.

Franz is discovering that his learning is cumulative; that the best next questions emerge from what he has already learned and organized in his head; that how he behaves in relation to his hosts can determine how much more he will be trusted to be told, at least about some things—and that he himself enters into the data he is gathering, as he must. Because of what he is doing, in contrast to what my other characters are doing, trust operates very differently, and for none so importantly as for Franz.

J.V., Ralph, and Yetta may feel in fleeting moments that they are at the mercy of Mercenaria and the Mercenarians; Franz *knows* that he is, that in some ways he must be. Unlike J.V., in his efforts to ignore where he is; unlike Yetta, who is already wondering what Thailand will be like; unlike Ralph, who decided long ago that trying to figure out where one is may derail one's creative impulses—unlike all of them, Franz is in real trouble.

Unlike them, he *is* learning to speak the language, he *has* gotten to know some people; in spite of himself, perhaps, he *does* care about what happens there to the people he has come to know—and lastly, he is stuck there. Of course, not really for very long—but longer than J.V., or Yetta; and certainly much less comfortably than Ralph. Ralph's days are much alike and end with a drink, a good dinner, and a comfortable bed. Franz's days are each different, ending at different hours, under different circumstances, hardly ever with a good dinner, never with a comfortable bed. Some of those days are really hard, you might think painful. And yet, Franz is beginning to notice that some of those same difficult days now end with faint stirrings of joy and mastery, unfamiliar but genuine.

Perhaps Franz is most like Ralph, in the problems he faces. If it turns out that he is not a competent ethnographer, he may decide that Ralph has a better route to success. We ethnographers know that occasionally a Franz tries to be a Ralph. Occasionally one even succeeds in being a Ralph while pretending to be a Franz. But it's difficult. It takes brains, and gifted wordsmithery, and seizing opportunities. As with all specialized skills, even shoveling muck or shucking oysters, wanting to be good at it is never quite enough.

I trust that it is apparent to the reader that Yetta, J.V., Ralph, and Franz—all of them figments of my imagination—have nothing to do with the real world or the craft of ethnography. But perhaps they can help us in thinking about anthropology. Like Yetta, we ethnographers, at least at first, *are* tourists—or distinguishable from them mostly by our pretensions. Like J.V., we too may sometimes see the ongoing life around us mainly as background: for our personal dramas, for our eventual academic success, or for the specifics of our work. We have scenarios in mind; often they do not play out. On one or another occasion, in one or another place, each of us is likely to have said to himself, "Holy cow, I didn't have *this* in mind when I came here!" One hopes we do not, like J.V., see *all* of the field, including our fellow human beings, mainly as background; or our performance merely as performance. That is a different profession.

Like Ralph, we may be given to fantasy and artistic creation. If we are very gifted we may decide at one point to forgo the work of research in order to give full freedom to our inventive powers—the more candid among us may admit, though, that is hardly what the Canadian Research Council or some dead Swedish capitalist gave us money to do. But if one picks ethnography over tourism, journalism, and art—chooses, that is, to be Franz, rather than Yetta or J.V. or Ralph, why *choose* such a career?

One of the most difficult experiential aspects of our work is the loneliness of the field. Some of the more fortunate among us are spared it. So what follows in this connection may only reflect one ethnographer's experiences—and here I am speaking particularly to ethnographers. But if others recognize it, then the "why" of choosing ethnography becomes a useful question.

I suspect at least some anthropology students do not decide to *be ethnographers* until they have been in the field, felt the pain it can give them, and appreciated the thrill of finding things out. So perhaps we decide to be ethnographers out of pride; or perhaps from feelings of responsibility about those who trusted us enough to support our work; or maybe because what's back home for us is in its own way even more unmanageable or disagreeable than the field—or maybe for all of those reasons. But one also hopes that, at least for part of the time, it's because the ethnographer believes in what he or she is doing and is thrilled by doing it. Some at least of what is being found out has never been found out before.

Discussion Questions with Sidney Mintz

ENRIQUE MAYER: A brief observation—it used to be okay to write a play, as you just did, with other characters of the sort we were encountering in earlier times, such as the missionary, the trader, and the anthropologist. The world has changed greatly.

SIDNEY MINTZ: I think that the changes in the characters we choose for such games reflect how the world in which we anthropologists do our work has changed. The figures I have hinted at with my comments—such as tourists, television reporters, and novelists—now turn up more commonly in the same places that anthropologists do. At one time television reporters and novelists and tourists were not commonly to be found in the same foreign locales as we.

The significance of travel for people has changed, too. There was a time when one might encourage the best undergraduates to seek opportunities to travel—say, to Guatemala, or Colombia, or some such land. I clearly remember how excited students would become at the idea; their jaws would drop with awe and eagerness, just thinking about it. Now you ask a nine-year-old child if he has ever been to Milwaukee, and he tells you he has been to Katmandu. The grandeur of travel has lost much of its luster, and that loss may even be a small part of our crisis: doing fieldwork is no longer an enviable privilege.

Before we go to other questions, though, I'd like to turn back to Dr. Hardin's remarks on our not starting our field experience by embroiling ourselves in struggles over reflexivity, subjectivity, and objectivity. I heartily agree. I think some patience or, anyway, restraint in tackling such issues is a good idea. It's probably better to defer such questions, at least until we achieve modest comfort in the relevant language and are befriended by a couple of local people, who seem prepared to put up with us. If we get too preoccupied at the start with the relationship between collecting data and where we, as individuals, fit into its collection, we may find that our self-concerns actually get in the way—we don't want to end up upstaging, or outtalking, our informants.

Bringing ourselves as individuals into the fieldwork makes good sense on some grounds. In the book *Worker in the Cane*, the life history I recorded, I thought it was necessary to bring myself into the story, even though I felt unsure and even uncomfortable about it. But getting into the story is not, I think, a matter of simple awareness, or of shedding our disdain, or of acknowledging any contempt we may have for the Other, or of "being political." I think it is likely to be much more complicated and delicate a matter than that. One good reason for the ethnographer to lie low in the ethnography may be simply that he or she can get more done that way. I don't think that has even been discussed.

In her remarks, Dr. Hardin referred to that book, *Worker in the Cane*. I had indeed described it as the hardest one to write, because of the personal elements involved. I was very slow in finishing it. I had done the first fieldwork on it years before, and it was finally published in 1960. When it appeared, there were just a couple of serious reviews. A young assistant professor writing his first book—yet another first book, and social science at that—was not likely to get much attention. But a couple of reviewers wrote quite seriously that though they liked parts of it, there was a problem with the book: I knew and liked my informant, and that meant that the book could not be truly objective.

In those days, it was the buttered side of the bread to think of anthropology as a *science*. When in her presidential address for the AAA in 1948 Ruth Benedict talked about anthropology and the humanities and looked at anthropology as something more than only science, her critics said: "That's ridiculous, she's talking about art. Anthropology is about exactitude, prediction, empirical truths—not about art." The regnant view was that you, the scientist, took the informant and put him on a slide, adjusted the focus, and then looked down upon him, carefully. So reviewers who took *Worker in the Cane* seriously said that the book might have been okay, had there not been such a problem with transference and countertransference. I had, they wrote, failed to capitalize on what was called "stranger value"—the impartiality that comes from being a stranger—so to be able to maintain a proper scientific gaze. Though no one said it in so many words, the implication was that if I had not acted as if I liked my informants, then the book would have been more objective.

Now, I mentioned that the book came out in 1960; oddly, it has not been out of print ever since. What's more, there have been some references to it in recent writing—not many, but a few—because, with the passage of time, it has come back into view. My mother used to say that if you put all of your old clothes in a barrel and turn it upside down when it's full, you'll be back in style—that's sort of what happens when people begin to read your first book again. Some now say that it's a good book, but this time there is a different problem. Now I am a representative of the United States, the imperialist power; and my friend, Taso, the guy I was not supposed to admit that I liked, comes from an infamous colony of the imperialist power that I come from.

So back in 1960, I was unfortunately too friendly; and now I am unfortunately not friendly enough. But keep in mind that not a word has been changed in the course of fifty years—it is the same book. What has happened, of course, is that *anthropology* has changed. In those days one was supposed to be very lab-coated, parsimonious, impersonal, scientific; and I was not sufficiently so. Now one is urged to be in the picture, heart on one's sleeve, loving, perhaps feeling guilty, and never to impose upon one's informants—and I am not sufficiently so.

But of course this debate—if we wish to dignify it as such—is as old as the hills. Of course we must debate these issues, figure out what each of us should do about reflexivity and objectivity. But let's not forget our fieldwork while we are debating, or defer it until we have solved the philosophical problem.

KAMARI MAXINE CLARKE: I'm wondering if you can comment on the ways in which anthropology has changed. Does the discipline call for a particular type of ethnographic fieldwork that relates to both local and global methodology? Can you comment on what anthropology is and can offer?

MINTZ: A good issue. The field certainly is very different now, and probably some new skills are needed. But some things are much the same. Let me talk first about the ways in which anthropology remains the same, in my opinion, before hazarding some assertions about the ways that it may have become different.

I have on occasion, as many of us have, been dropped into places where I didn't know anybody and didn't know much of anything about the local culture. Under such socially meager circumstances, one has to use what wits one's got, in order to begin learning. But what one learns and whom one learns it from are linked; and each learning episode may be an opportunity to build ties with informants who are becoming friends.

Several times when I've been stuck briefly in some place of which I was wholly ignorant, I've tried when I could to bring some person with me who spoke the local language and to get into some farmer's backyard. Such a visit affords the opportunity to point to a cultivated plant and to ask what it is. "What is it used for?" The farmer tells me. "When do you plant it?" The spring. "How long does it grow?" Six months. "Does it ripen before you pick it, or can you also use it green?" Yes, to both. "How do you dry it?" And so on. With a bit of luck, I can initiate a half hour's conversation with the man.

Now, in all likelihood, this is a man who has never before been asked a question respectfully by a stranger about something that he knows. No one—no big shot, no foreigner, no bureaucrat, not even the local agronomist— has ever before asked him about something that he knows, and they don't know—except, maybe, "What's the way to the nearest bar?" For maybe the first time in his whole life, this grown man is being addressed as an equal, in terms of his capacity to know. And I've discovered that after such a conversation, I can do fieldwork with that man.

That has not changed. Respect for other human beings is the fundamental basis upon which anthropological fieldwork has to be done. Some have done it at the point of a bayonet, and yes—for certain kinds of information, that works. But it should be self-evident that gathering data, some of it personal, cannot really be done effectively without some chemistry of acceptance. And so, I'd argue that if you start with what I have just told you, you can do fieldwork. Of course, being able to initiate such a dialogue does not make the fieldwork any easier, perhaps particularly if you cannot tell a pumpkin from a lima bean. But it's a way to begin, and that has not changed.

But now, what has changed? Let me tell another anecdote. I went to an American university campus, not my own, to teach one semester. And the day I arrived, a graduate student arranged to see me, even though I had not yet unpacked my bags. She was leaving for the field that day, and she said that she had to speak with me. She was going to a country I knew and planning fieldwork in a community I knew. She wanted my opinion about what she was undertaking, and we talked about it. In the course of our talk, I casually asked her where she was going to live, meaning in whose house, or by renting, or howsoever. But she replied by mentioning a large city, quite far from where she was going to do the fieldwork. So I asked, "Why are you going to live there?" And she reacted with surprise, almost shock, and said well, she couldn't possibly live in the community. I said "Why not? There are five thousand people living there, why can't you live there?" She said she couldn't because it would be an imposition on the people. So I said: "Surely you have a boyfriend?" And she said yes. I said: "Do you ever have an argument with your boyfriend?" And she said yes. I said: "Why don't you give him up, so as not to be an imposition? Do you have a mother? Have you never imposed upon her? Are you going to have children? Do you mean you cannot have any social relations because they might be an imposition on some of the people you relate to?" You can see that the interview did not go well. But underneath all of the words, hers and also mine, the basis for the rationalization is important and poignant—it is fear.

Fieldwork is frightening—or anyway, for me fieldwork is frightening. I suspect many anthropologists, maybe most, feel the same way. You mean live in that place? Be there at night? Use that toilet? Eat out of those plates? And indeed it can be hard; sometimes it can even be disgusting. But fieldwork is like that; it is what we have, perhaps unsuspectingly, chosen to do. To gather our information we should be with those from whom we must learn. We are not supposed to live somewhere hours away and commute, from nine to five, to the place where our informants live and work. We do not learn enough that way; we're not there for what may happen after dark that way; we're not so likely to get to know anyone as well that way. Seeing someone at many different points during the day and night, at work and at leisure, with family members and alone—all this helps to cement the relationship and can serve to increase trust and friendship. All of this is obvious, and so obvious that it hardly bears saying—but the interview ended badly. These are only anecdotes; yet it may be that students have changed, as well as anthropology.

REBECCA HARDIN: Can I recount a story from our anthropology department that I think speaks to some of Kamari's question? I am remembering a colleague and friend in my year who did a dissertation on sex tourism in [a beach resort]. I remember one of our advisers saying to her, "Okay, the proposal looks great; I can see it's just an observation, a network of interviews; I can see how the networks analysis is going to work with these women. But what about the clients; aren't you going to have to talk to some of the clients?" And my friend said, "No way, those guys are disgusting. And I don't want to have anything to do with them." It's a largely northern European clientele, a growing trade connected to all kinds of agreements having to do with visa status, immigration for women who go to Amsterdam; it's connected to all types of capital, bodies, and lives. The fear took a different face—it has to do with confronting those global networks and building those into a methodology. But I wonder how much you see those kinds of fears shifting as the very themes, topics, and people with whom we work are shifting.

MINTZ: Please let me say two quite different things, one having to do with our vastly expanded "field," and the other with who currently works alongside us in it. I wrote two books that are directly linked, one might say, to sugar. One was the life history of my friend, published long ago. The other is a stab at a general history of sugar with relation to Europe, and it was published much more recently—about half as long ago as the first. A former student of mine suggested to me recently that those books were very different, as well as produced in quite different eras, one being a recounting of an individual's life-course, and the other the history of a global industry. That is true, I suppose; but they seem to me rather more as if they were the same book, the earlier coming to rest in some manner within the latter.

In my thesis, finished in 1951, I tried to write down in brief form the way that the Puerto Rican sugar industry had changed in the preceding century. A couple of years later, I recorded the life history of a friend in the same community where I'd lived earlier. It was only when I was preparing that manuscript for publication that I realized that my friend's life was a kind of detailed chiaroscuro for that earlier historical account. Both of those books had a global aspect, because both were about the world sugar industry. But whereas the globe was irrelevant to anthropology at the time of the first book, it had become quite fashionable by the second.

I submit that the recent stress on globalization has been oddly ahistorical, discounting or ignoring important global phenomena of past centuries. To be sure, globalization in earlier centuries was occurring at different speeds from what is unfolding today. Moreover, it was not recognized by contemporary observers as being what it was. And finally, it was ignored by anthropology. Indeed. In earlier centuries it was happening even before anthropology had been born. A global sugar agro-industry, for example, has almost exactly five centuries behind it, and it led to the largest forced migration—of enslaved Africans—in world history. Its beginnings predated anthropology by centuries. Yet leaving it out of discussions of globalization by dating globalization from the last century, or from the present, could be read as an unthinkingly racist oversight.

Discussions these days of what is being called multisited ethnography as an aspect of globalization might profitably point out how anthropologists could have studied the Irish labor organizers who were "barbadosed" to the West Indies during Cromwell's rule in the seventeenth century. Perhaps even more to the point, they might have studied the "kanakas" who were "black-birded" in the Pacific at the very time that Malinowski was studying the Trobriands. But they didn't, because that was not yet considered among anthropology's tasks. All the same, discussions of multisited ethnography could profitably take note of the African miners who circulated from villages to mining compounds and back again throughout Africa south of the Sahara, and who certainly *were* studied by anthropologists, not that long ago. And so yet again, different, yes; but also in important ways, still the same anthropology as before.

One of the things that we anthropologists must acknowledge is that TV reporters and writers are moving into the difficult, demanding, dangerous, and at times almost suicidal areas where anthropologists once were the principal outsiders. This is one of the ways that I think our field is slipping away from us. If one has read the monograph by Philippe Bourgois on a crack neighborhood in the Bronx, for example, one gets a sense of how dangerous fieldwork can be. It is emphatically not my contention that this something that every anthropologist can or should try to do. We're not talking about *machismo* or some other adolescent difficulty. If one cannot do a certain piece of fieldwork, or does not want to, one should not do it. But I do think that we have given ground to people outside of our discipline because we have not been willing to do some tasks that are difficult for different reasons, physical danger only being the extreme case. Fieldwork opportunities are passed over for many reasons, and not just because they are dangerous—which I regard as an entirely justifiable reason for not taking them on—but because they are unglamorous, tedious, or dirty, or require getting to know a few people really well, or because we must impose on people, or because the people do not live up to our preconceptions about them. Those are among the reasons that strike me as not quite so justifiable. They are also among the unjustified reasons—as opposed to the justified reasons—for becoming more reflexive.

Of course it is in some way easier to invent a reality than to experience one. But as you know, imaginative genius is not all that common. I poke fun at Ralph's prolific imagination, but it is something most of us lack. It plays an important role in what Ralph gives us. We are not all Ralphs, and we are not all going to be able to become Ralphs. But not doing well as Franz does not mean one has carte blanche to try being Ralph on the same fellowship.

My characterizations are caricature, of course. But I think it may be useful to keep the distinctions they stand for in mind, as we assess the ways that anthropology's obligations have changed. TV reporters, tourists, and novelists have different goals from us, and we from them—not better, or less good, but different. And as the world changes, it's true that we anthropologists need to change as well. For example, we are now called upon more often to gather data in short spurts of effort. Yet we do not know enough, we anthropologists, about how to create the kinds of relationship we once prized with people we're only going to see for short intervals of time. To the extent that our fieldwork now involves multisited ethnography—I have already suggested that the novelty of this challenge may be slightly oversold—we do have to learn better how to interview intensively and quickly. Most of us never learned that because we had the luxury of seeing the same people in the field, day after day. To some extent that luxury is now often out of reach. If you want to study West African tourist junk salesmen on Fifth Avenue, you must work differently with your informants.

I suspect that fieldwork is always confronting us with the unexpected. My own case is typical. I did fieldwork on markets in Haiti and devoted a good year and a half to that work. I thought that I was going to interview market women in the marketplaces. That was among the silliest ideas I ever had. Market women in the market are working; most of the time they do not want some dopey foreigner bothering them with dumb questions, posed in bad Creole. I learned that what I had to do was live in a community from which marketers came, so that I could be with them before they went to market, and could go to market with them, and return to the village with them—and then talk with them at some length, at their leisure. There is nothing very mysterious about this. But we cannot always predict how even quite simple issues may alter the ways in which we work.

These are, I guess, some of the things that we have to learn in contemporary ethnography. And then, one way or another, we have to cope with the extremely difficult ethical and political issues that arise when we do work in our own society. A wonderful article by Bob Adams, published in the *American Anthropologist* more than thirty years ago, confronts exactly that problem. What is entailed when our discipline comes home and has to deal with the issues taking shape around the corner, rather than on some far-off island? There are many such methodological and substantive issues that we have to engage, and I don't think we've gotten quite there yet.

QUESTION FROM A STUDENT: I was an undergraduate anthropology student and prepared for fieldwork in Kenya. I found that anthropology was a reciprocal way of learning, as I was understanding a particular culture; and simultaneously I was understanding about myself. But after arriving at my field site, I ended up deciding I didn't want to be in anthropology. I was not prepared to be so intrusive in an unfamiliar setting. So I ended up deciding to pursue medicine as a career, and in the interim, while trying to get into med school, I ended up volunteering in rural North Carolina. I feel like I have come full circle, because the tools that I learned as an anthropologist have been such an advantage to me, when dealing with patients, patient care, and patient contact. Medicine is a career where most people are fully removed from the patients and do not see them as brothers and sisters. I always reflect upon how grateful I am that I did have anthropology as a building block for understanding people in a different way, though it's not in Africa.

MINTZ: I think that is a very useful and insightful comment. It indicates another way in which we as anthropologists fall down on the job in explaining to people the benefits of our kind of training—in just the way that you have explained it. *We* should be doing that, as well as you. *We* should be telling people that. We do not seem able to address our lack of fit with the modern world effectively; and I think it is an anthropological problem, or better said, perhaps, a problem for anthropologists. We anthropologists do not seem to appreciate our strengths and accept uncritically the greater persuasiveness of others.

Ask yourself who runs foundations in this country. The answer? Political scientists run foundations in this country, not anthropologists. Anthropologists are above running foundations in this country, while political scientists are not above running foundations. Something of the same has to do with our concepts and our terminology. Political scientists now use our word *culture*, for example, which had, and still has, a meaning. Their term is *political culture*. I confess that I do not know what it means; but political scientists do. Or consider what peasants are, or were. We used to study peasants; but we don't study peasants any more. Now agrarian studies programs study peasants. We anthropologists have been writing books about how there are no more peasants. Meanwhile, agrarian studies programs continue to study the people whom we have apparently written out of existence. Everything we come up with, we give away or throw away. It is odd; I think that we give our ideas away not because we cannot explain them, but seemingly because we are above explaining them.

There was a time in the history of this discipline when people—ordinary people without anthropology degrees, without any degrees at all—could talk to anthropologists. Today too many anthropologists are more comfortable talking to each other. In some important manner, we have turned our backs on what we once were. I firmly believe that in terms of knowledge about us humans, anthropology gave to the world what nobody else had. Philosophers did not tell us that human beings were equal, the world around. Political scientists did not teach us that. We were there to speak out when desegregation was in the air. We taught people how other societies, technically much simpler than our own, coped with danger and death, raised brave and kind children, honored wisdom, did well with what they had. But those are apparently no longer the things that interest us, nor are we much interested in teaching them to others. And I think that's too bad. The fact that so few people can easily read and understand what we write is an enormous disappointment to our ancestors, in my opinion.

HARDIN: I wonder about your characterization of Yetta and Ralph. They were fairly balanced, but not really. You don't like these people.

MINTZ: You're right that I don't like *some* tourists and *some* novelists! After all, I wrote the piece. Guess where I got the idea that Franz has to go the bathroom all the time. I wrote those lines, and it is I that you are listening to. I believe that what I have done to Ralph, Ralph would do to me. But my liking or disliking my characters is not really the point. Ralph enjoys a different freedom from Franz in what he creates; he creates it in a manner very different from the way Franz will write a monograph. My point is the different methods, constraints, and goals of Ralph and Franz. Though I confess that I am inclined to admire Franz more for what his work entails, I may actually admire Ralph more for his creativity. The real point is the difference between their objectives and methods. As for Yetta, I do not really dislike her; I grudgingly admire her, even while making fun of her. I think that with her zeal and *Lebenslust*, she might easily become a good ethnographer, in fact—not snobbish, willing to socialize with others, energetic, fearless. But she has not been educated to realize that. She might benefit greatly from meeting an old-fashioned anthropologist, I think.

HARDIN: Is there a relationship between that and being too good to explain it to people, I wonder. If we think about if there is a desire to distinguish ourselves from tourists, from novelists, from TV reporters. Can that backfire?

MINTZ: That's an excellent point. But there are significant distinctions among us as working scholars. And there also must be a remembering—at least for the ethnographers—of the difference between our own petty and egotistical needs, on the one hand, and what the fieldwork that we undertake requires of us, on the other. There is nothing immoral about fear, nothing contemptible about shyness. It is by the manner in which we handle our own problems that we discover whether we are serious about anthropology. Honesty, above all with oneself, is fundamental, whatever we may construct theoretically with the idea of reflexivity. I am convinced that Redfield, Benedict, and many others knew they were not great ethnographers. But they were awfully good anthropologists, all the same, possibly in part by virtue of their honesty with themselves.

They are among our ancestors. We are in a profession, and we had predecessors. We living ethnographers, here and now, have invented very little. Anthropology, and the doing of fieldwork, has been around for quite a while; a lot of people have long been doing the fieldwork, in an honest way. Much of the time, they knew what they were doing. Franz Boas, to name one, knew what he was doing. In his autobiography, W. E. B. Du Bois recounts how he was teaching at Atlanta University, and in 1906 the commencement speaker was this little Jewish fellow from New York, this weird little guy named Franz Boas. Boas came down to Atlanta and said that African civilizations were functioning in that part of the world a thousand years ago—that they had armies and metallurgy and weaving and philosophies. And Du Bois says in his autobiography that his jaw dropped in wonder, because he had never heard such things. In 1906, in Atlanta, W. E. B. Du Bois learned for the first time from this eccentric old German immigrant, with his dueling scars and accent, that Africa had civilizations.

You are right that when I caricature novelists and TV reporters, I am indulging myself. But who has to go to the bathroom all the time? I do. Who wastes time on his e-mail because he's afraid to tackle the hard questions? I do. I have tried to be as truthful about Franz the student as about his fellow strangers. The difference is that Franz—and I—want to keep on doing what we went somewhere else to do. We don't change professions, then and there. We do not decide to be novelists instead—unless we choose to leave one profession and to take up another, different, profession. We do not hide our fear by saying that we don't want to impose ourselves on others. We do not make up all that stuff. We do fieldwork—as best we can.

One hopes that we do it out of commitment. First of all, the people who provided the money—I don't think one should take the money and misrepresent why one took it. We owe them that. In addition, we owe the people whom we study the best that we can do. Beyond that, in my opinion we owe it to our ancestors, to the people who gave us anthropology, who built anthropology. We have an obligation to them. We should point out where they are wrong, but without spitting on them.

On one level these things do not really matter to me. I have tenure. I have written books. But I think it's important to say this as honestly and forcefully as I can because I am afraid that we may lose our profession. We have already neutralized much ethnographic reporting. Malinowski did some bad things in the field and seemed at times contemptuous of the peoples he studied. But he also wrote some of the best monographs ever written. That he was an egotist and supposedly an imperialist, and even the fact that he used nasty words in referring to native peoples, does not negate the value of the monographs he wrote, or the accuracy with which he reported. I think that many ethnographers, who misunderstood the relationship of the societies they studied to their own, and who may have even disliked or been repelled by their hosts, were nonetheless deeply impressed by the care, skill, and wisdom of the people whom they studied, and reported on their attainments by doing exacting and difficult ethnography. We have sometimes vitiated ethnographic reporting because we disliked the outlooks of the ethnographers, and this may be a costly error—particularly if it leads us to overvalue bad ethnography because we like the outlook of the ethnographer.

CLARKE: It seems like there is something else going around now. If we turn it around and think about the usefulness of ethnography as a research tool, then perhaps the incorporation of ethnography into literature and many other subfields, even journalism and feature stories, is actually the success of the profession in demonstrating how we need to use thorough methods that go beyond just spending a day and interviewing someone and getting results. Perhaps there is something else there that allows us to push beyond the boundedness of anthropology as a discipline.

MINTZ: I agree with you that the sorts of things that we have done have been illuminating for workers in other fields. It is good for them and good for us. But we have not been good at helping our fellow citizens grasp the fundamental lessons about humanness that I assume are shared knowledge for all of you. We have not succeeded in explaining clearly to our fellow citizens what we do. For the most part, if you ask others what the historians do, they know; but if you ask them what anthropologists do, they're not sure. We have failed to explain clearly and patiently the basis of our discipline. In this connection, I can recall distinctly, as we stood in the lobby of the convention hotel in Philadelphia many years ago, amid hundreds of fellow anthropologists, the late Eric Wolf saying to me, "Do you realize that three or four thousand people who call themselves anthropologists have come to these meetings, which they consider anthropological, and yet for the most part, they have nothing to say to each other?"

I thought that was true at the time, and think that it is probably still true. I believe that is because we do not have spokespersons who work with skill at making our work and our objectives, scientific and humanistic, intellectually accessible. We can do all the other things we do, too. But we should show that our profession has continuity and coherence, and that some objectives are held in common with those of other scholars and artists. I feel that we are not succeeding at those basics—still not, and not yet.

72

The Contemporary Desire for Ethnography and Its Implication for Anthropology

GEORGE E. MARCUS

Thirty years ago, when I began my career, it was a fairly straightforward, unproblematic task to communicate to a public in Europe or the United States what social-cultural anthropology was as a discipline—even though there had been strong rumblings of change from the 1960s. As part of a general perspective on humans, defined as a Western science in the nineteenth century, it was the task of twentieth-century social-cultural anthropology through the distinctive method of firsthand fieldwork observation and the associated genre of writing known as ethnography to create a comparative archive of the diversity of the world's peoples and cultures, and especially of the peoples who had been encapsulated and pacified by the various European and American colonialisms. So the study of the so-called primitive peoples—their kinship, religions, histories, languages—and the many more more-or-less masked versions of this originary task that have emerged and still haunt the notion of the mainstream of the discipline in the guise of "area studies" provide a "cover story" for anthropology to its publics.

Behind this cover, first during the 1960s and then more definitively in the 1980s, anthropology underwent critical self-corrections. Philosophies and theories of interpretation gave a sophisticated self-understanding to a field that was inherently, but also unreflectively, interpretive in its origins. Fieldwork was subjected to a critique of power. Ethnography, especially the ways it established authority

73

for its claims to knowledge, was subjected to a rhetorical critique. Most importantly, the post–World War II Cold War arrangements, which prolonged, at least cognitively, the organization of colonial regimes and territories, in the notion of the "Third World," have given way to conditions and ways of thinking and participation that simply lack authoritative compass or definition. This provides a great opportunity for anthropology, in terms of its originary goals and interests, but very little of the way it still represents itself is relevant to these new challenges, and most importantly, established ways of thinking about its still very relevant instruments—fieldwork, interpretation, ethnography, and commitment to creating knowledge through understandings of the meanings of subjects' discourse and actions for themselves—are in need of renovation.

Fed by a certain skepticism of its own past—to an extent far greater and riskier than any other social science discipline—anthropology is now remaking itself pragmatically by "muddling through" and, I think, successfully. There is still a vast public demand for what anthropology offers. The task ahead for anthropology is to re-educate the public about what it has historically offered as it remakes its instruments, methods, and commitments in new circumstances and with new demographics. Far from being the remnant of a colonial discipline, and then a Cold War one, anthropology promises to be a central producer of knowledge that in its own relations and modes of production incorporates that with which it objectively tries to come to terms as knowledge but that is as yet unnamable in the midst of millennial transition.

Recently, I have thought more about this task in, on the one hand, exploring the importance of discussing the pedagogy of graduate training of anthropologists, especially in reconceiving and adapting fieldwork for the sorts of projects that are more and more commonly undertaken by anthropologists- and ethnographers-in-the-making. And on the other hand, I have become more systematically interested in a certain present "crisis of reception" (in contrast to a "crisis of representation," the slogan that stood for the main thrust of the 1980s so-called Writing Culture critique). For me, the binds presented to anthropologists in the ways that the ethnography they produce is now received, and not received, most importantly drive innovation and rethinking of the classic ethnographic form and the norms that support it as an ideology of fieldwork practice, imparted loosely as professional lore. In the space available here, I want to consider the future of ethnography—so central to the identity of anthropology—caught between problems of reception and the challenge of a new pedagogy.

Let me first tell a story of a certain current politics in the practice of ethnography and how it led to my interest in these issues.

On the Contemporary Desire for Ethnography

The prosperity of ethnography as a mode of inquiry and constructing knowledge in anthropology has depended, especially over the past two decades, on the demand or desire for it outside its discipline. In the 1980s, this desire came from within the humanities in a wave of transdisciplinary critical refashioning. (Ethnography and the fieldwork situation were one of the important sites for reexamining issues of representation, the politics of narrative, the construction of subjectivity in text and everyday life, the multiplicity of identity, the political significance of struggles over meaning, and the power of the capacity for critical reflexivity.) At present, the source of this desire has shifted decidedly to major institutions undergoing transformations: governments, corporations, militaries, charities, universities, and markets. What made ethnography fascinating in the 1980s is very different from what fashionably is desired of it now. The issues or topics of the 1980s are either taken for granted, under the presumption that the lessons have been learned, or are lost in the seductive appeal to respond to desires to be informed by ethnography by either the powerful or the public who want effective and familiar stories of complex social transformations. (Witness the recent appearance of several series of manuals on every aspect of ethnographic research practices—formalizing the informal to offer a how-to method to the uninitiated; also new journals of ethnography with inclinations very different than the 1980s to overcome indulgent reflexivity with method and exactitude, and the expansion of ethnographic consultancies during the dot-com boom that have even survived the bust.) Ethnography functioned similarly before, but never with the cachet and approval it has now. But in this approval it is conventional, compliant ethnography that is most desired.

This difference between now and then in the desire for ethnography, which drives its production, creates an interesting current politics of ethnography as a knowledge form in terms of which I want to locate myself in order to offer the following remarks. Specifically, I am interested in possible strategies for critical ethnography that are still actively shaped by the issues raised in the 1980s but go beyond the traditional framings of ethnography (to which discussions of these issues then adhered) in order to address certain contemporary conditions of change for which institutions of political economy desire what ethnographic knowledge promises. But I am interested in doing ethnography, not on the terms defined by its new patrons, but on the terms of its own critically evolved debates and legacies since the 1980s. On the one hand, I think that ethnography should still be the medium for major discussions and debates about what is becoming of the social or cultural—and not let it recede much to what it was before—a subordinate, always slightly subversive, but legitimated method of social scientific knowing in aid of the macro-narratives of more prestigious or powerful others. On the other hand, I do not want to be—in fact, cannot be—closed to appeals to and parallel interests within the realm of powerful patronage in what ethnography offers. To locate myself between the two periods of heightened desire for ethnography requires indeed finding a source of possible critical independence among its most likely patrons at present in cultures of expertise, which requires seeing beyond, or not settling for, the resurgence of merely the old virtues of ethnography in the reform of the theories, projects, policies, and programs of its interested patrons.

Current challenges to the traditions of ethnographic process can be met by simple "muddling through," as many anthropologists would probably prefer. (The ethos of ethnography has always most comfortably developed in terms of ethnographers playing the role of double agents—providing formal results for patrons and colleagues but among themselves reveling in the serendipity and unpredictability of the fieldwork process—thus never investing too much in the thinking through of projected research.) Yet given the current politics of ethnography that I have just outlined, I think a much more explicit discussion about the norms and forms of ethnography is needed at this point, particularly in graduate training, but without the rigidity of conventional discourses on method with which such a discussion might be associated. I have chosen to do this in terms of the challenges of multisited ethnography (Marcus 1999).

On Multisited Ethnography

My own initiative in trying to come to terms with what ethnography is becoming and, from this, what it still could be has been developed in a proposal for multisited fieldwork. This has most often been sympathetically understood as a ratification for what is already happening to ethnographic research circumstantially, often involving the tracking or following of the dispersal of traditionally situated subjects of study within grids or geographies that are given by macro visions of, for example, the world system, capitalism, nation-states, and so forth. My intention, though, has been to use this proposal to explore a more complicated and ambitious range of issues about the reinvention of the practices of ethnography within its traditional mise-en-scène, true to the spirit of those practices, but different from their typical modes of implementation.

Here I give only a very abbreviated sense of my own preferred design for multisited fieldwork, because I want rather to emphasize what the implications of such a practice of ethnography would be in relation to the more conventional norms, forms, and pedagogies of ethnography widely in place. I do have a specific sense of multisited ethnography, but really I am more concerned to push ethnography broadly in this direction—where I think it is moving circumstantially anyhow. In this direction there are many specific designs and strategies of work that could be discussed and debated. My main interest is simply in getting such discussions and debates within the realm of an alternative practice of ethnography started and legitimated. In effect, this is the 1980s catching up with the new research agendas of ethnography within anthropology and other disciplines where it is promoted as well.

So briefly, in my own version of multisited research, which crosscuts various social fields, involving politics, law, science and technology, and financial markets, ethnography defines itself in close engagements with orienting cultures of expertise that are treated in the first instance as traditional objects of study. The point is to discover "the para-ethnographic" already present in the discourses and actions of expertise in their most reflexive and critical dimensions and then, in collaboration with, or independent of, these initial subjects, to move literally and ethnographically through the resulting, collaborative map and issues emerging in that orienting ethnography of expertise. Further, my supposition is that the para-ethnographic is at present less about the inside conditions or interior life of some group of experts (as would be the presumption in traditional ethnography) than about the nature of the social field, the connections of expert cultures to "elsewheres," the dynamics of broader processes, and this is what creates a potentially strong intellectual over-lapping identity or complicity between ethnographer in multisited space and expert counterpart/subject in the field.

The main point is not to presume that the issues and contexts of setting ethnographic problems are given beforehand in discourses and communities of knowledge that merely inform the siting of the ethnographic project. Rather, multisited ethnography finds these orienting contexts already in fieldwork. The sites and connections that define an ethnographic design arise, then, from an initial engagement with some situated "para-ethnography," alive among subjects, who, if not experts, are in some sense counterparts of investigators rather than purely "other" to them. This reinvention of identity of the informant, the role and ethics of his or her participation in the production of scholarly ethnography, and ultimately of the purposes and forms of independent ethnographic research, indeed the re-functioning of ethnography itself, are the issues at stake in proceeding with a multisited research design in this way. Many projects today in fact proceed like this, but what counts as in the field and out of it, who is a subject of ethnography and who merely informs ethnography, to what degree this is dominated by the expected written form that ethnography should take, are questions shaping ethnographic inquiry that are still very much guided by the older norms and forms of ethnography and fieldwork. The multisited proposal here is intended to suggest reinventions of this old model as they are identified in their trajectory of research in new terrains.[1]

So, in sum, the ethnographer would generate the field of fieldwork from within by the finding of para-ethnography; in new topic arenas—defined doctrinally and in self-conscious knowledge-making processes. This means a stronger sense of collaborations with expertise, and new relations and recognitions in terms of ethnographer-subject relations, a different sense of the reflexive positioning of the ethnographer, and the nature of ethnography as a project of critique. These are classic strains brought out in the old mise-en-scène of ethnography by the 1980s writing culture debates, now applied to much more decentered communities, networks, and processes.[2]

This version of multisited ethnography with the revision of the norms of ethnography itself as a goal suggests two problem areas on which I offer extended comments: the binds of reception of ethnography today and the remedy that multisited research suggests; and the idea of design rather than method in preparing graduate ethnographic projects as a means of considering pedagogic questions crucial to the reinvention of ethnography.[3]

On the Binds of Reception

I would argue that anthropology, or more generally the ethnographic mode of intellectual production, whoever produces it, is currently in a crisis of reception rather than a crisis of representation, as in the slogan for the earlier period of fashion and desire for ethnography. In the new topical arenas in which I am interested, ethnography risks being "production without reception," as a colleague working in the area of information technology and society has summarized the problem. The binds of minimal or else misrecognized reception of ethnography are what most pressingly drive experiments with form, especially within the strategies of multisited fieldwork. On the one hand, there is stereotypic reception (and a disinterest in its critical ambitions) on the part of its most prominent patrons currently; on the other, within the context of disciplinary communities, there is a summary and intellectually superficial reception of ethnography. In short: on the one hand, there is subordination; on the other, there is aesthetic response. In this way, the critical ambitions of ethnography are discounted. Its validity is not tested by a community of disciplinary reception sufficiently large— nor adequately intense—to be accountable.

To elaborate a bit, the crisis of reception is that for the most creative and ambitious ethnographic work of anthropologists in particular there is little or no constituency for it inside the discipline. There is nothing like the density of specialization among those committed to the tradition of ethnographic practice in the new topic arenas that is comparable to the discourse community that assimilated the production of ethnography of peoples and places in the classic period of modern anthropology. Individual works of ethnography are less probed and assimilated to the experiences of other ethnographers than they are appreciated in a summary way for what they do and do not achieve. Ethnography in its disciplinary contexts only really works, I would argue, not as case or example, but as an artifact to be pulled apart and imaginatively reconstructed. This sort of reception is almost totally lacking in fields like anthropology, which promote ethnography so that it lacks this basic sort of intradisciplinary intense critical assessment that it needs to prosper. And it is not clear to me at this point whether any such intense communities of detailed reception of ethnography will ever emerge again in anthropology or other fields.

The other source of reception for ethnography is among its primary patrons— humanists in the 1980s, business people now. But here ethnography has been and is now received stereotypically or else in a more limited way than in terms of what anthropologists think they have to offer in the framework of the ethnographic process. Ethnography since the 1980s has been the site for creativity, speculation, and the playing out of big arguments (the genre for envisioning the shape of emerging cultural ideologies from practices). Whether ethnography as such can or should bear this intellectual weight is another question, but the stark fact is that there are no or only weak readerships for ethnography on its own terms. It is often understood summarily as a case, at most, a finding that confirms or contradicts positions in ongoing, theoretical or policy debates, among the patrons of ethnography, be they humanists in the 1980s or political economists and business people now in both public and more private spheres. This is indeed an important use of ethnography to which those producing it can play, but it also frustrates the independent and complicated assessment of argument within ethnography's own process of production.

I want merely to suggest here that one move in response to these binds of reception of ethnography is in a further turn in the multisited design of fieldwork practice—a turn, I believe, that could have a transformative implication for the refunctioning of ethnography as a knowledge practice itself—away from the norms and forms that regulate it now. In the negotiation of fieldwork relationships across diverse communities and sites, multisited fieldwork in its coming into being suggests an active idea of reception in its very processes of inquiry. That is, the primary constituencies/readerships for the production of ethnography are also its diverse communities of subjects, and that the norms for producing ethnography should work out disciplinarily legitimate practices for incorporating this internal reception as the primary field of reception for ethnographic arguments produced within it.

It would be worth working through a range of scenarios whereby reception becomes an integral dimension of ethnographic writing and performance, such that now secondary readerships, including disciplinary and academic ones, come to play a quite different role in reception than their traditional, ultimately authoritative prerogative. On the one hand, of course, this notion that the ethically desired primary reception of ethnography be among its subjects is actually nothing new—it has been an informal ideal and measure of the virtuosity of ethnography throughout the classic period, only that the subjects were in fact largely silent, and their responses were only imagined and represented in the informal professional culture of ethnographers. (Also, it was this ideal that was made explicit and real in the constructs of dialogue and polyvocality that gave the 1980s critiques their particular edge.) In multisited research today in new topical arenas, this kind of engaged reception tied closely to the production of ethnography is something ethnographers tell in their informal discussions (that are similar to but quite different in emphasis and detail than the kinds of stories from the field that ethnographers used to tell). But as before, it lacks expression in the formal knowledge practices of ethnography. A thinking through of reception as integral to the production of ethnography in a very explicit and formal way would both overcome the seemingly inevitable binds of the established sources of reception that I have outlined and transform the way that ethnography is understood by the communities producing it. Thus, it is the binds of reception—the uncertainty now about whom ethnography is for—that drive the entire project of anthropology remaking itself in facing multisited conditions of fieldwork.

On a New Pedagogy: Design over Method

The specific notion of the design of multisited research has been serving me recently as a concept for replacing the usual notions of method, or in the case of anthropology, the valorization of the "learning by doing" approach to fieldwork. In anthropology, discussions of fieldwork often emphasize the beginning and ends of the process, rather than the crucial middle phases, when the ethnographer achieves some agency in terms of his or her purposes. They also conform to the practice of completely outlining the research process beforehand in a formal methodological way because of the requirements of social science proposal writing, even though any experienced ethnographer knows that the actual process is likely to be full of twists and turns, and the ethnographer even values these highly opportunistic factors.

In contrast to these norms of training and practice, the idea of design presumes a process of fieldwork well underway, the point at which the constraints and possibilities of a particular research situation are clear enough so that the ethnographer can actually impose a research design upon "the field" as it has emerged. It is at this phase of fieldwork in which thinking about working from expert social imaginaries to multiple sites of ethnography can be developed. So my notion of multisited ethnography is not the mapping of a prospective field beforehand in conventional research proposing, but an imagining beforehand of embedded research scenarios that are only relevant well into the process of fieldwork. The pedagogical problem is how to achieve these sorts of leaping-ahead thought experiments in terms of research imaginaries before the fieldwork.

But, I would argue that training for fieldwork quite traditionally occurred just in this way by reading ethnographies in thick contexts of preexisting area studies. To get "inside" an ethnographic text has always meant for anthropologists with an eye toward fieldwork to explore its prompts for thinking through scenarios with the material presented. The "scene" of reading here is precisely that point in fieldwork when the imaginary of readers engages with the material and in a sense "redesigns" it. So, written ethnographies have always been read most productively for new research imaginaries, as prompts, as shared scenario building among ethnographies of a common area. This sort of thick context and thus this sort of research design through the imaginative reading of ethnographies are missing now for ethnography with far more ambitious theoretical and critical tasks. The question is how to restore something of this thickness of discussion at present, or its equivalent, where the conception of fieldwork projects can occur more by design than method. Where in the ongoing activities of the discipline could such a marked reinvention of the ethnographic process explicitly occur? Not so much in the work of the mature scholar, governed by a proud rhetoric of opportunism and circumstance, but in the process of producing the career-making dissertation ethnography, the design of the first project. There is a space in graduate pedagogy here to work through pragmatically the sorts of proposals I have suggested.

But, first, we should oppose the deeply entrenched double-agent or double-faced ethos of fieldwork that I have mentioned, since it secures a half-hearted, conflicted commitment to formally discussing ethnography as a practice at all. In terms of the current politics of ethnography that I outline, when there is the move to formalize ethnographic method in all of its conventional ways, this double-facedness on the part of those who practice ethnography more critically, and with more theoretical ambition, is a very weak position indeed. (The two-facedness of the way ethnography is regarded professionally by its practitioners consists in something that must be presented as whole, in the beginning, while knowing that it is its unpredictability that gives it its intellectual power.) Contrast two typical documents of before and after: before, the proposal for funding that defines and maps ethnography as method, as instrument, versus after, the preface to many resulting published ethnographies of the same projects about how one has succeeded by serendipity and opportunity in a found project that turns out not like one suspected.

While my heart is with the latter, I feel that it stalls ethnography especially in the current space between the 1980s and 1990s demands for it that I outline. So I fall on the side of a more formal sense of ethnography, but not by making it more method in terms of what it has been, but through the notion of design that incorporates ideas about pedagogy with which I am dealing here. What is needed is not formal method, but some defined means of thinking through the research process in its most directive moments. Critical ethnography has to offer more than the demystification of dominant or official discourses and practices, demonstrations of the fallibility of reason, and proof of the intractable indeterminacies and flexibilities of social and cultural life. Or at least it has to offer these things within a thought-through framework of research for which I prefer the notion of design rather than method.

Finally, why specifically do I like the idea of design rather than method? First I should note that my experience of design process has come from my participation periodically as a commentator in the organized critique of projects in an architecture school, and I have been reading the work of scholars who have written on the design process in architecture both theoretically and practically. While there are things about the core practices of architectural design creation that I do not care for in their own context, including the overly formalist writing on the design process itself, still there are several aspects of this process that might very appealingly provide an alternative model for pedagogy in shaping ethnography training, something that yields a legible determinate project that is discussible at every stage, including the final product. Also the idea that design fully incorporates the notion of experimentation as part of its practice is attractive. Design is problem solving, but there are no absolutely closed final solutions—except of course that one is held accountable for the final product. Design is material, achieved, on the landscape, but the discussion and critique of it goes on, and it exerts influence on other designs in the future in interesting ways. Design thus produces something legible, precise, without giving up on the critically attractive notions of intractable multiplicity and flexibility that have overwhelmed ethnographic interpretation and argument in recent years.

While I do not have space here for a full discussion of design processes, the specific characteristic that I like is the fact that while one is responsible for generating a product, a building in the case of architecture, a corpus of writing, at present, in ethnography, one is held closely and critically accountable for it at every stage through the critique process. It would be interesting in this regard to think through the various aspects of work around designs—the charrette, the display and group critique, the methods of the classic atelier—in terms of the production of ethnography as integral to the research process. Given that many fieldwork projects begin with passing through and allying in complex ways with fields of expertise, these training events and practices would even blur the lines between the seminar room and the field site. In light of my previous discussion especially about ethnography now being production without reception in its disciplines (except for aesthetic judgment), a key point for me is that design is the one process of producing something—a form or a representation—that is intimately tied to reception issues at the same time. This echoing of multiple sites and the folding of reception into the production of design from its inception in training thus suggests a means of preserving many of the currently relevant principles of the 1980s critiques of ethnography as a surrogate for method and might be an interesting way of developing a pedagogy for the new forms and norms of ethnography as they are emerging.

"Being-there-ness" was such a prominent trope of the critique of traditional ethnographic authority and a guarantor of the more mundane desire for ethnography now. Well, today, a sort of occupation of the space of activism advocacy is what takes its place, especially in the new topical arenas. The experiential passion of presence in a field site is replaced by involvement in the public issues of a more diffuse social and cultural space. This is a mixed or hybrid kind of authority for those embedded primarily in the culture of academic scholarship, but it will never be clarified as a form of authority until ethnography as a research practice is renovated, rethought in terms of the sorts of challenges and desires that I indicate. The key critical fantasy and real possibility at the same time is the folding of reception into the space of inquiry that the ethnography evolves by design, begun as the emergence of a new pedagogy.

In the wake of the 1980s critiques of ethnographic authority, "being-there-ness" does not diminish in importance as a trope of ethnography, but its signification does change. It is no longer the sign for anthropology's special existential empiricism ("I was there, therefore I saw with validity and authenticity") but a sign for a special community of reception that validated the tropes of the scene of dialogue and collaboration that the 1980s critique promoted—that special community of the native by which ethnographers implicitly and imaginarily have always judged each other in informal professional relations. This was a powerful shift but one that could not be realized as actual reception (other than in the spate of focused anthropologist/other structured ethnographies that are still produced). In disciplinary discussions back home the community of reception among subjects (mostly those unreachable at home, fixed in the site of classic fieldwork) remained a chimera in ethnographic talk, but a powerful one. Only now in the complexities of multisited ethnography does reception become something more, a fulfillment of the revised "being there" trope of post-1980s anthropological authority in the scenes of the evolved field site of work with subjects here and there, near and far, but always substantively in touch and connected long after the report to the academy of ethnographers and others interested has been made. This suggests the new politics and ethics of participation, of being there, to be worked out in every multisited project as part of its design.

Discussion Questions with George Marcus

HAL SCHEFFLER: A question regarding the academic market versus wider markets. What are the possibilities and problems of ethnography as a commercialized publishing contract—that is to say, an output for which one is paid, like a report or mainstream account?

GEORGE MARCUS: I would argue that the alliances between ethnographers and consultants or knowledge workers in spheres of relevance are absolutely crucial. Because I've done ethnography of elites, I present such interactions and projects as an origin moment. You might argue that it is politically retrograde, but in multisited fieldwork you inevitably cross into relations with counterparts who are situated in such a way that they are producing intellectual representations that have an organic relationship to your own, but under a whole different set of constraints. For instance, they are trying to figure out a problem for a company, while you are worrying with it for other audiences and conceptual concerns.

REBECCA HARDIN: What about selecting or prioritizing among such partners, or even formally collaborating with them?

MARCUS: Of course, it's not any consultant that would work as a partner in most ethnographic projects. The politics of selecting partners in these domains of work are interesting and well worth more consideration than they are given in most anthropological training. Further, there are some practical strategies. If the person in question is an anthropologist, for example, that presents particular advantages and challenges. Let me explain.

Thinking back on the stages in my career it bears mention that there was a whole stratum of people pushed out of anthropology departments because there were no academic jobs in teaching and research. Many of these people became consultants in the 1970s. And I always remember their accounts of the attendant challenges and contradictions. There was a column that conveyed such voices in the American Anthropological Association newsletter, in fact. And the items they printed were very bittersweet; I always felt that these people were doing this work, but there was always another dimension to their engagement with the material and relationships before them. Then for a while there was a better academic job market, but it remained somewhat routinized, this other kind of job or career in consulting.

Actually academic anthropologists often needed the other, what used to be called applied anthropologists, for involvement as a kind of "native" or "local expert" in certain arenas, such as the study of elites, or corporations, or nongovernmental organizations. You could never replace the knowledge such anthropologists gained merely by doing fieldwork from an academic setting. And the questions then, ethically and interpersonally, become quite complex. Such experts would sometimes underwrite ethnographic texts or documents for scholarly "patrons," whoever employed them formally. And the reverse could happen; scholarly work would get woven into reports and summaries without being formally recognized or remunerated by professional organizations. So while there was potential for this kind of collaboration, it was also fraught. My argument is simply that for those of us who remain primarily within the academy, those other areas of anthropological activity are absolutely essential to developing academic projects. Whether you wind up working in a neighborhood or village with conventional subjects or not, moving through more practically oriented or professionally organized fields of representation is absolutely essential. The challenges arise in matters of collegiality across these divisions.

STUDENT: I would like for you to talk in more detail about the reception of our work and how it applies to knowledge making. How does it relate to notions of activism and applied anthropology?

MARCUS: Interesting questions: is it more applied anthropology or more critical anthropology that would lean more to the activist agenda? To answer that would mean several shifting terms would still need to be defined. I always say that applied anthropology is working for patrons in that indeed you have very clear constituents to whom you give over the whole ethnographic endeavor. It's not exactly that; it's a bit more theoretically rich because you actually have more independence than it might seem. But how the constraints of professional anthropologists versus the constraints of academic ones relate to activism is very unclear and worth more thought. I suppose that you would have to really think about variations within advocacy, which itself is a professionalizing set of fields. If the work by an anthropologist was really not for any profit, then would it be applied? Can we make categorical distinctions on the basis of whether something we do is less or more "for hire?"

KAMARI CLARKE: I am struck by how hopeful you are. I came to anthropology late in the game, and I have had a few surprises. I think in this idea of reception you're trying to rename or perhaps reclaim relations of productivity in particular ways. You take the risk of just not asking subjects to be constituents in new forms of knowledge. What of gaps between local knowledge and changes in the world? Might they not make for massive communication gaps on key matters? Do you think you're being too optimistic about the dynamics of reception? Is it an assumption of yours that the world has changed in ways that make that less problematic than for example in colonial or immediately postcolonial moments? Or do you feel that the critique of ethnography as a set of strategies for constructing authority in/through texts has basically done its work?

MARCUS: These are all really important questions. The idea is that you have that party of people who think the world has changed, and that party of people who doesn't think it has; neither one can prove it one way or the other. I tend to be with the party of people that think that the world has changed, but I really am very suspicious of hyped-up discourses about the nature of that change. Even if the world is very much like it was for the last several generations, you could still implement the changes I advocate here. There is nothing particularly high-tech about them. Rather, they remain close to that type of inclination of anthropology that seems necessary in order to reinvent.

I have this type of happy warrior view of where it may go, but the idea is that more attention to reception can be incorporated as such into a well-established discipline. You may be hopeless about the intellectual prospects, but it's a precious space that occupies a certain type of analysis that can be tentative and flexible and in that way it's very positive.

. . . It does require playing around with authority and moving toward our field's best inclinations in totally different conditions of doing work. Perhaps it is as superficial as the way that fashions change, though I tend to think that over time important decisions have been made. Some of them, in terms of the way we structure and regulate economies and conceive of progress and development, were either a success or failure of the 1980s and 1990s, depending on your point of view. In sum, I don't know for sure that the world has changed, but certainly the nature of anthropological projects has changed.

NOTES

1. Before moving on, I want to make three asides, or discussion comments, about this model of multisited ethnography:

a. While specific sources of my proposals here are elided in this essay, they arise from four kinds of engagements in which I have been intensively involved in a sustained way. One has been collaborations with Douglas Holmes in his work on the institutions of the European Union and the circulation of subversive, mainly right-wing political discourses in and around them (Holmes 2000). This is one specific project in which my version of multisited ethnography has been forged. Second are the interesting recent efforts to produce ethnographies of international financial markets in which the special challenge is to understand a very abstract sphere of circulation that has great social implication, but for which it is very difficult to establish a social context (Lee and LiPuma 2001; Riles 2001b). Third is a continuing interest in the ethnography produced in the field of science and technology studies, probably the most central, diverse, and long-established arena for developing in situ the generic issues I raise here (see, for example, Downey and Dumit 1997; Fortun 2001). And fourth, the predicaments of students in constituting fieldwork designs—a number increasingly involved in projects being forged experimentally by the work of established scholars like those I have just mentioned—have provided the most suggestive as well as pressing challenges for practical changes in the way ethnography can be conducted, a pedagogic concern to which I want to return later in this chapter.

b. I want merely to stipulate here the interesting debate that might ensue from my postulation of the "para-ethnographic" as a key construct in the design of multisited ethnography. This discussion would focus on the phenomenological bases of the recognition and accessing of such a dimension of subjects' discourse and actions as the "para-ethnographic"; it would focus on the nature and capacity of the faculty of practical consciousness and whether anything about it could ever be equated with "the scholastic point of view" (Pierre Bourdieu 1990), the domain of distanced reflective reason that we reserve for ourselves as academics; and if one were able to establish such collaborative relations with subjects on this level, what implications this would have for the whole project of ethnography where certain defining distances are closed between ethnographer and subject, at least in certain reaches of the domain of multisited fieldwork. Here, as I said, I choose to stipulate these interesting debates on which my whole proposal is based in order to emphasize the implications for the needed renovation of ethnography in its design and pedagogy. (Not only my proposal is based on these debates, but a whole school of interpretative theory within the American tradition of cultural anthropology in which the so-called native point of view has been valorized over the architecture of social relations as the emphasized object of study. In multisited research, the social is not ignored, but it emerges in fieldwork from a priority concern with subject models through a more active and explicit practice of collaboration in ethnography.)

c. This conception of multisited research could be identified as the fulfillment of a long delayed and desired anthropological study of elites. But any such sense of a research topic in anthropology as yet another addition in categorical coverage (first peasants, then workers, and now elites, etc. . . . .) is belated. The study of elites (and especially experts here) is part of a larger design or weave of research that integrates systemic (institutional?) processes into the everyday life and, generally, subaltern vision of ethnographic research. In terms of the theme of the conference at which these chapters originated, the study of elites or expert cultures (through a finding of and bonding with "para-ethnography") is at the heart of a distinctive and critical ethnographic approach to centers.

2. Recall here the strong images of these 1980s critiques—the central trope is field-work strongly enacted by dialogue—where the anthropologist's informing ideas and theories are challenged by informants—the relativization of the scholastic point of view à la Pierre Bourdieu by upgrading the intellectual capacity of subjects, in the terms in which the anthropologist is interested. This is to recall that one of the strongest images of the 1980s discussions is the idea of multiple authorship in any ethnography. The informant is more active than he or she was ever thought to be, involving a raising of the standing of native knowledge in its own forms, of the dialogue settings from which it is accessed, of relation-ships that generate ethnography with equal intellectual capacity on both sides. Aside from exemplary texts in subsequent years that made ethnography exactly this, the point, while provocative, remained ambiguous, unfinished, the implications for practice undefined, especially given the present context of multisited ethnography across many settings.

3. A third problem area would be how multisited research affects prominent styles of critical argument that ethnography now typically makes by closing the distance between ethnographer and expert subject.

Most often, critical ethnography has served to undo (demystify?) the common sense of established institutions, centers, dominant discourses, and elite practices, but such critiques are delivered from the distance of the "scholastic point of view" and often in sympathy with some subordinated, often silenced subject that gives shape to the moral economy of the ethnography. It is precisely this distance that is closed and this pure sympathy that is made ambiguous in developing the orienting design of multisited ethnography by some complicit engagement with the found critical dimension or potential already in play within expert practices. Thus, this standard strategy of critique is not an option. The danger then is that the ethnographer will actually be seduced by, or join, the intellectual game of the sphere of expertise with which she or he is engaged, thus eviscerating the project of critique altogether (by indulging the "going native" option). Anyone who studies corporate managers, scientists, policy makers, etc., by finding collaborative alliances within the field of study can easily slip into being a sort of adviser or taking up the role improvised for the ethnographer. I have seen this threat of seduction materialize in a number of projects where the researcher nearly joins the community of subjects as ethical adviser or house. This is an increasingly tempting role within such research, and it appeals both to a sense of new personal opportunity as well as to widespread desire for some sort of activist dimension to ethnographic work, along with the dissatisfaction with the anticipated indifferent or merely positive but not sustained reception to one's work by professional peers. The desire to shape work for those who really understand it and care about it not only leads to a possible shift in the nature of ethnography that maintains its professional boundaries by folding dimensions of reception among subjects into its results, but also threatens to motivate the ethnographer to work primarily with and for his expert subjects in developing a new technique for them, or a better analysis. So there is a potentially serious problem in how critical perspective is redeemed once one develops a complex relation with expert or elite subjects.

The other option is to explore the social fields that expert imaginaries in the course of practice evoke, in what I referred to as para-ethnography. There are many possible stories or outcomes of ethnography from this premise, but none that can return to the strategy of demystifying critique, although the danger of slipping into pure participation remains. It is the worldview, so to speak, of experts that is most wanted, their attempt to define a rapidly changing or evaporating social field intimately tied to and defined by their purposes. This is most often what the ethnographer wants too, but not only this. An evolution of fieldwork from orienting engagements with expertise also guarantees them as well independence from expert complicities. It is in the literal and figurative movements away from the orienting focus on expertise that makes the ethics of multisited research really complicated, but it is also through the ethical questions themselves posed by working through cross-cutting commitments that the reflexive and recursive shape of such fieldwork projects emerges. The knowledge product of ethnographic research must thus arise from contending with the complicities that materializing the multisited design of ethnography entails, and any focused object of critique secured by the distance of the constructed professional role of fieldwork can no longer be relied upon.

Part 2

Doing Transnational Ethnography

The Homeward Ship

*Analytic Tropes as Maps of and
for African-Diaspora Cultural History*

J. LORAND MATORY

I have been in love with Africa since I was five years old, partly owing to a book. Physically, all that is left of my *Illustrated Book about Africa* by Felix Sutton and H. B. Vestal (1959) is the front cover and the first thirty pages of text and vivid lithographs, along with the strips of masking tape with which my mother had, on multiple occasions, repaired it. Through these pages, I learned of the desert aoudad, the Egyptian cobra, the rock hyrax, the fennec, and the bustard, as well as the "jungle" okapi, few of which I had ever seen in the zoo. I then spent years searching for these creatures in American zoos, game parks, pet shops, and books. Nothing in the book, however, fascinated me as much as the "plate-lipped Sara women," the kente-draped Ashanti, the "blue-veiled Tuaregs," the Bedouin falconer, the leg-o-mutton-sleeved Herero woman, and the "Watusi" dancer with his red skirt, dance wands, and colobus-fringed headdress. I have since come to regard this indiscriminate merging of African ethology and ethnology as racist, but this book became the seed, or the roots, of my equally indiscriminate love for Africa and longing to embrace her.

Trips through Tropes

Yet that embrace came by the grace of multiple matchmakers. Before I ever flew to Africa, I met her through a Cuban *santera*—as the practitioners of the African-inspired Santería, or *Ocha*, religion are called—who taught Spanish at Howard University, in Washington, D.C. Five gold bangles on her arm quietly announced Dr. Contreras's devotion to and protection by the Yoruba-Atlantic

93

goddess Ochún. I suspected mystery in their meaning before I knew what they were, and so I reached out with an inquisitive touch. With serpentine speed and balletic grace, Contreras withdrew them just beyond my reach. Following the map laid out by Roger Bastide's *African Religions of Brazil* ([1960] 1978), I also stopped over in Brazil, retracing what he and William Bascom (1972) identified as the great arc of Yoruba influence in the Americas. Consequently, Yorubaland was the capital of the Africa that I sought.

My late sister and role model Yvedt also loved Africa. She followed her passion for African art—a passion stoked by the books and danced lectures of Yale University art history professor Robert Farris Thompson—and connected our family to a great black pilgrimage cycle, which, from the 1960s until the present, has made the journey to Africa almost as important a rite of passage for bourgeois African Americans as the tour of Europe has been for our bourgeois Euro-American friends. Before her time, in the early 1950s, my maternal aunt and her family had lived in Liberia. In the 1970s and 1980s, their ultra-modern New Jersey split-level was decorated with African sculptures, masks, and spears, some of it brought back from Liberia and much of it purchased at a Manhattan gallery called Merchants of Oyo. My Liberian-born cousin ultimately married a Nigerian, as I did, and now both lives and works bi-continentally. A paternal first cousin became Muslim and married a Senegalese man. And long before any of these events, my parents were introduced to each other by their Nigerian classmate at Howard University, a man who (like at least one other Howard classmate) repeatedly hosted my visits and my sister's to Nigeria.

Yet the role of Africa in our lives was never without controversy. Indeed, controversy was a structural element of that role. When I was eight, my little cousin Wade and I were raising a joyous clamor as we shouted and tumbled behind our grandparents' waterfront rambler in Norfolk, Virginia. But for his clothes, shoes, and momentary lack of an entourage, our grandfather looked like a Ghanaian Ashanti chief. Nonetheless, when he angrily threw open the sliding glass door of the house, he shouted, "Shut up that noise! You sound like a bunch of Africans!" With equal measures of innocence and artfulness, I replied, "But, Granddaddy, we are Africans!" He harrumphed and shut the door. I doubt, though, that he managed to resume his nap. Wade and I quieted down, at least for a while, but Granddaddy could hardly shut the door on my words or on the Africa in his back yard.

Despite his West African appearance, Granddaddy was an American Pentecostal bishop. Churches like the scores that he founded across the state of Virginia for the nationwide Church of God in Christ had, in Melville J. Herskovits's model, provided the prime example of Africanisms, or African influences on

American culture—that is, "shouting," or the form of transcendent exclamation and dance that reveal the presence of the Holy Ghost in the worshipper's body.

My past thirty or so years of research in West Africa, Brazil, and the black-ethnic populations of the United States have in many ways been devoted to the question of what makes me African American, apart from the chocolate-brownness of my skin, the fullness of my lips, and the social encumbrances that Granddaddy and I share with other descendants of enslaved Africans. The sort of cultural connections that seemed so obvious to Afro-Brazilianists and Afro-Cubanists and are so readily named by Brazilians and Cubans have been vigorously debated among North Americans. This chapter considers how our choice of scholarly language shapes real, human lives. How, in sum, does the cask of our descriptive discourse flavor the wine of our pan-American relationship with Africa?

Metaphors We Think By

Lakoff and Johnson's *Metaphors We Live By* (1980) argues that metaphors structure all of our language. They are pervasive. Metaphors can be semi-poetic, as are the following: "He shut the door on Africa," or "this book became the seed of my love for Africa." Alternatively they can be entirely mundane, as are these conventional expressions:

"Of course he's angry: You shot down every point that he made."

"Your claims are indefensible."

"He attacked every weak point in my argument."

"His criticisms were right on target."

"I've never won an argument with him."

All of these expressions embody the conventional metaphor that discussion is like war (Lakoff and Johnson 1980, 4). Any given metaphor—which compares one thing to another—highlights the similarities between the compared objects and hides the dissimilarities. Thinking of an argument as a war highlights its competitive nature and naturalizes the motive of mutual destruction between the participants. What aspects of argument might be better highlighted and enhanced if we compared an argument to, say, lovemaking? "Her thoughts brought me to an intellectual climax I could never have imagined." Or "His argument was forceful and clumsy. A more thoughtful argument might have fulfilled mine rather than tearing it apart."

Lakoff and Johnson say that metaphors are typically natural. For example, "I'm in an up mood" rests, in their opinion, on the tendency of well bodies to be vertical and of sick ones to be horizontal. I do not agree that metaphors are typically natural, but they are pervasive, even in our scholarly language. Let us call the metaphors in our scholarly descriptions and analyses "analytic metaphors." I have announced this chapter's concerns with some of the analytic metaphors and other analytic tropes that scholars have employed to highlight what matters in the cultural history linking Africa with its New World diaspora. Here I try to illuminate what is at stake in these linguistic frames.

For each analytic trope I discuss, I tell a story about the dimensions of cultural history that it highlights, as well as the equally valuable dimensions of cultural history that it hides, and, sometimes, the effect that its usage has had on the cultures so described. Hence, like others in this volume, this text might be construed as autobiography. However, and also like others in this volume, it is also a history, an intellectual history of multi-sited ethnography. A range of authors—including Kamari Maxine Clarke, Paulla Ebron, Aihwa Ong, and I—have made field sites of transnationally mobile populations and cross-border identities, rooting our analyses not in a priori theory and secondary references but in the messy currency-changing, language-switching, passport-inspecting, bribe-demanding, police- and customs-inspected, and boundary-filled world of physically itinerant lives.

As intellectual history, this essay excavates the underrecognized, under-examined, and under-exploited scholarly precedents of transnational ethnography in the study of the African diaspora, a task I share with the other contributors to a recent School of American Research collection (Yelvington 2006). As event history, this essay retraces the ignored Afro-Atlantic precedents of today's much-vaunted transnationalism. As autobiography, it narrates why it was difficult for me to overlook these intellectual and historical precedents.

This re-examination of the long-charted routes of black Atlantic cultural history offers both a theoretical model and a critique of the language we have used to describe newer transnational communities, as well as the forms of translocal, trans-ethnic cultural intercourse that have long shaped intra-African cultural history—along trade routes, at the convergence of Tutsi and Hutu, Hausa and Fulani, Bantu and "pygmy" or Khoisan, "Arab" and "African," and so forth. What do the metaphors that scholars use highlight and hide about these complex, mutually transformative interactions? And how do such metaphors reshape local social life on the ground?

Survivals

Melville J. Herskovits was once the whipping boy, but is now the preeminent model, of African American talk about our cultural connection to Africa. The metaphor of "survivals"—or recalcitrant leftovers from a people's historically original state—is the linchpin of his analysis. He asks, What aspects of

African culture "survived" in the Americas? Where did they "survive" and how? I argue that Herskovits's choice of an analytic metaphor begs the question of what he is looking for and where he will look to find it.

It was anthropologist and social evolutionist E. B. Tylor who first established the term *survivals* among the analytic metaphors of early twentieth-century anthropology. For Tylor, the term *survival* referred to the practices left over from lower stages of a society's evolution, which therefore provided evidence that the society had passed through that stage before reaching the present one. Likewise, for Herskovits, the term *survival* described the ancient and timelessly African practices left over—in any given New World black population—after acculturation to the dominant Euro-American culture.

This metaphor implies (and Herskovits's investigations assume) that Africa is the past of the American present. They assume that Africa is so unchanging and isolated from the rest of the world that twentieth-century Dahomean culture, for example, could provide evidence of the culture that reached Haiti in the eighteenth century and has survived ever since then. According to the "survival" metaphor, Africa is to the past as the black Americas are to the present.

Herskovits was one of a cohort of scholars in the 1920s and 1930s who employed this analytic metaphor and a host of its cousins, including "memories," "heritage," "retention," the sartorial metaphor of "vestiges"—which literally suggests clothing—and its metaphorical extensions. Hortense Powdermaker, for example, shared Herskovits's doubt that captivity had rendered African Americans—in an extension of the clothing metaphor—entirely "culturally naked" (Herskovits [1941] 1958, 29). However, these scholars did not all agree with Herskovits regarding the importance and depth of African "survivals."

Herskovits's major contribution was to amplify these metaphors by inverting the sartorial image of the "vestige." Hence, rather than the African American wearing his or her Africanness on the outside, he or she is said to contain or embody his or her inheritance as an unconscious "underlying logic" or "bent" within apparently Euro-American external forms, such as being filled enthusiastically with the Holy Ghost in the midst of Sunday meetings at Granddaddy's Church of God in Christ. Nonetheless, all of these analytic metaphors suggest that African Americans' contact with Africa is limited to the past and that the "survival," "memory," "vestige," or "retention" is like a self-existent, unchanging object bequeathed to the living by dead forebears.

This unchanging object will appear, over time, in different clothing or behind different masks, but the object remains the same. In imitation of Afro-Brazilianist Arthur Ramos, Herskovits called this re-clothing or masking "syncretism." The paradigm case is the Afro-Latin American "masking" of African gods behind the statues and lithographs of Catholic saints. For example, among *santeros* in Cuba and its diaspora, statues of Saint Bárbara, patroness of firefighters, are used to represent the Yoruba-affiliated god of thunder, lightning, and fire, Changó. By extension, Herskovits regarded "shouting" in black North American Protestant churches, like Granddaddy's, as a syncretic survival of an ancient African religious practice—that is, an instance of African spirit possession adapted to and hid behind a Western Christian name and conception of God.

Finally, all of these analytic metaphors suggest that the worn or embodied cultural heirloom makes little functional or structural difference in the lives of the heirs. No matter how much they "shout," African American Christians still form *Christian* churches. No matter how much like Africans they rhythmically sing and hoe the fields, the row still gets hoed and planted with the master's cotton or sugar.

Yet, in my observation, Africa does make a functional and structural difference in African American lives. For example, in more than a trivial sense, I am reminded of the role of Africa in Granddaddy's and my misunderstandings and self-understandings. Our gaze toward Africa and the images it revealed have been structural and functional in both of our lives, though perhaps to opposite effects. I am alive because of both ancient and modern Africa: the aforementioned connections at Howard University between my parents and Nigerian classmates in the 1950s. I married an African woman—another daughter of Oşun, according to one Brazilian priest's revelation—and my whole career is based on the study of Africa. Although he looked like an Ashanti chief, Granddaddy's relationship to Africa was litotic—that is, structured by the trope of negation.

We employ the trope of litotes when, in response to "How are you?" we reply, "Not bad." We say what we are not, allowing the listener to infer logically what we are. Most of the time, litotes suggest understatement, but not always. Blackface minstrelsy, for example, allowed Irish and Jewish immigrants—whose whiteness had long been doubted in Europe—to amplify their difference from the black anti-citizen of the U.S. republic and thereby ratify their own whiteness and worthiness of citizenship. The white pancake makeup around their eyes revealed their "real" whiteness underneath, in contrast to the blackness of the burnt cork on the rest of the face. Even black immigrants to the United States participate in this process of litotic self-fashioning. Many black immigrants endeavor to declare in word, accent, and deed, "We're not like black Americans," partly in order to discipline their children and to claim exemption from the racism that encumbers black American lives. Similarly, Granddaddy was not-African. He thought that his affirmation of African inferiority and his simultaneous denial of our behavioral likeness to Africans would lift from black Americans' shoulders the excuse for our oppression. Nonetheless, or really therefore, Africa remained central to his self-construction and mine. We could no more divest ourselves of our inward pre-occupation with Africa than we could remove our chocolate skins.

Moreover, contrary to the implications of the "survival" metaphor, both our respective understandings of Africa and Africans derived from contemporary sources—mine came from a book and his from missionary adventure tales and segregationist apologetics. Neither of our perceptions was an object handed down from the African forebears who disembarked at Jamestown or Charleston. Also contrary to Herskovits's model, then, the continuing role of African cultural history in our lives did not depend on our isolation and poverty, which Herskovits said were the usual conditions of African "survivals" in the Americas. So the above story speaks to what Herskovits's metaphor hid: that Africa is alive in the literary, religious, educational, and touristic lives of the urban and often the elite black Americas.

The next story speaks even more directly to Herskovits's assumptions. The locus classicus of Herskovits's African "survivals" in the United States is the Gullah, or Geechee, people of the South Carolina Low-Country and Sea Coast Islands. They have long been the focus of scholarly investigations into what remains culturally African about black North Americans. Various scholars have sought to explain the Gullahs' local subculture in terms of "survivals" of Gola culture, in what is now Sierra Leone. Indeed, in the second half of the eighteenth century, the rice planters of the Sea Coast Islands drew many of their workers from the rice-growing regions of Sierra Leone and Liberia, and the term *Gullah* might derive from the Sierra Leonean ethnonym "Gola."

On the other hand, captives had come to these islands from many other regions of Africa as well, and students of the local creole language variety also known as *Gullah* have identified an extremely diverse set of African origins in its lexicon and in its justly famous basket-making tradition. Thus, some leading authorities identify "Angola," a land far away from Sierra Leone, as the more likely source of the term *Gullah* (Rosengarten 1986, 1997; L. Turner 1949).

In my grandfather's day, Africanness was a source of shame, but now Oprah proudly receives the DNA evidence that she is ancestrally Kpelle, and Whoopi receives her Zulu ancestry with equal pride. As black North Americans have grown more willing to embrace Africa as a cultural model and emblem of collective identity, the "acculturation" of the Gullahs—that is, the decline of their distinctive language and crafts—has been reversed. For example, the "Africanness" of Gullah basketry has become its major selling point and a source of income for many craftswomen in coastal South Carolina, increasing the incentive of basket-sewers to produce reputedly African basketry forms (such as rice fanners) and even to wear African clothes.

However, it was Joseph Opala (Euro-American anthropologist and former member of the Peace Corps in Sierra Leone) who recently established the local conviction that Sierra Leone in particular was the source of the islanders' Africanness and the appropriate target of their "return" to the motherland. Moreover, the interest in this ahistorically specific tie was reciprocal. In 1986, Sierra Leonean president Joseph Momo paid a highly public visit to the Sea Coast Islands and encouraged the islanders to visit what he called their "ancestral homeland," which is precisely what a party of them did in 1989.

President Momo continued the American tradition of attributing the islanders' linguistic distinctiveness to their African roots, and he identified the similarity of the South Carolinian Gullah language to Sierra Leonean Krio, or Creole, as proof. Note that he drew no such connection between Gullah language and similarly named Sierra Leonean Gola language. Unlike Gola, both South Carolinian Gullah and Sierra Leonean Krio are predominantly English in their lexicons, since Krio initially came about due to the interaction among African American returnees to West Africa and diverse British-educated recaptives—that is, captives from other parts of Africa rescued by the British from slave ships bound for the Americas. Sierra Leonean Krio is also indebted to the language of British colonial administrators and Anglophone missionaries in Freetown. Thus, these Sierra Leonean and South Carolinian creole language varieties share features primarily on account of the parallel circumstances of their genesis, not on account of Gullah's being a "survival," "retention," "memory," "vestige," or "underlying logic" of Krio— much less of Gola or any Angolan language.

In sum, the shared features of the Gullah and Krio language varieties are highly ambiguous evidence of the Gullah people's Sierra Leonean or even African roots. However, given the shared will to recognize such linguistic similarities as the product of "survivals," Gullah has become a powerful emblem of a new "Kinship across the Seas"—between Gullahs and Sierra Leoneans. Despite the ambiguity of linguistic evidence in this celebrated case, Creole language furnishes the second most influential analytic metaphor—after "survivals"—in African diaspora cultural history.

Creolization

African Americanist cultural history is indebted to Sidney Mintz and Richard Price ([1976] 1992) for their "creolization" model. This model emphasizes the New World social institutions, organizations, and sanctioned spaces that made the practice of African creative models possible in the Americas. According to Mintz and Price, African American populations came to the Americas equipped not with whole and particular African cultures (like Gola culture, for example) but with the hodgepodge of beliefs and practices that the culturally heterogeneous "crowds" of Africans brought to any given New World locale. New, African American cultures formed in the spaces and around the aspects of social life where the dominant planter class allowed African American cultures to be distinctive.

Moreover, argue Mintz and Price, these newly African American cultures took shape quickly and enduringly—first, on the slave ships and then in the early years of any given American slave society. They formed quickly because they had to address the local need for people of diverse aboriginal cultures and languages who were laboring under the same plantation labor regime to communicate and cooperate immediately with their masters and with each other.

Mintz and Price's creole language metaphor, particularly when it is interpreted in the light of the white-dominant plantations that are its inspiration, suggests that African American cultures are internally systematic and bounded local systems. They are walled off by the slaves' immobility, the masters' restrictions, and the long-term stability of the resulting local social systems. No longer, after Mintz and Price, could we follow Herskovits in merely counting up the arbitrarily ordered and nonfunctional heirlooms that Herskovits traced to the African past.

In the 1980s, Brazilianists told a story about Afro-Brazilian religions that bears out many implications of the creolization model. In the Afro-Brazilian Candomblé and Xangô religions, as among Afro-Cuban religions, the Yoruba-affiliated denominations enjoy a prestige far out of proportion with their number of adherents (and out of proportion with the number of captives who arrived from what is now Yorubaland). Moreover, the Yoruba-affiliated denominations have been funded by the state and the bourgeoisie and protected from the police in many cases when other ethnically coded denominations have been denied funding and protection.

Yet, contrary to Mintz and Price's linguistically based view that such creole cultures form quickly and then endure, the Brazilianist literature of the 1980s suggests that Yoruba prestige is a late development and results from nothing aboriginally Yoruba but, instead, from the willingness of many Yoruba-affiliated temples to change their practices according to the aesthetic demands and political interests of their white patrons. For example, they had to disavow so-called black magic and wear white clothes instead of colorful prints. Moreover, by accepting the premise that they belonged to a distinct, African culture, they consented to their enduring marginalization from the state and the capitalist economy.

However, like Mintz and Price, the advocates of this interpretation of Afro-Brazilian religion—who include Peter Fry, Beatriz Gois Dantas, Jim Wafer, Diana Brown, Colin Henfrey, and Roberto Motta—assign a defining and structural role to the local, American political and institutional context in the formation of discrete, internally integrated, local creole cultures (i.e., patronage). This local integration of bounded, discrete cultures is analogous to structuralist visions of how languages work—that is, as closed, internally ordered, synchronic systems—hence the paradigmatic role given to creole languages in Mintz and Price's creolization model.

Collective Memory

I tell a somewhat different story about how the prestige and sponsorship of the Yoruba-Atlantic denominations came about. But let me introduce it with a reflection upon an analytic metaphor that regularly overlaps with the "creolization" metaphor. That is, the conception of "collective memory" and "forgetting" as the chief mechanism of sociocultural reproduction and the chief mechanism of diasporas' relationship to their homelands. Roger Bastide, Joan Dayan, Karen McCarthy Brown, and others have followed Maurice Halbwachs in arguing that the preservation of myths, for example, can occur only when the social relationships or places to which they refer or the institutions to which they are relevant remain intact. Bastide argues, for example, that the Yorùbá goddess Yemọja continues to be thought of as a mother in Brazil because lower-class Afro-Brazilian families tend to be what Bastide calls "matriarchal" ([1960] 1978).

Yet the failings of his "collective memory" metaphor are also instructive. It hides a great deal. For example, there are ways in which the reproduction of an image or the teaching and learning of a technique in society are not self-evidently forms of "preservation." They are as likely to be forms of appropriation, quoting, mockery, propagandistic nostalgia, and so forth. For example, when a child mocks her parent's order to "Hang up your coat, Janet! Hang up your coat!" she does not, in any simple sense, "remember" her parent's order. She displays her objection to it, rehearses future resistance to it, and gives a sign that she will "forget" to hang up her coat the next time she comes home. Likewise, virtually every African American movie these days makes a visual joke of a flamboyantly effeminate gay person. Only at a superficial level does the continual propagation of this image appear to "remember" the presence of gay people in our community. Its conspicuous intent is to ridicule, condemn, and marginalize that presence, and its conspicuous effect is less to reproduce that social role over time than to drive it underground.

Of course, few scholarly theorists are unaware of the nonliteral and sometimes deliberately distorting effects of recollection, but the term *memory*, with its usual, commonsense implication of involuntarism and disinterestedness, does little to clarify the highly political and nonliteral character of recollection, commemoration, and the reproduction of behaviors in their real social context. To the extent that it has a social reality or effect, all memory is *commemoration*—always selective, tendentious, selectively acknowledged, and acted upon in keeping with the interests of the powerful. "Memory" is too simple a metaphor for this process.

In an example more central to my argument, the following is the sort of "memory" that Afro-Bahian allies of the Candomblé articulated about Africa. Here I quote one Afro-Bahian who was interviewed by Donald Pierson in the late 1930s: "These people here in Bahia think Africans are all barbarous and uncivilized. They won't believe we write our language and that books are printed in it. . . . They don't know that in Lagos there are good schools, better than they've got in Bahia. Look at this [said Pierson's informant, pointing at the photograph of a school in Lagos]! Is there anything in Bahia as fine as that?" (Pierson 1942, 272).

I am not questioning the truth of this recollection, just pointing out the motivated and selective nature of recollection and its power in contesting enemy ideological positions. Thus, recollection—that is, the most literal type of memory—and, even more so, performances like commemorative parades involve a degree and type of nonliteralism and agency hidden by Bastide's "memory" metaphor.

Though Bastide understood Candomblé to be a socially structured but involuntary "memory" of Africa and 1980s ethnographers of Candomblé regard it as the product of white, bourgeois manipulation, these scholars were probably quite aware that leading figures in the nineteenth- and early twentieth-century Candomblé—such as Martiniano do Bonfim, Felisberto Sowzer, and Joaquim Devodê Branco—were transatlantic travelers who frequented Lagos and Porto Novo (Matory 2005). These travelers were often fluent in English or French, and like some of their counterparts in Afro-Cuban religion, many studied in Anglophone West African mission schools, where their teachers were Anglophone Africans.

On their return journeys from Lagos to Bahia and Havana, they carried with them not just the memories of a past Africa but also the cultural nationalism of late nineteenth-century Lagos, which was then a British colony. In Lagos, rising British racism during the 1880s and 1890s had inspired a lively literary and cultural movement called the Lagosian Cultural Renaissance, which documented the diverse regional practices that this movement would redefine as "Yoruba" culture and proclaimed the unique dignity of that culture.

This new "Yoruba" ethnic identity amalgamated a number of previously distinct cultural strands. The term *Yoruba* appears to come from a term that the

Hausa people used for Ọyọ, a savannah kingdom that would only later be amalgamated with the Ẹgba, the Ẹgbado, the Ijẹbu, the Ifẹ, the Awori, and so forth within the same, pan-ethnic identity (ethnic groups in what are now Nigeria and the People's Republic of Benin). This pan-ethnic identity probably first took shape in the slave forts of West Africa and on the auction blocks of the Americas. Many African American ethnic identities were named by maritime slave traders after the African port of embarkation, where captives of diverse ethnic affiliations were normally gathered together.

As Gerhard Kubik points out, the ethnonyms that came to describe Africans in the New World were initially little more than "trademarks" (1979). The bearers of these trademarks did not become ethnic groups for themselves in the Americas because they had always been that in Africa. Rather, they came to think of themselves as unified ethnic groups for a series of accumulating reasons. They did so, first, because people gathered from the same African port were, in the Americas, often selected by the same buyers for their similar technical skills and, second, because the Roman Catholic church often missionized them through trademark-targeted brotherhoods. What cultural similarities they discovered in the Americas had clearly not been salient or relevant to these populations in Africa.

The Lucumí in Cuba and the Nagô in Brazil were among those "trademark" groups that became ethnic groups for themselves for the first time in the Americas. Only much later did their ethnic counterparts in Africa receive the name *Yoruba*. They first received that name not in what is now called Yorubaland but in Freetown, Sierra Leone. Black missionary Samuel Ajayi Crowther cobbled together a new and hybrid dialect intended to be equally comprehensible to the Ọyọ, the Ẹgba, the Ẹgbado, the Awori, the Ijẹbu, and so forth, who, again, had never previously thought of themselves as a single ethnic group. Crowther and his collaborators reduced that language to writing—the first book in this language was the Bible—making it into an emblem of the new ethnic identity.

Much of its vocabulary came from the diaspora; the new capital of this new ethnic group—Lagos—was built by Afro-Brazilian hands in Brazilian architectural style. And just as the returnees helped to create Yoruba identity in West Africa, so did the products of West African cultural nationalism transform Latin American cultures. For example, the nineteenth-century founder of Afro-Brazilian studies (Raimundo Nina Rodrigues) and the twentieth-century founder of Afro-Cuban studies (Fernando Ortiz) read the publications of the Lagosian Cultural Renaissance and cited them as proof of Yoruba superiority to other Africans. They cited this literature in the defense of the Yoruba-affiliated denominations in Brazil and Cuba.

Rodrigues relied on the translations and interpretations of his informant Martiniano do Bonfim, who had himself introduced numerous innovations into

Afro-Bahian religious practice, based not upon what they learned in Ọyọ, the hinterland kingdom whose gods predominate in Brazilian Candomblé and Cuban Santería, but upon his own fictive elaborations of Ọyọ history. The occasion of this Afro-Brazilian priest's elaborations was a sojourn in Lagos between 1875 and 1886.

Martiniano's parents had sent him to attend a Presbyterian School in British colonial Lagos, and he was simultaneously being trained as a *babalawo*, or divination priest. When he returned to Bahia, he used his prestige and credibility to invent "African" traditions for which there had been no African precedents. For example, he fabricated an Ọyọ institution that would justify the founding of an Afro-Brazilian institution by the same name. At the Ilê Axé Opô Afonjá temple, he founded a set of offices called the 12 Ministers of Xangô—secular sponsors drawn largely from the unreligious Bahian bourgeoisie. Yet Martiniano claimed to be restoring Candomblé to its original form. Martiniano used this invention to confer distinction upon and to bring additional bourgeois sponsorship to his protégé—Mãe Aninha, whose temple then came to be regarded as the most "purely African" and unchanging of Afro-Brazilian—and possibly all African-diaspora—religious institutions.

The "survival," "memory," and "creolization" metaphors are insufficient to account for the most important elements of this history—the wishful, strategic, selective, border-crossing, and dialectical self-inventions that produce ethnic identities, not only in the black Atlantic world but everyplace else as well. Indeed, those analytic metaphors persuaded scholars who probably knew full well of the candomblecistas' transatlantic travels to overlook those travels or to ignore their powerfully transformative effects. Linear genealogy and bounded spaces of cultural autonomy—both implicit in the reigning family of African diasporist analytic metaphors—are less maps of real cultural history than declarations of future, nation-style independence.

Growing Pains: A Family of Metaphors in Conflict

As I noted earlier in this essay, the objects that fall under a given rubric condition ways of understanding those objects and, by contrast, other objects. Our ways of expressing knowledge and understanding exchange of knowledge shape knowledge itself: metaphors matter. Metaphors of plant growth and reproduction have furnished another family of metaphors of cultural history. Yet the plant kingdom furnishes a diverse set of forms from which to select, each suggesting a different vision of the units and flows that constitute cultural reproduction. Next, I will address a few of these forms and the productive controversies they have fertilized.

First are the popular "roots" and "diaspora" metaphors: both might be regarded as elements of what Deleuze and Guattari ([1980] 1987) call "arborescent metaphors." The term *roots* compares (1) the relationship between (1a) an ancestral or homeland culture and (1b) its descendants or diaspora to (2) the relationship between (2a) the roots of a plant and (2b) its trunk, branches, or leaves. The term *roots* suggests unidirectional, upward flow of the substances that constitute the plant's life and integrity. It suggests the temporal later-ness and superiority of the branches, along with the rudimentariness, primitivity, dirtiness, lowliness, and lack of refinement of the roots.

The term *diaspora*, too, is an arborescent metaphor in that it compares the dispersion of a people or way of life to the dissemination and germination of seeds. Diaspora inverts, without subverting, the premises that also underlie the *roots* metaphor. Imagined in terms of diaspora, the history of a culture involves the same unidirectional spread and temporal inequality that "roots" suggests. "Diaspora" also implies the unique authenticity, the unchanging nature, and the defining character of the homeland.

On the other hand, Deleuze and Guattari identify in "rhizomes" a non-arborescent plant morphology, a metaphor of cultural history that, in their view, is less beholden to the authoritarian presumptions of the state, and one that better illuminates the non-ancestral and crosscutting flows that shape any given nation or community. It was Paul Gilroy (1993) who first called attention to the virtues of this metaphor in African diaspora cultural history. However, "rhizomes" is not yet in wide enough use to reveal a clear pattern of assumptions in its scholarly usage.

In comparison to the arborescent metaphors, "rhizome" is intended, advantageously, to undermine the presumption of hierarchy and the centralization of legitimacy. It challenges the monopoly of rulers and of direct ancestors over the definition of cultural authority and group membership. Yet the biological source of this metaphor suggests a unity of organism rather than of process, an implication ill-suited, in my view, to the realities of cultural history. Culture does not come in temporally, geographically, or populationally bounded units. It is our metaphors and metonyms that chop it up into units and map a logic of collective being and action.

To my mind, any social units comparable to organisms in the history of circum-Atlantic movements and transformations of people and ideas—such as races, tribes, classes, nations, religious denominations, or the whole of the circum-Atlantic family of cultures and nations—are falling apart and regrouping on a daily, if not hourly, basis. That is, in any given hour, a person might act primarily in coordination with his or her nation and might, in the next hour, act in coordination with his or her race, ethnic group, or religion. Moreover, the criteria for belonging in any of these groupings is under constant debate.

The "rhizomes" metaphor might be adaptable to these facts. Severed segments of a rhizome system can form new and distinct organisms, but as far as I am aware, once a daughter organism has formed, it can never reunite as the same organism with its mother. Human social groupings can. Cuttings and graftings are human actions, inevitably distorted by the apparent clarity of plant metaphors from pristine nature.

"Rhizomes" inspired Paul Gilroy's reprise of several key analytic tropes from the existing African-diaspora literature—"syncretism," "creolization," "ethnohistory," and "black Atlantic" itself. In a most ironic case of the neglect of the lessons of African-diaspora scholarship, Gilroy appears to overlook the origin of these terms and concepts in a body of work that he dismisses—sometimes unfairly—as "essentialist."

The most memorable analytic trope that he draws from this literature is the "ship." Gilroy describes the cultural history of the African diaspora primarily as a discontinuous cultural exchange—as if conveyed by an anchorless ship—moving among diverse African-diaspora populations. Ships and other such vehicles moved African people and their descendants from place to place, during and after the slave trade, enabling them to influence each other across national boundaries. Books, records, and ideas moved similarly, undermining both the notion that what geographically dispersed African-diaspora populations have in common is mainly African "survivals" and the notion that African-diaspora cultures are self-contained and separated from each other by national borders.

Drawing examples primarily from the English-speaking black populations of England, the United States, and the Caribbean, Gilroy's *Black Atlantic* argues that the shared cultural features of African-diaspora groups result far less from shared survivals or cultural memories of Africa than from black Atlantic populations' mutually influential responses to their shared exclusion from the benefits of the Enlightenment legacy of national citizenship and political equality in the West. In charting the history of Anglophone black Atlantic culture, Gilroy's "ship" metonym prioritizes cultural exchange across territorial boundaries over the territorially divergent but uninterrupted "memory" of Africa posited by Bastide and followers of Melville J. Herskovits.

Yet Gilroy remains curiously comfortable with the notion of the African diaspora's continuous "memory" of slavery. For example, Gilroy believes that black Atlantic ballads about lost love symbolically commemorate slavery. But when genres inaugurated by one ethnic group, nationality, or race are adopted by another (such as soul music in Jamaica, reggae in Puerto Rico, or rumba in West

Africa and Congo/Zaïre), whose collective past is being "remembered," who is the rememberer? Weren't the regimes of slavery in the different "remembering" communities, nations, and regions different? Wouldn't the diversity of named musical genres suggest that the rememberers are diverse and at least partially constituted by nationality or locality?

Yet Gilroy, like transnationalism theorist Arjun Appadurai (1990), represents the territorial nation and the local identities it generates as contradictions to (rather than agents or optional objectives of) these ship-borne cultural crossings. Yes, local identities are in dialogue with each other across borders, but bounded identities continue to structure much of the dialogue. That is, the exchange of ideas, objects, and personnel certainly crosscuts national, ethnic, and other social boundaries. However, numerous and powerful social actors retain a stake in defining and policing those boundaries and in speaking for the populations conditionally confined by them. The power to speak on behalf of a group, to protect its monopoly on certain resources or means of livelihood, and to determine access to those resources and means keeps collective identities passionately alive and impossible for cross-cultural interlocutors to ignore. The contents and boundaries are ever-changing—often under the influence of boundary-crossers—but the elaborately drafted obituaries of nation-state, race, and tribe are not ready for publication.

The fact of extensive exchange across locales and populations should not blind us to the fact that reifications of the bounded social group—such as those implicit in arborescent metaphors and other organic metaphors of society (i.e., representations of society as a living body)—perform real and powerful work on behalf of the social and political actors who invoke them. And no actor can ignore these social facts, in even the most translocal of interactions.

And if, for Gilroy, "collective memory" usefully highlights something about Afro-Atlantic people's relationship to their past, why is the "memory" of Africa selected for denial in Gilroy's model? The credibility of this representation of black Atlantic cultural history relies less on disproof of Africa's role than on a silence about it. I offer, then, the briefest summary of an alternative analytic metaphor in the cultural history of the black Atlantic, one that begs no questions about the tropes and touchstones that people can use to think their collectiveness into being.

Dialogue

My metaphor of a black Atlantic "dialogue" (Matory [1994] 2005; 1999; 2005) suggests that Gullahs and Sierra Leoneans, Yoruba people and the

New World worshippers of the gods that became Yoruba, African Americans, black Britons and Jamaicans, and light and dark Brazilians are not discrete systems or cultures but participants in a continuous, mutually transformative dialogue. No local population is an isolated collective rememberer of or heir to a self-contained national past. Rather, collectivizing recollections and other performances are responses to the claims of other self-proclaimed classes of actors.

Ethnic or national groupings articulate the boundaries that separate them not insofar as they have historically been insulated and isolated from one another but insofar as they have engaged in dialogue and confrontation with each other. The metaphor of Afro-Atlantic dialogue places traditions—or strategically constructed genealogies of cultural reproduction—into a context beyond nation and region, into a larger, transoceanic context. Local cultures do not result merely from inheritance or from the local inertia of quick-forming, slow-changing systems. Rather, actors produce their cultures in dialogue.

Yet that dialogue is not a conversation among equals. It draws together more powerful and less powerful actors. Relative wealth, linguistic proficiency, nationality, and unequal access to the means of communication and reward distinguish one class of actors from another. On the other hand, the "dialogue" metaphor does posit one type of equality: temporal equality. It posits the radical coevalness (see Fabian 1983) of Africa, Latin America, and the United States in a dialogue that, even following the conclusion of the slave trade, has continually reshaped all of these regions. In other words, Africa is not to its diaspora as the past is to the present. Rather, Africa is an ongoing interlocutor in the cultural history that shapes us all—no less in North America than in Latin America and the Caribbean.

Equally evident is the fact that metaphors through which we think of our African American connection to Africa shape how we live our lives. For me, a Yoruba proverb sums up this phenomenon well: "Ewe ti d'ọṣẹ"—"The leaf has become the soap." Though it usually refers to how long-resident outsiders become insiders to the community, it also suggests that a leaf wrapping that once gathered up and shaped a quantity of soap eventually disappears into that soap ball, and only the historically wise are aware that the shape of the soap ball derived not from the soap but from a now-invisible leaf. Such is the role of analytic tropes in reshaping the social realities that they once only poetically described. It is when the metaphor dies that it becomes the most inescapable map for a lived reality.

Hence, in the 1970s and 1980s, the "roots" and "survivals" metaphors offered African Americans a new way of imagining and interacting with Africa. These metaphors modeled and mimed our increased willingness to dress, marry, worship, and conduct religious or heritage tourism in ways that we understood to reflect a timelessly African past. A new understanding of our "kinship across the seas" persuaded us—in the Free South Africa Movement and the movement to stop the atrocities of Sudanese Arabs against that country's black population—to intervene in the African present.

However, the "survival" and "roots" metaphors also have a way of turning real Africans into Afrocentric cardboard cutouts no more real than the "Ubangis" in Tarzan movies. They leave us surprised by the complexities of modern African life, naive in our disregard of cultural differences, and nonplussed by West Africans' failure to recognize the so-called slave forts of the coast as our Auschwitz—holy ground not to be contaminated by beautification or commercialization. Unlike African American heritage tourists, many Africans think of the slave forts as the sites of all sorts of profitable commerce, past and future.

Now that many of us not only study and travel to Africa but also have African immigrant neighbors and spouses, I ask you to imagine how much more productive the dialogue might be if we recognized its rich precedents—precedents that have involved as much commerce, musical exchange, mutual religious conversion, and transatlantic struggles against European domination as survivals of a four-century-old past.

White Africans

I conclude with one further story of a cultural process poorly highlighted or comprehended by existing analytic metaphors of African or African American cultural history. In the early 1980s, Nigerian diviner Wande Abimbọla, Afro-Puerto Rican *santera* Marta Vega, and Afro-Brazilian Candomblé priestess Mãe Stella attempted to form an international coalition based upon their and their followers' common worship of the *orişa*, or Yoruba gods. This unification effort was based on the long-standing premise that these traditions shared common African "roots" and, therefore, a common African essence. For this reason, in the view of Mãe Stella and many followers of this movement, it was time to eject the Roman Catholic saints from Candomblé and Santería, or Ocha.

Tensions first arose when Africa's definitional centrality as the roots of *orişa* religion seemed, in Abimbọla's view, to suggest that the venue of *orişa*-worshippers' world conference should return in alternating years to Ile-Ifẹ, the mythical origin of Yoruba civilization. Vega argued, on the contrary, that the conferences should begin in Ifẹ but then circulate among six American *orişa*-worshipping capitals before then returning to Ifẹ. The ranking authorities in each of the American locales objected to a further entailment of Africa's centrality—that Abimbọla and other Nigerian-born priests were more authentic in their practice and therefore, in general, possessed greater religious authority than the American priests.

Mãe Stella and Marta Vega decamped from this arrangement once its hierarchical implications became clear. They redefined themselves functionally not as Africans (or inferior American facsimiles thereof) but as a *candomblecista* and a *santera* (and as superior exemplars of those categories). The collectives most willing to accept their redefinition as "African" were those with the least seniority and status within the American systems. For example, the Italian-Brazilian *candomblecistas* of São Paulo, who have only recently converted from the more hybrid Umbanda religion, not only fully embraced Abimbọla's authority but are also the most likely among the American worshippers to wear African clothing during their rituals.

The "roots" metaphor suggests that the worshippers of African gods around the Atlantic perimeter are of one and the same organism or family. And it would seem to legitimize Abimbọla's unique authority, while the "survival" metaphor invites a restoration of the putatively lapsed integrity of the shared heritage, lending further support to Abimbọla's authority. The "collective memory" metaphor would do little to explain the African-centered conduct of the Italian-Brazilian converts to Candomblé, but it could do equally potent work (1) to justify either the discreteness of each local tradition of *orişa* worship or, alternatively, (2) to legitimize the Nigerian priesthood's centrality and unique authority. I have heard priests employ this metaphor in both ways. On the one hand, in the 1970s and 1980s, Abimbọla (1976) and other Yoruba scholars praised priests in the diaspora for having "remembered" an extraordinary amount of Yoruba language and liturgy, thus confirming the unity of a transnational religious community in which Abimbọla and other Yoruba priests were presumed to possess such great transhistorical memory—and enduring mastery of their shared, ancient religious origin—that he was qualified to mete out such generous praise. Indeed, his largesse was proof of his leadership. On the other hand, I have heard the discourse of "collective memory" used to resist Abimbọla's assertion of global leadership. The mulatto *babalao*, or divination priest, and president of the Yoruba Cultural Center of Cuba, Antonio Castañeda Márquez, told me in 1999 that his encounters with Nigerian *babalawos*, including Abimbọla, proved that colonization had caused the Nigerian priests to forget much of the tradition that Cuban *babalaos* had, through secrecy and literacy, managed to "remember." Contrary to what he surmised, from previous experience, was Abimbọla's intention, Nigerian priests had no authority over the Cubans.

Contrary to the assumptions implicit in the "roots," "survival" and "collective memory" metaphors, the world community of *orişa* worshippers is held together as much by a metahistorical vocabulary of debate—much of which it has come to share with the anthropologists—as by an objectively shared origin, practice, or recollection of the past. This debate is a form of "dialogue," but so are the moments when worshippers from diverse locales choose to highlight the sameness of similarly named gods, their shared autonomy from Christian authority, and "Yoruba" religion's unique worthiness of respect among black Atlantic religious traditions.

Applied to this case, the "creolization" metaphor aptly captures the historical importance of diverse subordinate groups' mutually transformative interaction in the context of Euro-American dominance. However, with its assumption that African American cultures are essentially local phenomena requiring local explanation, the "creolization" metaphor entirely overlooks that translocal context of local identity-making, collective self-legitimization, and the struggle for authority. Far more than "survival," "roots," "collective memory," "creolization," "ships," and "rhizomes," the "dialogue" metaphor renders the ironic completely comprehensible. Sometimes, the whitest among us—like Antonio Castañeda Márquez and the Italian *candomblecistas* of São Paulo—become the most African. Such is the power of metaphor in self-fashioning, and such is the power of "dialogue" over mere "roots," "survivals," and "collective memories."

Diasporic Dreaming

"Return Reproductive Tourism" to the Middle East

MARCIA C. INHORN

The Ethnography of an Emerging Global Technology

In 1978, Louise Brown, the world's first in vitro fertilization (IVF) baby, was born in England. In 1980, the first Islamic *fatwa* on medically assisted reproduction was written, allowing IVF to be undertaken by infertile married Muslim couples. In 1986, the first IVF clinics opened in three Middle Eastern Muslim countries, Egypt, Jordan, and Saudi Arabia. In 1988, while still a medical anthropology graduate student, I arrived in Egypt in an attempt to understand the infertility experiences of poor urban women seeking biomedical treatment in a public maternity hospital in Alexandria. This particular hospital aspired to offer IVF to Egypt's poor; thus, women were clamoring to the clinic from all over the country. Indeed, by 1991, the hospital's first IVF baby was born (Inhorn 1994). In that same year, intracytoplasmic sperm injection (ICSI), a variant of IVF designed to overcome male infertility, was introduced in Belgium. And by 1994, IVF physicians in Cairo had brought ICSI to Egypt, creating massive demand for this new assisted reproductive technology (ART). In 1996, I returned to Egypt to study the experiences of mostly elite infertile Egyptian couples who were seeking access to both IVF and ICSI (Inhorn 2003). Many of these Egyptian couples were transnational labor migrants to the petro-rich Arab Gulf who were returning on "IVF holidays" to Egypt. Although the term *reproductive tourism* had yet to be coined by the media, it was clear that Egyptian couples were crossing international borders in their "quests for conception" (Inhorn 1994).

113

By 1999, what had been a majority Sunni Islamic ban on third-party reproductive assistance—that is, no sperm donation, egg donation, embryo donation, or surrogacy—was effectively broken when Iran's leading Shia Muslim ayatollah issued a *fatwa* allowing donor technologies to be used as a "marriage savior." By 2000, clinics in Shia-dominant Iran and Lebanon had begun to offer third-party reproductive assistance to their infertile patients. In 2003, I relocated my study to Lebanon, where I found burgeoning demand for donor technologies, especially egg donation, among infertile Muslim couples (Inhorn 2012). Not all of these couples were Shia Muslims or Lebanese. Indeed, numerous Syrians, Palestinians, and couples from other Middle Eastern Muslim countries were arriving in Beirut on secret "IVF holidays" to use IVF or ICSI with donor eggs. In addition, infertile Lebanese couples were flocking back to Beirut from the diaspora. Having fled the country during the fifteen-year (1975–90) Lebanese civil war, they were "coming home" to make their "test-tube babies" in a place of cultural comfort.

Having observed these Middle Eastern "homecomings," I decided to relocate my study of assisted reproduction to a "sending" community in the heart of Arab America. My field site was Dearborn, Michigan, an ethnic enclave community with the largest number of Arabs in North America (Abraham and Shryock 2000). There, I found numerous Middle Eastern infertile couples who were dreaming of making an IVF baby "back home" in the Middle East. Over five years (2003–8), I studied these couples' longings for children, as well as their diasporic dreams of pursuing affordable ARTs in the Arab world. In 2007, I traveled to the Middle East's only "global hub" city—namely, Dubai in the United Arab Emirates—to follow the return trips of Middle Eastern infertile couples from the diaspora. In Dubai, I found not only diasporic Middle Eastern returnees but also hundreds of infertile couples from around the globe, engaging in what scholars and media pundits were now calling "reproductive tourism," "fertility tourism," "procreative tourism," or, more neutrally, "cross-border reproductive care" (CBRC) (Gürtin and Inhorn 2011).

In short, what began as a medical anthropological study of infertility among Egypt's poor emerged over time into a multisited ethnographic investigation of an emerging global technology and its uses in the Muslim Middle East. In my ethnographic studies of ARTs, the term *emergence* has special resonance. As defined by Raymond Williams (1978, 125), emergence involves "new meanings and values, new practices, new relationships and kinds of relationship [that] are continually being created." In the world of assisted reproduction, *emergence* is everywhere. First, the technologies themselves are emergent—for example, ICSI evolved as a subtle but revolutionary variant of IVF (Inhorn and Birenbaum-Carmeli 2008). Almost as soon as these new technological variants arrived, they globalized rapidly

(Inhorn 2003), creating new local markets and consumer demands (Spar 2006). Bioethical discourses surrounding these technologies—for example, whether donor technologies are permissible—are also emerging, in the Islamic world as elsewhere (Inhorn and Tremayne 2012). Furthermore, in the past decade, the global phenomenon of "reproductive tourism" has definitely emerged, with infertile couples criss-crossing the globe in pursuit of twenty-first-century, high-tech conception.

In the Middle East, a phenomenon of what I call "return reproductive tourism" is also emerging. Namely, diasporic Middle Eastern couples who are infertile often dream of making a test-tube baby "back home" for a variety of cultural, moral, and psychological reasons. In this chapter, I attempt to capture the motivations and dynamics underlying return reproductive tourism to the Middle East, based on ethnographic research undertaken in four different Middle Eastern "sending" and "receiving" communities. Only through such a multisited ethnographic research strategy would the dynamics of return reproductive tourism become clear to me.

George E. Marcus (1995) was the first to coin the term multisited ethnography to describe qualitative research that "moves from its conventional single-site location . . . to multiple sites of observation and participation that cross-cut dichotomies such as the 'local' and the 'global,' the 'lifeworld' and the 'system'" (Marcus 1995, 95). According to Marcus, such multisited research is particularly useful when examining "the circulation of cultural meanings, objects, and identities in diffuse time-space" (96). Reproductive tourism lends itself especially well to multisited ethnographic approaches, including what Marcus calls "tracking" through space and time. In my own ethnographic research, tracking routes of ART circulation has included following the spread of ARTs from Euro-American sites of invention into "receiving" sites such as Cairo and Beirut, where Middle Eastern IVF physicians have opened their clinics, offered new services, and catered to reproductive travelers. My ethnographic research has also involved listening to the stories of hundreds of Middle Eastern ART seekers in diverse locales before, during, and after their reproductive travel.

Most Middle Eastern ART seekers are practicing Muslims, and thus they are very concerned about "following the religion" in the creation of human life (Inhorn 2003, 2012). Medical anthropologist Arthur Kleinman (1997, 45) has invoked the term *local moral worlds* to capture "what is at stake in everyday experience." Local moral worlds are perhaps best exposed in the realm of medical decision making. When patients confront emerging health technologies such as ARTs, which in some way challenge their deeply embedded religious traditions, the "local moral" becomes abundantly apparent. The emergence of ARTs in the Middle East has provided an example par excellence of local moral worlds "in motion." To wit, infertile Middle Eastern Muslim couples living in diasporic communities must now make very difficult decisions about "what is at stake" in their quests for conception. In many cases, the stakes are high and the quests are transnational in nature. In this chapter, I illuminate the importance and character of this emerging phenomenon of return reproductive tourism within the burgeoning Middle Eastern diaspora of the new millennium.

Return Reproductive Tourism

To begin, I offer a concise definition of *return reproductive tourism*, which is characterized by three distinctive features: (1) it involves return to a "home" country of origin to undertake ARTs, (2) it involves a "holiday" visit to family in the home country, and (3) it is motivated by a set of factors that are different than those usually cited in the scholarly literature on reproductive tourism (i.e., restrictive laws, religion and ethics, costs, lack of services, shortages and waiting lists, safety concerns, category exclusion, lack of privacy, poor quality of care, poor success rates) (Gürtin and Inhorn 2011).

Return reproductive tourism is undertaken by expatriate populations, or those living outside their countries of birth. These expatriates may include, inter alia, immigrants, guest workers, political exiles, and refugees, all of them living in what have come to be known as "diasporas" (Dufoix 2008). Such diasporic populations number in the millions around the world and are heavily represented in the Western countries of the European Union, North America, and Australia. These diasporic communities may confront their own infertility problems, and may face the need for ARTs. But, instead of relying on "host" country ART resources and services, members of these communities undertake return reproductive tourism to countries of origin.

I focus on return reproductive tourism to the Middle East, among Middle Easterners living outside of the region and among the region's own internal migrant populations. In focusing on Middle Eastern diasporic communities and their quests for ARTs, I forward three major arguments. The first argument is historical: Even before the term *reproductive tourism* was coined at the turn of the new millennium, many infertile Middle Eastern diasporic couples had been returning to the Middle East since the arrival of ARTs in the region in the late 1980s (Inhorn 2003). This pattern continues unabated in the twenty-first century. Second, this desire for ARTs "back home" is linked to cultural and psychosocial factors so far rarely mentioned in the literature. Finally, for some diasporic infertile couples, the term *reproductive exile* is a more accurate descriptor of their ART-seeking

116

experiences (Inhorn and Patrizio 2009). Many Middle Eastern infertile couples are political exiles and refugees. Having left their home countries because of war and political violence (Inhorn 2008; Inhorn and Fakih 2005), some of these couples remain "stranded"—unable to return home because of ongoing political violence, fear of death, lack of return visas, and lack of ART services in the war-torn home country. However, most of these refugees and political exiles lack sufficient economic resources to undertake ARTs in the host country. They are a particularly tragic group of reproductive and political exiles who deserve our scholarly and activist attention.

Middle Eastern Diasporas

Originally, the term *diaspora* referred to geographically scattered religious groups living as minorities among people of other faiths. However, between the 1970s and 1990s, the term *diaspora* was greatly expanded to encompass most contemporary forms of out-migration. As noted by French scholar Stephane Dufoix in his book *Diasporas*, "'Diaspora' has become a term that refers to any phenomenon of dispersion from a place; the organization of an ethnic, national, or religious community in one or more countries; a population spread over more than one territory; the places of dispersion; any nonterritorial space where exchanges take place, and so on" (Dufoix 2008, 2).

For centuries, the Middle East has been a site of both diasporic concentration and dispersion. For example, Armenians fleeing the Ottoman Turks settled in ethnic enclave communities in Lebanon, Syria, and Egypt. Similarly, the Druze, a persecuted Shia Muslim minority subgroup, fled to the high mountains of Lebanon, Syria, and what would become the state of Israel in 1948. In more recent years, the region has been home to significant internal and external migration because of three historical processes: (1) mid-twentieth-century decolonization movements across the Middle East and North Africa, some of it associated with bloody violence (e.g., Algeria); (2) uneven regional political economies, related largely to the varying regional dispersion of oil wealth; and (3) political violence and outright war occurring in many Middle Eastern nations over the past sixty years (Gelvin 2005). This includes ten military interventions by the United States alone, including its two recent wars in Iraq and Afghanistan (Inhorn 2008). In 2011, most of the revolutionary uprisings across the Middle Eastern region have involved violence and the flight of refugees, especially from Libya and Syria.

Not surprisingly, these three major factors—decolonization, uneven political economies, and political violence—have led to massive population movements within the Middle East and beyond. The Middle East and North Africa have the largest percentage of migrants in the world and the world's highest proportion of internally displaced persons (IDPs) (Mowafi 2011). It is probably fair to say that no other region of the world has been more affected by the population disruptions and diasporic dispersions associated with political violence. Over the past two decades in particular, fifteen of the twenty-two Middle Eastern nation-states (roughly 85 percent of the region's total population) have suffered in protracted conflict situations (Mowafi 2011). However, this figure does not include the new situations of political violence emerging since the 2011 "Arab spring."

Among the most significant patterns of violence-related internal migration within the Middle East are: (1) the expulsion of Palestinians from Israel in 1948, with movements into Jordan, Lebanon, Syria, and Palestinian enclaves in the Arab Gulf; (2) the exodus of Lebanese to a variety of Middle Eastern countries during the Lebanese civil war (1975–90), subsequent Israeli occupation of southern Lebanon (1990–2000), and the 2006 Israel-Lebanese "summer war"; (3) massive Egyptian labor out-migration, first to Iraq during the 1980s Iran-Iraq War (followed by their expulsion at the time of the first Gulf War) and then to most countries of the Arab Gulf over the past two decades; (4) political exile of nearly half a million Sudanese to Egypt and the Arab Gulf because of Sudan's ongoing civil war; (5) two waves of Iraqi refugees, first to Saudi Arabia (with subsequent resettlement in the United States) after the first Gulf War (1990–91) and then more than 4.8 million Iraqi IDPs and refugees moving to Syria, Jordan, and Lebanon in the aftermath of the 2003 U.S.-led invasion of Iraq; (6) 6 million Afghan refugees fleeing to Pakistan and Iran in the aftermath of the Soviet invasion of Afghanistan (1979) and since the 2001 U.S.-led war in that country; and (7) on a more mundane level, movement of hundreds of thousands of educated professionals from resource-poor Middle Eastern countries to the booming Arab Gulf economies.

What is perhaps less realized is the extent to which Middle Eastern diasporic populations have simply fled the region altogether.[1] Of the estimated 15 million Lebanese worldwide, only 3.5 million live in Lebanon today. Nearly 7 million Lebanese are estimated to live in Brazil alone, and nearly one-half million in the United States, where they make up the single largest group of Arab Americans. Lebanese ethnic enclaves can also be found throughout the world, including in most parts of Latin America and the Caribbean, in French-speaking West Africa (particularly Côte d'Ivoire, Sierra Leone, and Senegal), and Europe, Australia, and Canada. Of the estimated 11 million Palestinians worldwide, 6.6 million are refugees and nearly one-half million are internally displaced persons. Nearly 1 million Palestinians live outside the region, mostly in Chile, but also in a variety of Latin American and Western countries. Following the 1979 Islamic revolution, 4 to 5 million Iranians left the country, primarily going to North America (both the

United States and Canada), Europe, and Australia. Since the 1979 Soviet invasion and the 2001 U.S.-led war in Afghanistan, Afghans now constitute the world's largest refugee population, with more than 3 million Afghans fleeing to other countries, including 200,000 who have received asylum in the West. Sadly, the number of Iraqis who have received political asylum and resettlement in the West since 2003 is estimated at only 60,000, according to the United Nations High Commission for Refugees and the U.S. Citizenship and Immigration Services.

In addition to these "violence-created" diasporas, millions of Middle Easterners have also fled economic poverty in resource-poor countries. Nearly 18 million Syrians are estimated to live outside the Middle East, primarily in North America, Europe, South America (particularly Brazil, Chile, Venezuela, and Colombia), Australia, and Africa. Between 7 and 9 million Turks now live in Europe as "guest workers," including nearly half of them in Germany alone. Approximately 4.5 million Moroccans live abroad, with two-thirds of these in Europe. As the former colonial power, France is home to 1.6 million Moroccans, but large populations of Moroccans also live in Spain (767,000), Italy (500,000), the Netherlands (350,000), Germany (200,000), and the United States (200,000). Because of France's history of colonialism in North Africa, millions of Algerians and Tunisians have also migrated there, especially during the 1992–2002 decade of Islamist political violence in Algeria. Nearly one-half million Egyptians, both poor laborers and educated professionals, have migrated to the United States, Canada, and Italy. Finally, hailing from one of the world's poorest nations, nearly 600,000 Yemenis live outside their country, mostly in India and parts of Southeast Asia (e.g., Singapore), but also in the United Kingdom (80,000) and the United States (12,000). Inside the country, 7 million Yemenis live in hunger, yet Yemen has granted refugee status to 164,000 Somalis since the Somali civil war, which began in 1988 (Mowafi 2011). Unofficial estimates of Somalis in Yemen put the figures at 1 million, further exacerbating poverty, unemployment, malnutrition, and now political violence in the country.

The Multisited Studies

Given the massive scope of this Middle Eastern diaspora, it is important to understand how Middle Eastern expatriate communities deal with their infertility problems and attempt to access ART services, including through return to home countries. As noted earlier, this chapter examines the phenomenon of return reproductive tourism to the Middle East based on ethnographic studies of infertility and ART-seeking in four different Middle Eastern locations, as summarized in table 1.

Table 1. Middle Eastern study populations

Year of study	Country of study	Country of origin ("home")	Country of current residence ("host")	Number of "return reproductive tourists"	Primary type of diasporic population studied
1996	Egypt	Egypt	Arab Gulf countries	18 of 66 (to Egypt)	Egyptian labor migrants, mostly middle-class professionals
2003	Lebanon	Lebanon, Syria, Palestine	Sub-Saharan Africa; other Middle Eastern countries; North America; South America; Europe; Asia	37 of 189 (to Lebanon); also 20 Syrian reproductive tourists (to Lebanon)	Lebanese war refugees, who permanently resettled in host countries
2003–8	United States (Detroit, Michigan)	Lebanon, Syria, Palestine, Yemen, Iraq	United States	3 of 95 (2 to Lebanon, 1 Iraqi refugee couple to Bahrain)	Lebanese, Palestinian, and Iraqi war refugees; Syrian and Yemeni labor migrants; mostly recent resettlement in the U.S
2007	United Arab Emirates	50 countries in South Asia, Middle East, Europe, sub-Saharan Africa, Australia, US	7 Emirates of UAE, plus 17 countries	219 "reproductive travelers" (to UAE)	Temporary reproductive "tourists" to UAE, as well as labor migrants to UAE, mostly middle-class professionals

The first study, undertaken in 1996 in two major, private hospital–based IVF clinics in Cairo, Egypt, involved 66 ART-seeking Egyptian women and 27 of their husbands, many of whom were currently living outside the country, mostly as middle-class professionals in the Arab Gulf. Of the 66 women patients interviewed, 18 were living abroad with their husbands in the Gulf. The primary host country was Saudi Arabia (10 of 18), but a number of Egyptian couples were also living in the smaller Gulf countries of Oman, United Arab Emirates (UAE), and Qatar. This initial study was intended to examine the introduction of ARTs in

Egypt and included couples suffering from female infertility, male infertility, or both (Inhorn 2003).

The second study, undertaken in 2003, was based in two major IVF clinics in Beirut, Lebanon, one in a private university hospital and the other in a private stand-alone clinic. As an ethnographic case-control study of male infertility and ART-seeking, 120 infertile men (cases) and 100 fertile men (controls) were interviewed, as were 44 of their wives. Most of the men were Lebanese, but 20 were Syrian, and 11 were Palestinians either living in Lebanon or in the Palestinian diaspora. Importantly, nearly half of the men in the study (exactly 100) had spent extended periods of their lives abroad, in exactly 50 different countries of residence. At the time of the study, 32 of the Lebanese men were living abroad, including 11 in sub-Saharan Africa (Côte d'Ivoire, Sierra Leone, Senegal, Nigeria, Gabo, Ethiopia); 10 in other parts of the Middle East (Saudi Arabia, UAE, Kuwait, Yemen, Egypt, Tunisia); 5 in North America; 3 in South America (Brazil, Panama); 2 in Europe (Netherlands, Switzerland); and 1 in Asia (Taiwan). In addition, all 20 of the Syrian men in the study had traveled with their wives to Beirut to seek cross-border ART services, as had 5 of the Palestinian men living in the Arab Gulf (Abu Dhabi and Dubai) and Central Asia (Kazakhstan). In total, 57 of the 220 men—or exactly 25 percent—were undertaking cross-border reproductive care at the time of the study. Of these, 37 men—or 17 percent of the total study population—were engaging in return reproductive tourism to Lebanon, primarily to undertake ICSI for male infertility but also for their wives' infertility problems (Inhorn 2012).

Following the Lebanese study, a five-year research project (2003–8) on infertility and ART treatment seeking was conducted among the Middle Eastern diasporic population in southeastern Michigan, the largest ethnic enclave of Middle Easterners in North America. According to the 2000 census, more than 400,000 Arab Americans live in so-called Arab Detroit (Abraham and Shryock 2000), which represents nearly 30 percent of the entire U.S. Arab American population. Most of these Arab Americans live in Dearborn, a southwestern suburb of Detroit, which has been dubbed the "capital of Arab America." Arab Americans living in Dearborn are mostly Lebanese, Syrian, Palestinian, and Yemeni migrants and refugees. But, since the first Gulf War in 1991, 80,000 Iraqi refugees also settled in this ethnic enclave community, with thousands of new Iraqi refugees arriving since 2003. Within this community, the study was based in an Arab-serving IVF satellite clinic in Dearborn, where 95 Arab Americans—55 men and 40 women, including 31 couples together—were interviewed. Most of the Arab Americans in the study were from Lebanon, Iraq, and Yemen (in that order), but several Palestinians, Syrians, and one Moroccan immigrant were also included (Inhorn and Fakih

2005). As in Lebanon, the initial focus of this study (2003–5) was on male infertility and ICSI but later included couples with female infertility problems.

The final study was undertaken in 2007 in the UAE, then a booming Arab Gulf country. This study was focused specifically on the phenomenon of reproductive tourism. It was based in the UAE's largest private IVF clinic, located on the border of the neighboring emirates of Dubai and Sharjah. There, in-depth ethnographic interviews were conducted with 219 reproductive travelers, representing 125 infertile couples hailing from exactly 50 countries. The majority were Indian, followed in rank order by Lebanese, Emiratis, British, Pakistanis, Sudanese, Filipinos, and Palestinians. The ART treatment and travel trajectories of these couples were explored, including, in some cases, return reproductive tourism to a variety of Middle Eastern countries (Inhorn and Shrivastav 2010).[2]

Return Reproductive Tourism
to the Middle East

As noted earlier, the phenomenon of return reproductive tourism began long before the term was ever coined. In the 1996 Egyptian study, a pattern of return reproductive tourism was noted among mostly middle-class and upper-middle-class Egyptian labor migrant couples, who were returning from the Arab Gulf during their annual summer leaves. Because the Arab Gulf states are unbearably warm during the summer months, many migrant couples return to Egypt during July, August, or September. During this one-month holiday back home, infertile Egyptian migrant couples may attempt a single ART cycle in an Egyptian IVF clinic. As a result, IVF clinics in Cairo are packed with return reproductive tourists during the summer months (Inhorn 2003).

According to Egyptian migrant couples in this study, three major factors underlay their transnational treatment quests: (1) the greater affordability of ART services in Egypt versus the Gulf countries, (2) the greater trust in Egyptian medicine over medicine in the Gulf, and (3) the perceived ease and comfort of undertaking ARTs in a familiar environment, including staying temporarily in one's natal home with supportive parents. Thus, these visits to Egypt were in some sense "IVF holidays," in that they combined dimensions of treatment seeking with pleasure and relaxation.

On the other hand, virtually all of the Egyptian couples in the study emphasized that undertaking IVF "back home" often ruined their annual vacations. These visits to Egypt included the stresses of hormonal injections; daily trips to IVF clinics for follicular monitoring; costly and time-consuming surgical egg retrievals and embryo transfers; and, in many cases, the perceived need to hide the

IVF cycle from most, if not all, family members. Because ICSI to overcome male infertility had just been introduced to Egypt at the time of the study, it was especially shrouded in secrecy (Inhorn 2003). Thus, couples with an infertile husband were often simultaneously attempting to maintain complete medical privacy and achieve "holiday-like" merriment with family members. Balancing levity with medical embodiment of ARTs—all during a single summer month in Egypt—was often profoundly difficult to achieve. It is also important to note that, in some cases, labor migration in the Gulf had preceded the discovery of the couple's infertility. However, in other cases, couples had chosen to migrate to the Gulf precisely because they needed the higher incomes necessary to generate cash for ART seeking back in Egypt.

In the second study in Lebanon, which focused on male infertility, a similar pattern of return reproductive tourism for ICSI was discovered. As in the Egyptian study, some Lebanese men were working as temporary expatriates in the Arab Gulf. However, most were permanent residents of other countries, having fled during *al harb*, "the war," which lasted from 1975 to 1990. During the civil war period, almost one-third of the Lebanese population fled the country, especially young men, whose families wanted them to avoid conscription or militia involvement. Many Lebanese youth were sent to the Arab Gulf to work. Others were sent to live with family members or friends already residing outside of the Middle East, particularly in West Africa.

Of the 32 Lebanese return reproductive tourists interviewed in Beirut IVF clinics in 2003, their reasons for returning to Lebanon were quite similar to those offered by Egyptians. In general, they cited (1) increased affordability of ARTs in Lebanon, especially for those living in North America; (2) increased trust in Lebanese medicine over medicine in the host country, especially for those living in other Middle Eastern countries; and (3) desire to experience an ART cycle in the midst of a supportive family environment. However, for Lebanese living in West Africa, they were essentially "forced" to return to Lebanon because of a lack of ART services in their host countries. Sub-Saharan Africa is a major region of the world where ART services are relatively absent. Of the 191 WHO member states, only 48 had medical facilities offering ARTs as of 2006 (Nachtigall 2006). ART facilities are absent in the majority of the 34 sub-Saharan African nations, which are struggling with life-threatening diseases such as HIV/AIDS, neonatal and maternal mortality, malaria, and tuberculosis (Okonofua 1996). Although Lebanese diasporic communities in West Africa are often comparatively affluent, ARTs are simply not available in host countries. For example, with 100,000 Lebanese living in Abidjan, the capital of Côte d'Ivoire, the city hosts a Lebanese hospital with Lebanese physicians. However, there is no IVF clinic in that hospital or in the country as a whole. It is also important to point out that, as of 2011, political violence in Côte d'Ivoire does not bode well for the diasporic Lebanese community in that country.

In Arab America, on the other hand, the situation was reversed. ART services are readily available. However, the average price of one ART cycle in the United States is greater than $12,000 (Spar 2006). There are very few American "mandate states," which provide either full or partial ART subsidization to state residents. Furthermore, very few U.S. insurance companies cover the complete costs of an ART cycle. Thus, most Americans pay for ART services entirely out of pocket, which is why less than 1 percent of infertile Americans ultimately conceive through IVF and related technologies (Spar 2006).

This was certainly true of the infertile Arab American couples in the Dearborn study. With few exceptions, most of those interviewed were either war refugees or political exiles from Lebanon and Iraq, or economic refugees from poor rural communities in Yemen. The vast majority of these infertile Arab Americans were impoverished, working in unskilled positions without medical benefits. Many of them could barely pay for office visits (at $150), let alone the cost of a single ART cycle (Inhorn and Fakih 2005). Among the total group of nearly 100 interviewees, only 19 ICSI cycles had ever been undertaken—but 6 of these had been tried by one upper-middle-class Lebanese couple, twice in the United States and four times through return reproductive tourism to Lebanon. Among the remaining 13 ICSI cycles, two had involved reproductive tourism to the Middle East (Lebanon, Bahrain). The rest had been performed in the United States under great financial duress. Couples in the study had taken out bank loans or loans from friends and family, had sold wives' bridal gold or family land back in the "home country," or put the entire cost of the ICSI cycle onto a credit card, going deep into debt in the process.

Indeed, financial duress was a major theme of these Arab American interviews, as was the deep demoralization of ICSI failures. From the 19 total ICSI cycles, only two children—both sons of Iraqi refugees—had been born, one as a result of travel to an IVF clinic in Bahrain, a small Arab Gulf island nation near Iraq. It is important to note that at the time of this writing there were no functioning IVF clinics in most of Iraq, including in the capital city of Baghdad. Iraqi couples who require ARTs must travel to Mosul, a Kurdish-dominated city in the northern territory of Iraq, where Kurdish is spoken as the first language. Those Iraqis who can afford to do so may travel to the neighboring countries of Syria, Jordan, and Iran, each with its own active ART sector (Abbasi-Shavazi et al. 2008). Although once renowned for its medical infrastructure and high level of medical expertise, Iraq has experienced the decimation of its medical system during the current war period, including the targeted killing of medical personnel by militia groups and the subsequent flight of most qualified physicians from the country (Inhorn 2008; Inhorn and Kobeissi 2006). Many of these physicians have settled in neighboring Middle Eastern countries, such as Syria, Jordan, Lebanon, and Egypt, and a few have been given political asylum in Western countries, including the United States.

Diasporic Dreaming: Return Reproductive Tourism Back Home

Why do diasporic Middle Eastern infertile couples dream of making a test-tube baby back home? Over the series of studies described above, five major factors "pulling" infertile diasporic couples back home have become apparent. A sixth factor—perceived cultural discrimination—serves as a "push" factor for some couples, who believe that they are either treated unfairly or neglected in a host country's medical system. Interestingly, none of these factors are the ones repeatedly cited in the cross-border reproductive care literature (i.e., laws, religion and ethics, costs, lack of services, shortages and waiting lists, safety, category exclusion, privacy, quality of care, success rates). This list of standard factors emphasizes the push toward travel: namely, couples feel forced out of their home countries by various restrictions, constraints, and pragmatic reasons such as comparative costs. With return reproductive tourism, on the other hand, the desire to travel is fueled by a number of pull factors, which are described below with accompanying ethnographic vignettes.

MEDICAL "EX-PATRIOTISM"

Middle Eastern expatriates living in diasporic communities abroad often maintain both patriotic and nostalgic attachments to home, even if they have never lived in the home country. Such patriotism may be manifest in feelings about the relative superiority of home-country medical services versus those in the host country. Such medical "ex-patriotism" (Inhorn 2003) is clearly found among both Egyptian and Lebanese expatriates, who are often convinced of the superior medical professionalism and "experience" to be found in home country ART clinics. Among Egyptians, this medical ex-patriotism is rooted in the fact that Egypt was one of the first three countries to initiate ARTs in the region, as well as Egypt's long history of medicine and large number of medical schools. As a result, many Egyptian expatriates declared Egyptian ART services to be more "professional," "advanced," and "experienced" than in host countries, including the Arab Gulf.

Interestingly, these were the same three adjectives used by Lebanese expatriates to describe Lebanese ART centers and physicians. Even though Lebanon was a relative latecomer to ARTs—opening its first centers nearly a decade later than Egypt because of delays caused by the civil war (Inhorn, Patrizio, and Serour 2010)—prewar Lebanon was often touted as the "Switzerland of the Middle East," and Beirut was compared to Paris. Prewar Lebanon was known for its excellent medical education and services, with a highly functioning medical system and many Western-trained specialists. According to most Lebanese expatriates, Lebanon's spirit of entrepreneurialism and resilience could never be thwarted. Thus, they trusted the postwar medical system in Lebanon, including its fairly new ART clinics (begun in the mid-1990s), more than they trusted ART services in their host countries. Interestingly, this was true even among Lebanese expatriates living in Europe and North America. Many of them touted the better "experience" of Lebanese IVF physicians over American, Canadian, or European counterparts. As one Lebanese man living in Dearborn told me: "Don't forget! In Lebanon, they've got experience for this one [ARTs] better than here. For this one [ARTs], Lebanon probably has better experience than the U.S." A Lebanese women living in Dearborn explained: "Medicine in Lebanon is, what do you say? It is like 'progressive,' and I trust them." Another Lebanese expatriate put it even more strongly: "Honestly, Lebanese medicine is number one in the world! We're confident one hundred percent."

Such patriotic pride in one's country and its medical system is a compelling reason for many Middle Eastern infertile couples to return home. Even Iraqi refugees spoke with pride about Iraq's prewar medical field. One young Iraqi refugee couple reminisced about their country in this way. According to the husband: "We both left Iraq when we were young, and so we really don't know how the medical field is now. But they were very good, sincerely good, and [there were] a lot of very good Iraqi doctors, very smart doctors." His wife added, poignantly: "I would like to go and visit, but maybe not now. Not until the war is over. I would love to go back home to Iraq. But if you want to go back home and you see your country and feel bad all the time, you will just go there and get depressed."

LANGUAGE OF MEDICINE

A second major factor compelling return reproductive tourism is a linguistic one: namely, undertaking a cycle of ARTs involves a complex "ontological choreography" (Thompson 2005), accompanied by an arcane medical language. Learning this medical language is difficult enough for many infertile couples who are natives in the country of treatment seeking. However, for Middle Eastern diasporic couples who speak Arabic as their first—and perhaps only—language, the thought of going through the complexities of an ART cycle in an unfamiliar linguistic register is incredibly daunting. Thus, many of these couples prefer to return home in order to speak the same language as ART staff and, hence, understand the medical terminology, instructions, and explanations delivered to them. In the Arabic-speaking world, the vocabulary and language of ART medicine is delivered to patients in Arabic that is rich with "seeds," "planting," "spermatic animals," "microscopic injections," "babies of the tubes," and the like (Inhorn 2003).

The importance of familiar medical language in one's native tongue cannot be underestimated. This is especially true for monolingual Arabic speakers. In the Dearborn study, for example, exactly 40 percent of those interviewed spoke no English whatsoever or managed to get by in barely functional "broken English." This was especially true of Yemeni migrants, especially Yemeni wives, many of whom were illiterate in both Arabic and English. For Iraqi refugees, especially those entering the United States in the aftermath of the 2003 invasion, most infertile couples in the study were still struggling with English. Even some Lebanese, the most "acculturated" group of expatriates in Detroit's Arab community, were not proficient in English, especially if they had fled Lebanon in the aftermath of the 2006 Israeli-Hizbullah summer war.

As many of these monolingual Arabic speakers explained, they had come to the particular study clinic because of its Arabic-speaking physician and clinic receptionist. Several couples in the study had actually traveled great distances across state borders to access the particular Arabic-speaking clinician. For example, following an eight-hour drive, an Iraqi refugee couple explained: "We came here from Nashville because the doctor is Arabic. When we ask him about our case, he understands us. But the doctors in Nashville don't." The husband added: "We tried too much in Nashville, with three different American doctors. We met a nice American woman doctor who tried to help us. But I'm coming here now because at least we can speak Arabic, and it takes someone who can do that to really understand our problem." Similarly, a young Lebanese woman who had flown to Michigan from Mississippi commented: "I live with my husband in another state, but I came here just to see the doctor, because I need an Arabic doctor. It doesn't matter if he's Lebanese or not, but I just need to understand everything in Arabic. I can talk English, and I can understand, but the questions about these medical things are going to be easier for me in Arabic."

CO-RELIGION AND MORAL TRUSTWORTHINESS

In addition to linguistic similarity, many Middle Eastern couples want to receive ARTs from a physician of a similar religious background. For most Middle Easterners, this means seeking out an ART practitioner who is a Muslim. The reasons have less to do with a sense of Muslim moral superiority than with the belief that a Muslim co-religionist will understand the particular Islamic bioethical considerations surrounding ARTs. These Islamic guidelines are rich and complex (M. Clarke 2009; Inhorn 2003; Inhorn and Tremayne 2012; Serour 2008). To reiterate a point made earlier, the dominant Sunni branch of Islam—constituting nearly 90 percent of the world's Muslims—disallows any form of third-party reproductive assistance, including egg donation, sperm donation, embryo donation, or surrogacy. For Shia Muslims, on the other hand, third-party reproductive assistance has been allowed by Ayatollah Ali Husayn al-Khamene'i, the Supreme Leader of the Islamic Republic of Iran. Hence, donor technologies and surrogacy are now widely practiced in Iran and also in Lebanon, which has followed the Iranian lead (Abbasi-Shavazi et al. 2008; M. Clarke 2009; M. Clarke and Inhorn 2011; Inhorn 2006; Inhorn 2012; Inhorn and Tremayne 2012).

For Sunni Muslim ART patients, then, the major moral concern is avoiding any kind of third-party donation, either intentional or accidental (i.e., through medical negligence). Sunni Muslim ART patients are often concerned about finding a Sunni Muslim physician who runs a clinic where donor technologies are never employed. Issues of moral trustworthiness are clearly at stake. A Sunni Muslim physician, it is argued, will understand patients' fears about "mixing" (of gametes and embryos). A Sunni Muslim ART practitioner will be particularly morally trustworthy in this regard, paying special attention to the labeling of specimens, the laboratory handling of gametes, and the transfer of embryos, in order to avoid at all costs the "three Ms"—mixtures, mix-ups, and mistakes. Furthermore, because of moral injunctions against "touch and gaze" across genders, some pious Sunni Muslims prefer an ART practitioner to be female, so as to avoid the "male gaze" in the intimacy of a gynecological setting.

A Lebanese labor migrant explained his wife's reluctance to attempt IVF with a well-known Indian Hindu physician practicing in the UAE. "My wife still had the feeling, 'How am I going to start treatment with a non-Muslim?' First of all, he's a man, but she prefers a lady [physician]. Second, he's non-Muslim. She mentioned it one time . . . and then she didn't mention it anymore. It was a kind of anxiety; she was not feeling comfortable because he is not Muslim." He added: "Her family [members] are religious, and they practice the religion, and they are sharing her decision about the need for a Muslim doctor." Because of his Syrian wife's desire for a co-religionist, this Lebanese migrant, who was living in Dubai, flew to Lebanon five times over a period of six years to undertake ICSI, never achieving a single pregnancy. In desperation, his wife finally agreed to try ICSI with the Indian doctor in the UAE. Fortunately, they succeeded on their first attempt, bearing a healthy ICSI daughter.

DONOR PHENOTYPE

Shia Muslims, too, often want a co-religionist and ideally a female Muslim ART physician, particularly if they are religiously pious. However, for those Shia Muslims who accept the idea of third-party donation, they are often concerned about achieving phenotypic similarity with the donor, which, they argue, can be better achieved by returning to the home country. A donor of similar phenotype is desired mostly for the sake of the donor child; a child who looks "Arab" or "Middle Eastern" will be believed to be the biological offspring of the infertile couple. This, in turn, will prevent future uncertainty, curiosity, skepticism, or ridicule, especially given that donor technologies are a relatively recent innovation in the Middle East (ca. 1999) and are not widely accepted by the Muslim majority.

Having said this, both Iran and Lebanon, the only two Muslim-majority countries in the world where donor technologies and surrogacy are practiced, are becoming the sites of donor-driven return reproductive tourism, as well as more general cross-border reproductive travel among Middle Eastern couples of all religious backgrounds who are seeking donor gametes and surrogacy. In general, egg donation is much more widely accepted than sperm donation, and sperm donation is more common than surrogacy (Inhorn 2012). In Iran, embryo donation is also widely practiced, although less so (if at all) in Lebanon. Nonetheless, both Iran and Lebanon are becoming known in Middle Eastern circles as sites of third-party reproductive assistance. Increasingly, infertile Middle Eastern couples of all religious backgrounds—Sunni, Shia, Druze, Catholic, Orthodox, and Protestant—are traveling to these two countries to access donor gametes, particularly donor eggs.

For example, during the 2003 Lebanese study, 11 couples were using donor gametes, including 6 couples who had traveled to Lebanon for this purpose. Three were Syrian reproductive tourists, 1 was a Palestinian couple living in Dubai, but 2 were Lebanese return reproductive tourists living in Kuwait and the United States. These 11 couples were religiously diverse: 4 Sunni, 3 Shia, 1 Druze, 1 Maronite Catholic, 1 Greek Orthodox, and 1 Armenian Orthodox. In 10 of the 11 cases, donor eggs were being sought. Only one infertile man in the study—a Shia Muslim who followed the clerical directives of Ayatollah Khamene'i in Iran—had actually accepted donor sperm, in this case, from a Lebanese medical student.

In short, the Shia Muslim permission of donor technologies emanating from Iran has served to weaken the Sunni Muslim ban on this practice, thereby initiating a new form of reproductive tourism back to the Middle East, which is driven by donor phenotype. A Lebanese-Palestinian couple attempted to explain their desire for an egg donor who resembled either the light-skinned "white" husband or the olive-skinned "brown" wife. According to the husband: "People here will say it's okay. Nothing's wrong, because I am white. Also, if my wife does not get a white child, it's okay. I'm white, but she's brown, so if the baby is brown, it's no problem. But if the baby is coming Filipino, then that's a problem, and I will refuse it! That means that one man who is Filipino slept with my wife! Or that's what people will say if my wife uses eggs from a Filipino." Clearly, in this couple's local moral world, both the baby's future and the wife's moral reputation are at stake, which is why achieving donor phenotypic similarity is deemed crucial.

COMFORTS OF HOME

In addition, many husbands are concerned that their wives experience ART conceptions under optimal circumstances, surrounded by the tender loving care of family members, especially wives' mothers. In the Middle East, mothers and daughters are often extremely close, deeming each other to be "best friends" in life (Inhorn 1996). Thus, if there is a single family member who knows about a couple's ART seeking, it is generally the wife's mother, and often the husband's mother as well. Not surprisingly, Middle Eastern IVF clinic waiting areas are often crammed with elderly women, who are there to support their daughters and sons through the trials and tribulations of the "operation" (as egg retrievals and embryo transfers are called).

Not only is such maternal support deemed psychologically comforting, but many diasporic infertile Middle Eastern couples maintain an ardent belief that they will become pregnant if they can somehow manage to try ARTs back in the home country. Return reproductive tourism back home is deemed more "relaxed," more "familiar," and more "comforting"—in short, much less stressful than attempting to access ARTs in an unfamiliar host country clinical setting. This belief in the psychosocial benefits of simply being "at home" while pursuing ARTs is an important factor and a repeating theme among reproductive tourists of all kinds. Indeed, in the study of reproductive travel undertaken in the UAE, most travelers were adamant about the "comforts of home" and the importance of being in the home environment, if possible, when undergoing an ART cycle (Inhorn and Shrivistav 2010).

A young Lebanese couple, married for six years, had been unable to become pregnant since arriving as immigrants to Dearborn, Michigan. They were frustrated by their diagnosis of unexplained infertility and were seriously considering returning to Lebanon to undergo IVF. As the husband explained: "Actually, I was thinking of going back to Lebanon, because she believes that better doctors are over there, and also that she can get pregnant 'by her family.' Her mother is over there. Her father passed away, but her mom is there and she went to a few doctors to ask about my wife's case. If [my wife] went back there, it's better for her. Her mom, she also thinks that if [my wife] goes there, she can get pregnant." He added: "It's not an issue of money. IVF *is* cheaper there, but it is more about what she believes. She's never been back to Lebanon since she got here in 2003. Psychologically, this could be a good reason to go back."

DISCRIMINATION

One of the reasons why Middle Eastern infertile couples may want to return home is that they do not feel comfortable in host country ART clinics. Subtle and not-so-subtle forms of cultural discrimination may be at work, especially for Arabs and Muslims in a post–September 11 world (Inhorn and Fakih 2005; Inhorn and Serour 2011; Shaheen 2008). During the studies in Lebanon and Dearborn, several cases of outright medical discrimination were reported during interviews with infertile couples. For example, a Shia Muslim man living in Lebanon had been seriously injured in a car accident. He sought emergency medical care in Lebanon but was referred for rehabilitation to the United States. Unfortunately, he was denied an exit visa by the U.S. Embassy in Beirut, because he lived in the Hizbullah stronghold of Baalbek. His lack of full recovery had left him partially paralyzed and impotent, thus requiring ICSI with testicular aspiration in order to conceive.

In a somewhat different case, a Lebanese refugee living in the Netherlands was denied referral for ICSI by his Dutch primary care physician following a diagnosis of azoospermia. The Dutch physician, who was not an infertility specialist, deemed azoospermia to be "hopeless," and he repeatedly refused to refer his Lebanese patient for further fully subsidized medical evaluation within the Netherlands. Eventually, this Lebanese man accrued enough money to return to Lebanon, where ICSI with testicular aspiration (costing $5,000) led to the birth of a healthy son. At the time of his interview, this new father was justifiably angry at "those Dutch doctors." He described his plan to petition the Dutch government for reimbursement of all his treatment and travel expenses and was collecting the necessary documents from the Lebanese ART clinic.

Other examples of discrimination—or at least profound lack of cultural sensitivity—abounded. For example, a young Yemeni couple, married for eleven years, described their dream of seeking ARTs back in Yemen, if they could only afford it. The wife lamented the discrimination they had faced at the hands of American physicians. "Some doctors in Yemen are so-so, but some are good and specialized. I wish I can go to Yemen [for ARTs], because it is not the same as here." She continued:

If the doctors here were Arab, we can trust them more than Americans. When we went to the doctor [from a town in Michigan], he was an American male. We told him that we want a child, and he told us:

"Why are you coming?!"

"We want pregnancy."

"You're young! *You* are babies!"

"No, I *want*."

"What *we* think about *you*—we think *you're* babies."

"No, I'm *not* a baby."

In this dialogue, the physician's blatant misrecognition of a young Yemeni couple's justifiable desire to have a child after eleven years of marriage is all the more egregious because of the perceived name-calling—telling an adult couple that they are "babies," too young to be parents. The Yemeni wife in this story is remarkable for defending herself—in English—to the offensive American male physician. In so doing, she claims her right to be perceived as an adult and a potential mother of an American child.

Conclusion

This chapter has attempted to capture ethnographically the emergence of a new phenomenon, return reproductive tourism to the Middle East. Across the Middle Eastern diaspora, infertile couples often dream of making a test-tube baby back home, for a variety of cultural, moral, and psychological reasons. These reasons—including medical ex-patriotism, the language of medicine, co-religion and moral trustworthiness, donor phenotype, the comforts of home, and discrimination—are rarely highlighted in the scholarly literature on cross-border reproductive care. Thus, further ethnographic investigation is definitely needed, in order to assess the dynamics of return reproductive tourism to other regions of the world beyond Euro-America.

Of particular concern in my own research are the needs of "stranded" Middle Eastern refugee populations, who are constrained from seeking ARTs back home but who may face economic constraints and cultural discrimination in host communities. Indeed, three issues continue to haunt the Middle Eastern diaspora at the time of this writing: (1) ongoing forms of political violence, which have forced so many Middle Easterners into refugeeism and exile in host countries; (2) the many constraints, economic and political, that prevent them from returning to their home countries to seek ARTs; and (3) the levels of discrimination faced by Middle Easterners in post-9/11 Euro-America, including in medical facilities

(Inhorn and Serour 2011). As a result, diasporic dreams of Middle Eastern test-tube babies are unrealistic for many infertile but stranded refugee couples. How to best address the health and welfare of refugee populations—those who have been forced to travel to save their own lives—will be a major challenge for future ethnographers of the Middle East, particularly in the aftermath of America's War on Terror in Iraq and the "dark autumn" that seems to have emerged from the Arab spring.

NOTES

This chapter is an expanded version of my article "Diasporic Dreaming: Return Reproductive Tourism to the Middle East," reprinted with permission of Elsevier from *Reproductive Bio-Medicine Online* 23 (2011): 582–91. I wish to thank the journal editor, Martin Johnson, as well as Zeynep Gürtin, both of the University of Cambridge, for facilitating publication of the special issue on cross-border reproductive care, in which this article first appeared. I also extend my thanks to Kamari Clarke and Rebecca Hardin for inviting me to contribute to this edited volume. Profound thanks go to the hundreds of Middle Eastern men and women who have shared the details of their reproductive lives and travel with me, thereby making my multisited ethnographic research possible. Similar thanks go to the ART practitioners in Egypt, Lebanon, UAE, and Arab America who have welcomed me into their clinics. This research has been generously supported over the years by the National Science Foundation's Cultural Anthropology Program, and the U.S. Department of Education Fulbright-Hays Faculty Research Abroad Program. I am very grateful to these programs and am extremely sorry that the Fulbright-Hays program is no longer in existence as of this writing.

1. These figures have been compiled from a variety of United Nations and Web-based sources.

2. In each study, interviews were conducted in either Arabic or English, depending upon the preference of the interviewee. The interviews were generally unstructured and followed a basic interview guide constructed by me. In all of the interviews undertaken in Lebanon and in about half of those in Detroit, a semi-structured reproductive life history interview was also administered to all of the men in the study in order to understand their experiences of male infertility and ART seeking. In general, interviews lasted about one hour, although they ranged in length from one-half hour to three hours. All interviews were conducted in private rooms, usually within the clinics and occasionally in research subjects' homes. In the initial stages of research in both Egypt and Lebanon, a local research assistant was present. However, most interviews were conducted by me alone. All research subjects were asked to read and sign an informed consent form in either Arabic or English. Consent for human subjects' research was received from institutional review boards (IRBs) at my home institutions (Emory University for the 1996 study, University of Michigan for the 2003–8 studies).

Part 3

Ethnographies in Emerging Sectors

Toward a Critically Engaged Ethnographic Practice

KAMARI MAXINE CLARKE

The recent debates over the appropriateness of embedded American anthropologists serving U.S. military interests in Afghanistan and Iraq have raised some of the most controversial issues in American anthropological ethical circles today. Among Africanists, the most recent debates over the U.S. Army's involvement in various outposts throughout Africa have been especially urgent, raising concerns about the extent to which ethnographic knowledge should or should not be used to serve the interest of AFRICOM, one of six of the U.S. Defense Department's regional headquarters. My own dilemma related to the practice of ethnography, and its application emerged when I received an e-mail from a U.S. Army Study office agent inviting me to participate in a one-day seminar titled "Extremism in West Africa: Groups and Conditions That Enable or Inhibit Them." The meeting was described as setting out to consider the "potential activities of extremist groups" in West Africa with the goal of brainstorming with other "knowledgeable people about the possible directions these groups may take in the future." The objectives outlined aimed to protect the innocent through educating decision makers on the frontlines who may benefit from the insights of experts in academia. This attempt by governments to gain intelligence from its specialists has its history in the formation of anthropological studies. The backlash has been known to have contributed to the colonization of occupied peoples and, as a result, has led to the development of a widespread anthropological public in which the overarching presumption was that ethnographers should be engaged in technologies of data procurement that study or protect marginal groups or serve the disenfranchised. Such standards of anthropological purposes took shape with the historical emergence of anthropological inquiry in which previous generations were engaged in conflicts over colonial ethnography and a range of anthropologists were involved in mounting wide-scale reactions to power abuses as a result of Nazism. Thus, for many, ethnography and its ethical uses are understood in terms that distinguish the "powerful" (read: the U.S. Army) from the "powerless" (read: civilians, often in the global South, but also those marginalized in the North), and many identify ethnography as meant to protect those who are disenfranchised. Those locals seen as engaging in the destruction of others have been identified as those who are not to be studied; they exist below the ethnographic radar and are neither to be understood nor protected. However, determining "who is the disenfranchised" is a complex endeavor, for it often involves going beyond individual actors to look at root causes of violence in which further exploration makes evident that guilt or innocence go beyond the enactment of individual violence.

In keeping with Laura Nader's (1972) provocative article "Up the Anthropologist," it is clear that contemporary anthropological studies have taken the call to move beyond studying the underclass or the traditionally identified "innocent" informant. The new genealogies of ethnography—postcolonial, international institutions, governmental and nongovernmental—are such that ethnography is now being used as much in corporate domains, spheres of political governance, and judicial, NGO (nongovernmental organization), and war contexts as for the lives and practices of disenfranchised farmers and divinatory healers. These new uses of ethnography are being deployed to capture the complex study of emergent markets through corporate and unregulated domains, military terrains, the creation of Rule of Law regimes, and the management of more diverse local populations, and new ethnographic techniques are being developed that involve at times more participant observation and engagement through the increasing number of PhDs in anthropology who are pursuing other professional degrees. A case in point is my own post-PhD return to further professional training when in 2002–3 I pursued a MSL (master of studies in law) at Yale Law School. There I developed an understanding of the technical foundations of law—the same principles of law in which first-year law students at Yale were being trained. This allowed me to get firsthand insights into the making of legal minds who would go on to be engaged in the widespread export of American jurisprudence as well as to participate in different ways in advisory roles for legal, nongovernmental, and governmental projects.

Today, increasing numbers of legal anthropology students are engaging in legal and political anthropology circles, studying law and using their legal training to do engaged work with NGOs, state bodies, or international institutions such as the World Bank, World Health Organization (WHO), and others. Yet the anthropological development of legal anthropology emerged from a multilayered trajectory that tended to separate legal practitioners from legal scholars. The first significant body of scholarship concerning the contemporary development of legal anthropology came from E. Adamson Hoebel's (1954) "neo-evolutionist" perspective, which located transformations in the law as adaptation to changes in the means and relations of production. He argued that all societies followed a single path of development, from primitive (e.g., hunter-gathering) to more advanced economic modes (e.g., agriculture, industry). This evolutionary trajectory was soon overtaken by a new anthropological preoccupation: that of disputes.[1] Laura Nader's "Village Projects" dispatched graduate students to small-scale societies to collect data on dispute processes (see Nader and Todd 1978) and stimulated a florescence of related studies (see, for example, Roberts 1979; Moore 1978; Mather and Yngvesson 1980–81; Felstiner, Abel, and Sarat 1980–81; Canter 1978; Collier 1988; Starr 1978, 1989, 1992; Yngvesson 1985, 1988). In this body of work disputes were conceived of as processes, and emphasis was placed on the individual disputant and his or her decision-making process. By the end of the 1970s, dispute processing had become the dominant subject of legal anthropological inquiry and had established new directions in legal pluralist theory.

Contemporary changes in law-making are profound, and ethnographic approaches are becoming equally innovative. Anthropology, a discipline of inquiry concerned with the understanding of human phenomena, has over time clearly demarcated fields of appropriate study—from the subaltern or marginalized to institutions of corporate power, to judiciaries and transnational formations. But it is also a discipline of ethics-making in which its history of non-intervention in local politics is a vestige of anthropological histories of desired objectivity and neutral data procurement. Today, though cultural anthropology lies somewhere between humanities and social sciences, its professional principles have been central in debates about and constraints to its own disciplinary purview. This reality of the merger between theory and practice, objectivity and subjectivity, continues to shape the basis for new projects and the tools that ethnographers bring to bear to the fieldwork terrain. In this regard, attention to legal pluralism and the type of training that ethnographers bring to the field is growing, particularly in regard to those with joint advanced degrees and professional degrees.

In the development of legal anthropology, a range of cutting-edge scholars have conducted ethnographic studies that explore multiple legal formations in newly developing transnational realms. With publications in the late 1990s and early 2000s, from scholarship by Annelise Riles (2001a, 2001b), Sally Merry (2006), Richard Wilson (2005), Susan Hirsch (2006), Jean and John Comaroff (2006), Laura Nader (1972, 2002), among others, legal scholars and anthropologists began to use ethnography to examine the ways that global and local connections are mediated by political institutions, organizations, and practices, as well as by agents working on behalf of state institutions. Significantly, subsequent generations of anthropologists—Donald Brahman, Jed Kronkite, Galit Safarty, all scholars and legal practitioners—represent a new generation of ethnographers who are versed in both ethnographic scholarship on particular institutions/cultural practices in particular regions and in professional training. In this case, it is legal training with the goal of understanding the circulation of law and the study and practice of it. By mobilizing forms of inquiry that not only highlight spaces of legal engagement but also put into practice a form of ethnography of international relations, this new grouping of young scholars is increasingly conversant and engaged and is carving out a new domain of praxis. It is this new method of inquiry that highlights ethnography as embodied practice that is at the heart of the development of a new form of contemporary ethnography.

Given the increasing merging of professional and scholarly ethnographic projects, and the increasingly active role of ethnographers of law, medicine, corporations, and the state, intervening in disciplinary engagements with a range in practical expertise has enabled ethnographers to contribute to social action in ways that could be conceivably imagined as educational and even progressive. For unlike the past in which ethnographers of Africa were hired to document strong supple rural systems under stress, today contemporary popular culture worldwide has produced an image of Africa as a site for aid, of possible violence, and of victimization. Thus, ethnographers of the region are under demand to document and help analyze conflict of various kinds. In my case, in response to the invitation by the U.S. Army, I complied and attended the meeting with the hopes of using ethnographic insights to shed light on my impressions about setting up AFRICOM throughout the African continent. I modified and expressed my knowledge in ways that protected the interests of my informants. I shared insights on macro politics of violence in West Africa but was careful not to disclose personal names and group information that might negatively affect the populations with whom I work.

This chapter uses this personal experience to consider the complexities of such engaged ethnographic projects as they are related to rethinking of the public face of ethnography and interrogating the paradoxes of action and inaction central to the moral and ethical codes in the field. One case to consider is that of the violence and poverty in the Sudan; another pertains to the reconfiguration of the post-colonial state and the violence that we study as trajectories of our inquiry but rarely as trajectories of our intervention. The Nuer of the Sudan—a key anthropological object—has long served students of anthropological inquiry. However, as we see with changes in the region, Sudan's "local people," many who were are at once "victims" of colonialism, have also become killers engaged in the restructuring of the postcolonial state; the same is true in Uganda, where child soldiers have been heavily involved in war efforts in the North but are themselves victims of childhood abduction (see Clarke 2007b). At root is the "new scramble" for African resources: international corporations, whose missions go well beyond the state, working alongside various state and nonstate actors to engage in the procurement and trade of arms in exchange for mineral resources. These forms of violence go well beyond explicit forms of embattlement: they represent both the forms of symbolic power (Bourdieu 1991) that maintain violence of the postcolonial condition as well as the forms of violence within which ethnography participates. At issue is the complicity of ethnographic inaction, even as ethnography requires a modicum of action through which to document and theorize social problems. But also at issue are the corporate actors whose purposes often operate within the orbit of commodity extraction and material self-interest.

My central intervention involves recognizing that even no action—say, no assignment of responsibility to offending companies themselves—is itself an action. To answer what it means for anthropologists as "social critics" to be engaged in documentation efforts that not only have explanatory power but also connect that power to praxis, we first must contend with the conception that the seeming absence of public action is far from neutral. The key here is to recognize how the establishment of anthropological principles delimiting the performance of ethnography in contexts of war is clearly a political act—one that makes legible particular practices that foreclose or enable ways of thinking about the legitimacy of action. I suggest that first we rethink what it means for ethnography to represent political spheres; in so doing we not only follow the lead of many who have put to rest the fiction of the apolitical ethnographer but also consider how ethnography might be seen as a mechanism of engagement. As I argue, it is important to redefine the principles at the core of our discipline—including our code of ethics—recognizing that though the history of anthropological engagement has been engaged in the documentation and protection of "local" peoples as the "authentic" voices to be protected and understood, this is not the only subjectivity to be protected and understood as part of the anthropological project. We need to rethink the ethics of our research in domains that go beyond simply "protecting the names of our subjects" as the basis for ethical consideration. Such explorations involve critically assessing the ideological assumptions and moral codes that shape our established theories and their alternatives, exploring potential sites for new insights, and interrogating what they protect and why, in order to use the tools of the discipline to engage in principled engagement or intentional non-engagement.

I suggest that like the new training trends of students engaged in joint professional training and anthropology, we articulate the need for learning multiple field languages—languages of law or medicine or business—that govern the fields within which we work. This involves recasting the study of subaltern identities, difference, and the processes by which these identities are constructed by embracing the shift away from these theorizations as the end point of an engagement and moving toward new ways of opening the discussion with proficiency in the field logic in which we claim scholarly specialization. Meeting this challenge means reflecting the relationship between theory and praxis as the basis for mainstream anthropological inquiry as well as exploring the range of imbricated inquiries that influence research, writing, and practice—our codes of regulation and our modalities of inquiry.

I recast the role of ethnography as a technology of knowledge and power whose methods are able to capture the complexities of ruptures and entanglements, histories of violence of all forms, and make suggestions concerning the lessons that might be learned from the uses of ethnography in complex social contexts. And, just as ethnography has responded to the challenge of understanding new engagements with transnational connections, neoliberal governmentality, and empire and has fostered the burgeoning study of various appendages, so too does understanding violence in those field sites involve new considerations for how we rethink the role and limits of anthropological ethnography by exploring the ways that knowledge-producing mechanisms, such as ethnography, are enmeshed alongside relationships that need to be thoroughly explored and at times considerations of engagement rethought.

The kind of ethnography that I suggest as constituting an engaged anthropology addresses the conceptual distinctions made between theory and praxis: the perceived gap between embedded, empirical work—central to the core of methods, but with ghosts of objectivity and neutrality that often sideline the place of engagement—and that of "applied anthropologists," stereotyped as not theoretical, to whom such engagement may be surrendered. This compartmentalization is a falsity; it has no place in contemporary contexts of an unfurling new world order, in whose presence anthropology has a far from public face, and which risks becoming divided between those in ivory towers and those who are exiled from academia because of the work they do. Instead, what is needed more than ever is a relationship between theory and praxis—the practical application of social theory in such a way that enables transformative possibilities, possibilities that move us from merely documenting or disengaging to taking the practice of ethnography to its limits. That is, to use our field knowledge and technical advisory capacities to attend to social inequalities.

Such an approach to *engaged anthropology* follows a tradition of engagement with a broad-ranging genealogy from the history of applied anthropology to public anthropology, to anthropology and activism, to the anthropological study of the military. Yet there is no one definition for engaged anthropology. It has specific meanings that take shape out of the contexts in which their dilemmas emerge. As such, the critical spaces of intervention are diverse and are embedded in the particularities of the histories, politics, and power relations co-constituted within relevant spheres of engagement. The foregoing outlines one such example of the particularities of history, politics, and sets of power relations within which a particular axis of engagement might be manifest through possibilities productive of freedom.

Contemporary Ethnographic Engagements and Histories of Violence in Africa

At the close of the Cold War, a growing arms trade began to fuel African conflict zones in which rebel groups were vying for regional power. Throughout the 1990s, in regions such as Sierra Leone, Côte d'Ivoire, the Democratic Republic of the Congo (DMC), Rwanda, and Uganda, these conflicts and their resolutions, despite obvious connections to global trade circuits, found little international support for mitigating the colonial and economic production of war lines that were soon to explode, especially in comparison with the significant international brokering of the end of the Cold War and the formative international justice interventions at the end of World War II. What resulted were extreme disparities in the lived worlds of national communities in which there developed perceptions of rich African leaders and business people closest to postcolonial power participating in the disenfranchisement of a growing underclass. In some sub-Saharan African countries, large segments of the population were subject to various forms of violence and death at the hands of particular ethnic or religious groups. And today, many suffering from poverty remain external to regimes of health and the amassing of wealth, while a small number remained at the center of new nodes of power. With the changing nature of state governance in which we are witnessing the reconfiguration of the African postcolonial state, African governance is being increasingly controlled by nonstate actors, transnational circuits of capital engaged in economic speculation and investment, and a range of new enforcement domains where the management of violence is being shared by larger Rule of Law institutions, and brokers of violence.

In relation to the latter—the rise of paramilitary power—though over ten civil wars have been fought on the African continent over the past two decades and have been facilitated by the management of new paramilitary enclaves, many of these struggles, often fought in the name of ethnic strife and religious politics, have actually been rooted in mineral resource management, which economic speculation and capitalist logic have encouraged. As a result, the African continent now leads the way in innovating various forms of international criminal adjudicatory forms such as hybrid courts and international tribunals set alongside various national and "traditional" justice and truth and reconciliation forms. Moreover, the signing of international treaties is increasingly being economically linked to democratic restructuring mandates. Indeed, multiple brokers—including postcolonial state actors in Africa and elsewhere—are vying to control the terms of governance and competing with not only state actors but also NGOs and paramilitary forces. Thus, African states that have signed and ratified treaties such as the Rome Statute for the ICC are actually experiencing the weakening of their capacities to protect their borders, manage their populations, and control their markets and currencies (Hansen and Stepputat 2005, 32), even as regional competitors strengthen their attempts to consolidate power for resource control.

What we are seeing in some contexts, like that of the Sudan and the regional areas in and bordering the DRC, are very powerful paramilitary states in which it is not neoliberal policies that are at play in the regulation of these economies but what Janet Roitman (2005) refers to as alternate regulatory domains in which very powerful arms and military brokers harness power through highly formalized underground economies. In response to these and other perceived paramilitary as well as Islamic nodes of governance and power in Africa, in October 2008 the U.S. Pentagon launched the U.S. Africa Command (AFRICOM) as part of a global agenda for the U.S. War on Terror and as a means to control religious extremism, state collapse, and so forth—all part of broader contemporary issues. AFRICOM is the first African command, but there are already significant command centers in the Middle East, South Asia, and elsewhere. With an interim headquarters likely in Stuttgart, AFRICOM would establish five small new military bases "in North (possibly Tunisia), West (either Ghana, Liberia or Senegal), East (likely around the current U.S. taskforce in Djibouti), and southern Africa (perhaps Botswana) with a further chapter in Addis Ababa" (De Lorenzo, McNamee, and Mills 2007). And though there is broad-based consensus by panels of experts—in which I have been involved—engaged in the intellectual rationale or rethinking of such centers that their presence will create more problems than they would solve, the path is being charted to add to the already established post-U.S. American Embassy bombing in Kenya and Tanzania, and in general, the 9/11 U.S. military presence on the continent.

Today, a base of 1,800 troops has already been established in Djibouti as well as bases in the recently created (2005) Trans-Sahara Counterterrorism Initiative (TSCTI). An additional 4,200 troops spread throughout Egypt and other North African regions are within striking range; there is also a U.S. military presence in Chad, Mali, Mauritania, and Niger. In 2005, the initiative was extended to cover Algeria, Senegal, Nigeria, Tunisia, and another fleet permanently stationed in the Gulf of Aden. Its primary objective is being identified by many analysts in the region as related to oil procurement and limiting any Chinese influence over the supply. U.S. government officials maintain that these deployments are related to the realities of Africa's weakening state capacities and its lack of military forces to deal with significant challenges to its resources. Clearly, with the U.S. Army's formation of a newly established (2004) intelligence and research wing articulating its interests in Africa and other world regions as related to the protection of U.S. security, these are not simply matters of poverty and humanitarianism. Rather, the research wing is engaged in dialogues with various Northern academics—social and political scientists, historians, and especially anthropologists—in order to anticipate and look out for its own interests.

Accession to these U.S. and U.S.-led military plans and operations has divided African leaders and policy makers on the continent, where there is also tremendous opposition. This is seen in the rejection of a U.S. military presence by the South African and Nigerian governments and the vows by the leaders of Mozambique, Botswana, and Zambia to resist the setting up of U.S. bases in their countries. Yet, unlike Middle Eastern and Eastern European scholars whose engagement with such regional issues has been much more salient in the past twenty years since Cold War interventions in Africa ended, Africanist anthropologists have been late to intervene. The recent announcement of plans for AFRICOM has also spurred debates in the academic world regarding how the United States should engage Africa and how best to shape American foreign policy strategies. These debates have brought into play two dueling approaches: one advocating further U.S. bases and a higher-profile presence in Africa for more direct military action, if needed; the other contesting such militarization and instead promoting non-military interests in Africa. At the intellectual center of U.S. military expansionist policies are conservative think tanks such as the Heritage Foundation, the American Enterprise Institute (AEI), and the Center for Security Policy. President George W. Bush hailed AFRICOM as ultimately bringing "peace and security to the people of Africa" as well as promoting "our common goals of development, health, education, democracy, and economic growth in Africa" (U.S. White House 2007).

The Political Economy of Northern Interests in Africa

AFRICOM is said by many to have been designed shortly after Ugandan miners found "black gold" in the western region of the country and Tanzania announced the availability of commercially viable oil deposits along its coast. The recent organization of successive meetings of such academics with the U.S. Army's research wing in mid-November 2007 in an attempt to understand Africa's Northern, Southern, Eastern, and Western geopolitical regions is a case in point. But in response to this call, a loosely convened group calling itself the Network of Concerned Anthropologists circulated a petition calling on anthropologists to pledge their nonparticipation in U.S. military activities by refusing to engage in research and other activities that contribute to counterinsurgency operations in the War on Terror (Network of Concerned Anthropologists 2007b).

What are the terms of anthropological engagement here? The above anthropological initiatives speak to the central concern of this chapter: the connection between ethnographic knowledge and engagement (praxis),[2] with engagement at times being located as principled non-engagement. The popular anthropological engagement against U.S. military action or intervention in various places that anthropologists study has tended to range from public protests, teach-ins, and educational research to petition writing and circulation; but it has not transcended the liberal parameters of democratic discourse. Such (non)engagement is deemed principled because of a seemingly principled obligation to victims of war—as if, in many cases, the perpetrators of war are not themselves also conflicted actors embattled in practices whose deep causes are often far from evident and in need of further inquiry.

According to Marshall Sahlins, the U.S. military focuses on portraying anthropology's practical contribution as "collecting cultural data for winning local 'hearts and minds'—which is again aid to serve the goal of improving American counterinsurgency and pacification efforts. This is also described as inculcating respect for the local culture among U.S. military personnel or even as providing a sense of cultural relativism." As he observes: "Of course it is the opposite of cultural relativism—cultural cynicism one might call it—since the object is to appropriate the cultural practices of others to one's own purposes, notably the purpose of dominating them."[3] This, like various other AAA statements against the U.S. war in the Gulf states, Afghanistan, and now Iraq, suggests the importance of disengaging from military operations.

Sahlins continues by noting "the priority of the military mission over the welfare of the local people" and states that "[t]his kind of relation to the local people would hardly get through an IRB review on human subjects." His rejection of such engagement with the military aside, there is an unstated assumption here, one worth making explicit because of its widespread relevance in anthropological circles: that these "local people" are not also members of militias committing violence—or even presidents or other high government officials, whether they came to power through military coups or democratic force. These "local people" thus tend to be portrayed as being on the same side. This is an unuseful assertion and one that can be detrimental to determining the forms of possible ethnographic engagements.

American Anthropology and the Politics of Ethics: The AAA Code of Ethics

The American Anthropological Association (AAA) has its own Code of Ethics: adopted in May 1971 as "Principles of Professional Responsibility" and amended in November 1986, it was redrafted during January 1995 to March 1997 by the Commission to Review the AAA Statements on Ethics. The first draft of the new code was discussed at the May 1995 AAA Section Assembly meeting; the second draft was discussed at the November 1996 meeting of the AAA Section Assembly. Open hearings on the code were held at the 1995 and 1996 annual meetings of the AAA, and the commission solicited comments from all AAA sections during this period and debated their significance for inclusion. The document was finalized and approved in June 1998. Like many American professional codes, the AAA Code of Ethics recognizes that members carry with them their own ethical principles and presumptions; its public statements of morality assume that the code represents shared principles. As it states in the Preamble (§I),

> Anthropological researchers, teachers and practitioners are members of many different communities, each with its own moral rules or codes of ethics. Anthropologists have moral obligations as members of other groups, such as the family, religion, and community, as well as the profession. They also have obligations to the scholarly discipline, to the wider society and culture, and to the human species, other species, and the environment. Furthermore, fieldworkers may develop close relationships with persons or animals with whom they work, generating an additional level of ethical considerations.
>
> In a field of such complex involvements and obligations, it is inevitable that misunderstandings, conflicts, and the need to make choices among apparently incompatible values will arise. Anthropologists are responsible for grappling with such difficulties and struggling to resolve them in ways compatible with the principles stated here.[4]

In ethnographic fields of inquiry, we are told that the purpose of this code is to foster discussion and education, and though the AAA will not adjudicate claims for seemingly unethical behavior, we anthropologists are to take the principles of the code as tools to promote the development and maintenance of ethical frameworks "for all anthropological work" (end of §I). However, it is clear that in a rapidly changing world, in which different anthropologists engage in a variety of activities, the assumption that a professional organization can and should broker such ethical power is naive at best. Instead, it is useful to see the code for what it is: yet another instrument of governmentality—the organized practices and technologies through which subjects are governed. It is an instrument through which to make sense of the world theoretically and practically and to govern action using a range of mentalities, techniques, and rationalities.

In the Introduction (§II) to the 1998 Code, anthropology is defined as "a multidisciplinary field of science and scholarship, which includes the study of all aspects of humankind—archaeological, biological, linguistic[,] and sociocultural. Anthropology has roots in the natural and social sciences and in the humanities, ranging in approach from basic to applied research and to scholarly interpretation." Here it is clear that the foundations of the discipline remain deeply empirical. The AAA's view of that discipline follows:

> As the principal organization representing the breadth of anthropology, the American Anthropological Association (AAA) starts from the position that generating and appropriately utilizing knowledge (i.e., publishing, teaching, developing programs, and informing policy) of the peoples of the world, past and present, is a worthy goal; that the generation of anthropological knowledge is a dynamic process using many different and ever-evolving approaches; and that for moral and practical reasons, the generation and utilization of knowledge should be achieved in an ethical manner. (§II)

In the realm of research, the first principle is that anthropologists

> have primary ethical obligations to the people, species, and materials they study and to the people with whom they work. These obligations can supersede the goal of seeking new knowledge, and can lead to decisions not to undertake or to discontinue a research project when the primary obligation conflicts with other responsibilities, such as those owed to sponsors or clients. These ethical obligations include:
>
> • To avoid harm or wrong, understanding that the development of knowledge can lead to change which may be positive or negative for the people or animals worked with or studied

- To respect the well-being of humans and nonhuman primates
- To work for the long-term conservation of the archaeological, fossil, and historical records
- To consult actively with the affected individuals or group(s), with the goal of establishing a working relationship that can be beneficial to all parties involved. (§III.A.1)

The subsequent second to sixth principles highlight the importance of anthropological researchers:

2. do[ing] everything in their power to ensure that their research does not harm the safety, dignity, or privacy of the people and animals with whom they work, conduct research, or perform other professional activities. . . .

3. determin[ing] in advance whether their hosts/providers of information wish to remain anonymous or receive recognition, and mak[ing] every effort to comply with those wishes. . . .

4. obtain[ing] in advance the informed consent of persons being studied, providing information, owning or controlling access to material being studied, or otherwise identified as having interests which might be impacted by the research. . . . It is the quality of the consent, not the format, that is relevant. . . .

5. adher[ing] [in covenantal relationships] to the obligations of openness and informed consent, while carefully and respectfully negotiating the limits of the relationship.

6. not exploit[ing] individuals, groups, animals, or cultural or biological materials [and] recogniz[ing] their debt to the societies in which they work and their obligation to reciprocate with people studied in appropriate ways. (§III.A.2–6)

The AAA Code of Ethics has become quite relevant in contemporary anthropological debates post-9/11, since the United States is at war in the Middle East and the U.S. Army has increased its engagement with anthropologists, among other researchers, experts (e.g., linguists), and policy makers, resulting in the formation of the Human Terrain System (HTS) Project. News of the HTS and its relation to the U.S. military war of aggression in Iraq has shown how the deployment of new measures of governance has far exceeded the study of Iraqis for the sake of understanding, in order to rewrite Iraq's national constitution and reorganize its "civil society." The new measures appear to involve the formation of various types of military units to better control, monitor, or organize new forms of state building, which entails finding more effective strategies for military action.

This phenomenon has raised a range of heated debates among AAA members, as well as in general communities at large, and the Executive Board deemed "that the HTS project raises sufficiently troubling and urgent ethical issues to warrant a statement from the Executive Board at this time."[5] As a result, on October 31, 2007, the board, under the leadership of Alan Goodman, released a statement of resolution concluding:

> (i) that the HTS program creates conditions which are likely to place anthro-pologists in positions in which their work will be in violation of the AAA Code of Ethics and (ii) that its use of anthropologists poses a danger to both other anthro-pologists and persons other anthropologists study. Thus the Executive Board expresses its disapproval of the HTS program.

The statement made clear that anthropology "is obliged to help improve U.S. government policies through the widest possible circulation of anthropological understanding in the public sphere" and to engage in the "development and implementation of U.S. policy" through the democratic process. It is in this way that "anthropology can legitimately and effectively help guide U.S. policy to serve the humane causes of global peace and social justice." The board's disapproval of HTS in particular was "[i]n the context of a war that is widely recognized as a denial of human rights and based on faulty intelligence and undemocratic principles." It was thus presented on ethical grounds, owing to "grave concerns" with the currently articulated HTS project, which it called "an unacceptable application of anthro-pological expertise."

The conditions of ethical concern were enumerated as follows:

1. "As military contractors working in settings of war," anthropologists would have trouble sufficiently distinguishing themselves from the military, thus placing "a significant constraint on their ability to fulfill their ethical respon-sibility as anthropologists to disclose who they are and what they are doing."
2. Given their "responsibility for negotiating relations among a number or groups, . . . HTS anthropologists may have responsibilities to their U.S. mili-tary units in war zones that conflict with their obligations to the persons they study or consult."
3. The ethical imperative of voluntary, informed consent is compromised, since "HTS anthropologists work . . . under conditions that make it difficult for those they communicate with to give 'informed consent' without coercion, or for this consent to be taken at face value or freely refused."
4. There is a "risk that information provided by HTS anthropologists could be used to make decisions about identifying and selecting specific populations as targets of U.S. military operations"; this "would violate the stipulations in the AAA Code of Ethics that those studied not be harmed (§III.A.1)."

5. The program's conflation of "anthropologists with U.S. military operations . . . may create serious difficulties for, including grave risks to the personal safety of, many non-HTS anthropologists and the people they study."

These rationales highlight the challenges of ethnography in violence-related operations. Conflicting loyalties, the lack of informed consent, the vulnerability of local populations, and the reality of personal danger for the anthropologist are offered as reasons not to support such uses of ethnography and anthropology. A program like HTS is said to offend key tenets of protection in the AAA Code of Ethics, which are very much in keeping with the establishment and maintenance of the rights and protections for all humans enshrined in the Universal Declaration of Human Rights (UDHR), and with the related assumption that to contravene those principles is to remove the existence of those first-generation rights. As we see in the next section of this chapter, the assumption that these rights should at all times override second-generation rights, such as economic and cultural rights—the right to live free from poverty and in the context of the full expression of one's social world—must be critically rethought.

AFRICOM and Principles of Professional Responsibility

Constructed when anthropology was an elite discipline, the 1971 "Principles of Professional Responsibility," now known as the code of ethics, set in place not only social rules to protect local peoples from the abuses of colonial states but also the structures of accountability to the peoples whose lives were being studied. The recent AFRICOM initiative raises parallel concerns. The details of future military and nonmilitary conduct of the Africa Command are unknown. That body's management wing will be controlled unilaterally by the Pentagon, putting the participation of African-based governance and its local communities secondary to the operation of the initiative. At the time of this writing, the AAA Executive has not directly ruled on AFRICOM itself. However, the mobilizations of the ad hoc Network of Concerned Anthropologists, and their commitment to disengagement from military participation, highlight a key trend in anthropological engagement. This trend—starting with the 1980s break from serving as the "handmaiden of colonialism" and progressing to anthropologists' engagement in oppositional and antiwar positions—represents a new trajectory for the second half of the twentieth century and the basis for twenty-first-century organizing.[6]

The issues are far more complicated, however, than these oppositional movements suggest. For instance, such positions do not take into account the complex location of power and the structures of domination whose inscriptions go well beyond those directly engaged in enacting violence. Still, anthropologists have often been involved in the documentation of those data sets that can be disclosed, since their ethical responsibilities have been harnessed by a public set of principles—to protect local peoples, to maintain their anonymity. As the Preamble to the AAA's "Principles of Professional Responsibility" states, the goal of ethnography is to study the "processes and issues affecting general human welfare," yet to anthropologists they do "damage neither to those whom they study nor, insofar as possible, to their scholarly community. Where these conditions cannot be met, the anthropologist would be well-advised not to pursue the particular piece of research" (AAA 1986).

But what of the need for ethnographies of war written from the other side? Resource wars and new imperialist interventions are connected to disclosure and alliances (or not) with subjects in interesting ways and remains an important component of understanding and addressing root causes of violence of all types. Carolyn Nordstrom's *A Different Kind of War Story* presents an ethnography of a war zone, making clear that "an ethnography of war is not the same as the ethnography of the effect of war on a particular locale" (1997, 78). Here, although we get the story of violence from various ambits, and diverse notions of political violence are explored, it is the suffering of the articulated victim to be protected that looms large. But what of the story of men from Serbia who voluntarily participated in the wars that followed the breakup of the former Yugoslavia—or of men who fled those wars (Milicevic 2006)? How might participation in war be explained through the eyes of volunteers or draft dodgers? And what of victims turned killers, such as those child soldiers in Uganda now submitting testimony in which they explain their inculcation into the military countermovement? What of the U.S. Army soldiers or Marines fighting the U.S. War on Terror—one of the most imperialist resource wars of our time—whose stories remain to be fully incorporated and represented in ethnographic accounts? What of the smugglers and paramilitary intermediaries in the work of Janet Roitman (2005)? Yet these are not the types of subject with which anthropology traditionally been engaged. Rather, it is often the voice of Western sympathies with "victims" that have been articulated through popular ethnographies of the 1980s and 1990s. The voices of "perpetrators" themselves have yet to be fully engaged and developed.

What kind of engagement, then, might be at the center of an anthropological intervention that goes beyond public social criticism? I ask not because I have a principled disagreement with the ethical-political position taken by the AAA but because the history of anthropological ethnographies of war reflect a range of the widespread positions taken by the AAA professional organization that purports to serve a wide spectrum of people differently located in the landscape of knowledge production and political causes. To establish terms of ethnographic and professional engagement that delimit action based on core principles that are not shared by its broad and diverse membership is to represent the problematic roots of anthropology in which its role as executor for colonialism represents the elite or the local underclass of a given group or society. It seems to me that through a rethinking of the underpinnings of the code, the first step is to engage in the revival of study of inequalities that were once at the center of 1960s British social anthropology (for instance, see the Rhodes-Livingston Institute) or 1970s U.S., French, and UK Marxists once at the forefront of political economic concerns that formed the basis for social inequalities. Today, what is key is incorporating a lineage of engagement that takes seriously the insights of social criticism and also examines the complexities of power articulating the complexities by which seemingly "local people" are on opposing sides of many issues.

It is clear that ethnographic ethics have historically been institutionally concerned with the lifeways of "local peoples," always locating that which is "local" as those underprivileged whose circumstances resemble an absence of power. This one-sidedness points up the limitations of the field and the need to push beyond such boundaries. Yet American anthropologists are no different, and it is important that we recognize how and why anthropologists are engaged in different political positions for different ends. Some have loyalties to Iraqi, Sudanese, and Rwandan former perpetuators of violence—even "freedom fighters"—and see this affiliation as a political entitlement.

In the remainder of this essay, I focus on the first principles "deemed fundamental to the anthropologist's responsible, ethical pursuit of the profession"—principles pertaining to "relations with those studied" (AAA 1986). A reflection on the difficulties of determining distinctions between victims and perpetrators, those in need of information and those whose privacy should be protected, highlights the central problematic in boycotting such advisory meetings and explains why I accepted the offer to share some of my ethnographic knowledge with U.S. Army decision makers. I end by highlighting the limits of the AAA Code of Ethics in capturing the new terrain within which contemporary ethnographers might engage. This final section addresses what an engaged anthropology might be like in contexts where we are attempting to understand particular paramilitary operations alongside new supranational institutional forms of governance in which innocence is not clear cut.

Toward an Anthropological Approach to Ethnographic Engagement

Anthropologists have traditionally had minimal impact on social inequalities, though they have often reacted conscientiously and dutifully by opposing war efforts of abusive states, signing petitions, and issuing platform statements through the AAA Executive. Mark Goodale (2009) has written significantly on the absence of American anthropology in the public engagement of the creation and popularization of the Universal Declaration of Human Rights, given the field's objection to principles of universalism and the fear that the globalizing impact of such principles would negatively affect local communities.

The profession has changed significantly, and in order to reflect the realities of inequality and violence in the social worlds we study, it has also been engaged in reconceptualizing violence in social and political domains and representations of it thereof (see Hansen and Stepputat 2005; Das 1985, 1990; Kelly 2006; Appadurai 2006). For with postcolonial interlocutors engaging in the production of anthropological and ethnographic knowledge as well as in the perpetuation and silencing of violence, easy criticism of inequality and affiliation of local/marginal/dominated/black/brown categories are far more complex. By reflecting on anthropology's history in the exposition of inequality as a theoretical agenda, but whose critical engagement has mostly hovered over its objects—as mere commentary—these efforts have not contributed to the reduction of the very violence that it studies. As we know, social violence and its threats do not represent a sociocultural exception to be studied outside of local cultural processes. Rather, they are central to the making of the everyday, to be studied and understood in relation to the workings of religion, ethnicity, and the economy. It has been well established in contemporary literature that violence is intrinsic to modernity—the modernity of poverty, of race, of sexual exploitation, of science, that which designates victims. It is the modernity of the contemporary present and should not be disengaged or disarticulated from study.

Nevertheless, today, both in and beyond the academy, ethnographers have been under increasing pressure to engage in various social projects and with diverse publics—the military, corporations, and judiciaries. These demands of advocacy and participatory research may challenge ethnography, on the one hand, yet appropriate it for new social uses, on the other. However, to what extent do anthropological ethics restrict the spaces of investigation, collaboration, and even transformative praxis in war-torn contexts in which many militia members are both victims and perpetrators? How might a rethinking of AAA ethical codes turn a constrained yet narrowly engaged anthropology into a field of vibrant theory and praxis, one whose ideological positioning is less ambiguous and, where relevant, more directed toward various forms of social action? What does it mean for American anthropologists to move toward a more engaged anthropology at a time when U.S. American military clout is being exercised globally both to support various perpetrators of violence and to defend some of its victims? And how do contemporary engagements with violence of all forms—social, economic, political, symbolic, explicitly physical—need to be situated in a variety of emerging social fields?

In his seminal work, *When Victims Become Killers*, Mahmood Mamdani (2001) has established popular terms for interrogating the complexities of complicity of those who engage in violence, stressing the need to look actively to the ways that colonial inscriptions and their contemporary manifestations are part of the explicit enactment of this violence. In the Sudan—as in other postcolonial and sub-Saharan African contexts where the complexities of agency and complicity of violence are at once so deeply historical and so clearly embedded in related contemporary "dilemmas"—the specter of the victim rests alongside a range of institutional and individual phenomena. But the burgeoning resource extraction mechanisms and the military might deployed to protect them through force can no longer remain apparitions—specters of a sort that loom in the shadows, but whose effects are always present and are embedded in particular political economic arrangements.

In the past decades, anthropologists have written ethnographies that document the complexities and histories of competing sides of conflicts in order to understand structures of power without significantly intervening in the substance of study. While thus preserving our interest in the relationships between culture and power, they have conserved the status quo. The insights of ethnography as a discipline have rarely moved beyond social criticism; social activism is often left by the American academy to those development organizations or human rights NGOs engaged in the achievement of political and civil rights, or to the political scientists or journalists who often represent the face and controversies of public policy. These realities have gravely reduced the relevance of anthropology in a world of complex social dynamics. Our toolkit of ethnographic methods—the long-term and detailed forms of collecting data that emerge from the voices of a people—has neither served nor protected the disenfranchised; nor does it have the structural design to do so. For while over the past two decades institutions such as the World Bank, the corporate sector, social work institutions, and political scientists have looked to ethnographic methods for its explanatory power with the culture concept, more recent ethnographic reflexive inquiries or theoretical and complex articulations about the transnational and global arena are often not the insights that our legal, activist, political science, and journalistic collaborators look for as they, too, search for deeper meaning (Paine 1996).

During World War II, however, Ruth Benedict was engaged in pursuing both theoretical and public goals related to social struggles (Benedict 1946; Benedict and Weltfish 1943). As a public anthropologist, she was involved in the integration of theory and practice by articulating relativism (Benedict 1934) as a new way of understanding cultural differences within particular fields of social behavior. By connecting praxis and analysis, she articulated what she saw as narrow and discriminatory approaches in American society.

The resurgence of Marxism during the 1960s–1980s provided scholars with a similar set of tools with which to articulate the politics of inequality (Harvey 1990). The resurgence of the Frankfurt School's approaches to the relationship between theory and practice (see, e.g., Horkheimer and Adorno 1947) led to the development of a critical agenda through which not only to envision social change but also to participate in it through engaged scholarship. Yet these critical agendas were so mired with modernist thought that their assumptions were rooted in inequalities through the very practice of naming and conceptualizing social problems. Any questions often stopped short of disturbing the social inequalities that were at the center of inquiry.

The turn to poststructural and postmodern theories provided an avenue for the rethinking of presumptions of modern social categories. What many saw as the loss of the political (Harvey 1990) actually provided the tools not only to rethink subjectivity and presumptions about objectivity but also to ask different types of question. The questions being asked today have more to do with the ways that complex agents—in the Global South as elsewhere—within similarly situated social groups are differently positioned. Understanding these different social positions has been central to understanding the complex ways that power is embodied, as well as the ways that ethnography participates in its circulation through the production of knowledge and its connection to social action. Yet many would insist that poststructuralism makes action impossible since each construct is a reconfiguration of domination of sorts that does not help to pinpoint complicity. However, when violence is seen as a form of politics and action and its study is taken up both as a way to document and understand such actions as central to daily life, then collaborating with others in order to mitigate against tyranny in an age of extremism, resource wars, and current agendas of imperial intervention presents an important grounding for merging theory and praxis.

But to highlight some of the most central issues of our time—those at the core of violence and resource extraction—by only illuminating the processes by which these practices are taking shape is to embody a space of theorization that has its place in the contribution of scholarly knowledge. To keep ethnographic insights in the domain of observation is to participate in the complicity of its reproduction in which one documents various forms of violence and powerlessness by providing the means through which to measure its significance. For what often remains unfettered are those cycles of inequality that we condone—the rights of some to live and prosper, the lack of responsibility for those we let die. One such social field is that of government militarization domains—postcolonial, former colonial, and even those social worlds that are part of current American forms of military encroachments. In this regard, how are social and political fields of violence becoming more complexly enmeshed or their interdependence more exploited by political actors outside of anthropological domains in which religious and family values, electoral politics in the United States, and American military lives are at stake? In this regard, how are anthropologists to engage such social and political forces? Answering these questions involves making central principled forms of engagement and non-engagement explicit to the ways that we articulate the violence of everyday life. For central to this are core issues related to the political economy of Northern interests in resources in places such as sub-Saharan Africa and other regions in the Global South, the Middle East, and Latin America. Thus, in linking anthropological pursuits with public engagement, it is essential to bring various forms of epistemology—academic and nonacademic, Northern and Southern—into conversation.

Toward an Engaged American Anthropology

A more engaged anthropology must incorporate into our understanding of violence the realities that shape how and why people (perpetrators and victims alike) are ideologically and pragmatically aligned; but it must also mean taking steps before injury occurs—not simply afterward, through theaters of justice or AAA statements. The types of military action in Iraq or in the Sudan that offend our moral consciences should provoke more than the signing of proclamations pledging disengagement with American war efforts. Anthropologists must be willing to take positions, to engage with key government policy and decision makers on both sides of the aisle, and to see the various social processes (democratic or nondemocratic) in which those differently positioned in those processes are engaged as a basis for potential new rationalities productive of more equitable social worlds. For when disengagement yields no action, and when war continues with or without anthropological interventions, anthropology as a discipline participates in perpetuating the violence we once criticized.

There is no formula for engagement. Yet the options for engagement are countless, and the possibilities must go well beyond non-engagement with military forces as the basis for praxis. The considerations vary with the contexts at hand and should not remain embedded in a fixed professional code-based dictate. In this regard, ethnographers can document empirically the realities of social power—enfranchisement, inequality, and power abuses—in order to intervene before and during conflict contexts. Instead, with empirically grounded insights, collaborative action is possible through critical engagement, through praxis. The form and structure of the problem should be identified in ethnographic insights and should shape how those findings might be used to participate in locally relevant politics. Collaborative action, larger forms of mobilization, strategic forms of writing and documentation are all relevant and useful strategies for consideration. Others abound and can be generated through internal processes of negotiation and assessment. For those interested in such uses of critical theory, considerations for action range from the contextual relevance, the potential impact and transformative possibilities, the pinpointing of domains of support, and the highlighting and consideration of relevant threats.

The discipline stands only to benefit from unraveling the basis for social injustice by taking public positions that are legible within relevant fields of social and political power. And the production of scholarly theory that is critically and reflexively informed by efforts to rethink and generate new perspectives on social criticism and practice are key. The link between state making and life-protecting mechanisms for the protection of innocence are not always straightforward. There is no place where this is made more obvious than in conditions of war. The ugly realities of war-engaged violence are not simply about the embattlement of those visibly wounded. War is about the use of violence to achieve particular ends—often land, resources, and the power to construct the rules of law and procedure related to procuring and controlling those resources in legal terms. And at times those who are the most complicit in brokering conditions for conflict—such as international and national governments—can be the most legally protected. This is the case in sub-Saharan Africa, where the colonial history of anthropological knowledge and the realities of engagement (or lack thereof) have failed to transcend the empirical conclusions that have characterized our discipline from the beginning. Thus, the site of an engaged ethnography is actually the site of the convergence between an engaged practice of knowledge making and sharing, with a highly circumscribed decision-making process that considers how one shares that knowledge, on whose terms, and for what purpose. These queries are vital for exploring the way we ask and answer questions and the ways that we revisit the intellectual and practical histories that have not only influenced our practices but have also enabled various sites of inequalities to flourish.

NOTES

Thank you to Ariana Hernandez-Reguant, Hudita Mustafa, Sally Merry, Ida Susser, Setha Low, Michael Gnat, Rebecca Hardin, Tina Palivos, and Lieba Faier for their input during the writing of this text. An earlier version of this chapter appeared in *Current Anthropology* 51, S2 (October 2010): 301–12. © 2010 by The Wenner-Gren Foundation for Anthropological Research. All rights reserved. Reprinted by permission of the University of Chicago Press.

1. Gulliver's *Social Control in an African Society* (1963) built on the work of Llewellyn and Hoebel (1941) and Gluckman (1955).

2. *Praxis* is a central term popularized by early Frankfurt school scholars to highlight the necessary inter-interrelatedness of theory and practice as a form of engaged politics.

3. Marshall Sahlins, in blog dated November 7, 2007, re: "AAA Board Statement on HTS," http://aaanewsinfo.blogspot.com/2007/11/aaa-board-statement-on-hts.html; his comment was posted at 10:56 a.m. the next day (accessed December 26, 2007).

4. "Code of Ethics of the American Anthropological Association," approved June 1998, http://www.aaanet.org/committees/ethics/ethcode.htm (accessed December 26, 2007). All subsequent quotations are from this version.

5. American Anthropological Association, "Executive Board Statement on the Human Terrain System Project," October 31, 2007, http://www.aaanet.org/pdf/eb_resolution _110807.pdf (accessed February 28, 2012). All subsequent quotations are from this version.

6. The phrase "handmaiden of colonialism," often nonspecifically attributed to Claude Lévi-Strauss, was popularized by Talal Asad (1973). James Hooker used a similar construction, "handmaiden of colonial governments" (Hooker 1963, 455).

Global Assemblages of Business Knowledge and Corporate Ethnography in Hungary's New Economy

CSILLA KALOCSAI

In today's economy, corporate professionals develop identities as transnational managers with entrepreneurial qualities not merely within the confines of the multinational companies where they work but also within a much wider network in which business knowledge circulates. A case in point is Hungary, where I studied the changing workstyles and lifestyles of young urban professionals in transnational business between 2002 and 2004. After the collapse of socialism, not only did economic liberalization foster the influx of multinational corporations but post-1989 Hungary also witnessed the entry and transformation of many corporate educational institutions and actors that produce and mobilize Western business knowledge and practices. Traveling in clusters, these new institutions and actors form a complex transnational apparatus of expertise—to expand Nikolas Rose's term (1992, 1996). This apparatus includes global consultancy firms, foreign and local management gurus, expatriate managers, (inter)national business schools, local corporate training firms, English- and Hungarian-language business media, as well as various management conferences and workshops. Its development has also boosted human resource departments within transnational corporations. By the time I started my research in

160

2002, most of the foreign gurus and expatriate managers had left the country or became business school professors. However, business knowledge institutions have multiplied. In this chapter, I turn to one of the most significant and prestigious forms of management education, international business schools. I analyze them in conjunction with transnational companies to examine how these institutions interact in their efforts to redefine corporate learning and refashion corporate subjects.[1]

Although the important question of how capitalist enterprises make people into workers and shape their identities has long been debated (e.g., Allison 1994; Freeman 2000; Kondo 1990; Ong 1987), my intervention follows from shifts in contemporary corporate ethnography that considers changes in managerial subjectivities and forms of sociality as encroachments of market values (e.g., Dunn 2004, 2005; Fisher 2004, 2006; Hoffman 2006; Ong 2005, 2006a, 2006b, 2008). This nascent corporate inquiry relies on Foucault's theory of governmentality (1979)—"a form of activity aiming to shape, guide or affect the conduct of some person or persons" (C. Gordon 1991, 2–3)—and on the scholarship on its most current avatar, neoliberal rationality, which highlights shifting relations among government, market, and individuals and how they reconfigure the citizen-subject as an enterprising self and an entrepreneurial actor (Rose 1992, 1996; see also Brown 2003; C. Gordon 1991). The investigation of entrepreneurial ethic turns the ethnographic lens to corporate professionals positioned at various key nodes in the global circuit of business culture in different parts of the world. Although Elizabeth Dunn's 2004 ethnography on the transformation of property and corporate regimes and their various effects on persons and values in postsocialist Poland constitutes a study of a single company, others shift their focus from the corporate interiors to the corporate exteriors and look at job fairs and talent exchange centers (Hoffman 2006), changing corporate women's networks (Fisher 2006), and management consultants and business schools (Ong 2005, 2006a, 2006b). By including international business schools and local corporate training firms in my corporate ethnography, I seek to complement this literature and contemplate how these studies change the ways we think both about corporate ethnography and the corporate form.

Building on their work, I look at the intersection of commercial and educational practices, examining how Hungary's transnational corporations are aligned with global educational institutions to circulate knowledge about how to conduct business in the new economy on the one hand and how to craft, channel, and organize the personal capacities and selves of corporate managers on the other. Here Aihwa Ong and Stephen Collier's conceptualization of global assemblages (2005) is particularly helpful. Exceeding the concept apparatus, the notion of assemblages—that is, the complex interconnections of global forms with other contingent elements, not reducible to locality or structural effects—helps me to recast the corporation, challenge its fixed boundaries, and show its multiple determinations (Ong and Collier 2005). The edges of corporate power are thus fuzzy, but within those blurred borders between trade and training are important emerging patterns of self-formation and social change.

To put it simply, transnational corporations are tangled with various forms of business expertise, both socialist and postsocialist, to retool corporate professionals into cosmopolitan, entrepreneurial selves in contemporary Hungary. Accordingly, this chapter traces relational and historical connections through the assemblages of global business knowledge not only to reveal radically reconfigured sites of knowledge production and circulation in a country like Hungary but also to show how particular vernacular forms of meanings in that context are being rearticulated alongside and in relation to hegemonic, universalizing forms—often in both simultaneous and strategic ways.[2] I therefore take the notion of assemblage a step further to show how it can be understood both as a metaphor and a strategy for constructing contemporary corporate ethnography that focuses on both linkages and disjunctions, continuities and ruptures in new forms of geopolitical arrangements across the globe. Conceptualizing corporate ethnography as an assemblage helps move beyond the ethnographic tradition of exploring a single company that dominates the field. Echoing the work of Hardin and Remis (this volume) on the interface of nongovernmental organizations (NGOs) and corporations, I thus contribute to the ethnography of corporate encounters with other sectors while also using ethnography to make sense of the experimental alterations and repetitions of the corporate form in changing economic conditions.

Taking a cue from Ong's work on neoliberalism as exception (2006b), instead of positing the contemporary neoliberal order as totalizing, I show how various hybridizing practices in a postsocialist state like Hungary reconstitute the vernacular through cosmopolitan discourses "whose power is increasingly drawn from presumptions about universal personhood globally and the regimentation of interconnected spheres of knowledge and influence" (Clarke 2007a). Such hybrids endow both entrepreneurial subject making and business knowledge formation with a vernacular genealogy and provide grounds for problematizing notions of rupture and continuity prevalent in political, corporate, popular, and analytical discourses on neoliberalism. More specifically, my approach in this chapter emphasizes uneven continuities and discontinuities between socialist and neoliberal institutions, actors, technologies, and ethics. In other words, the "rapid emergence" of new business knowledge institutions and personnel on the one hand and the "quick" adaptation of entrepreneurial ethics among corporate managers on the other cannot be understood without distinct socialist legacies in Hungary, such as socialist leadership training programs and socialist vernacular notions of entrepreneurial self and sociality.

In what follows I take issue with two strategically positioned but contradictory discourses that emerged in the rapidly changing world of 1990s Hungary. One is a dominant corporate discourse that emphasizes the influx of Western business culture and the cosmopolitanism of the entrepreneurial subject, eclipsing both Hungary's socialist leadership programs and the complicated history of socialist entrepreneurship. The second is a dominant political discourse that claimed that Hungarians have always been entrepreneurs, and that thus casted socialist entrepreneurs as worthy citizens capable of transforming both themselves and the Hungarian economy into capitalist ones (Lampland 1995; Sik 1994), while the postsocialist governments of the time implemented structural adjustment programs. An emphasis on the continuous process of liberalization, however, overlooks the particularities of the socialist economy and obscures the specificities of neoliberalization.

To complicate this genealogical approach to neoliberalism, in the next section, I thus tell the story of an international business school in Budapest, tracing the vernacular forms and actors of socialist corporate knowledge that remained important in launching and (re)constructing the "new" global apparatus of business knowledge in Hungary. In the third section, I explore socialist entrepreneurial ethics, anchored in Hungary's first and second economies of the 1970s and 1980s, and illustrate how it provided a ground upon which new neoliberal ethics could take root and hybridize. And then in the last section, I examine how these new, albeit hybrid, structures and technologies of corporate education spread protocols for Hungarian business professionals and attempt to produce "new," more appropriate kinds of subjects. By modeling corporate ethnography as an assemblage, this chapter thus argues for the uneven connections and disconnections in business expertise and entrepreneurial ethics that have emerged between liberalizing socialist and neoliberalizing postsocialist times. Hence, the value of ethnographic research in an era of transnational corporate dominance and crisis is the ability to unpack these complicated interactions and thus to make sense of new global regulations and restructurings.

Tracing the Global Circuit
of Business Culture

"It is not by chance that MBA, the highest ranking degree in the business world, is not translated into Hungarian, since western business culture is the standard, the paradigm, and it is still the crutch," begins an article in a 1996 issue of *Figyelő*, the Hungarian business weekly, reviewing master of business administration (MBA) schools in East-Central Europe. Accordingly, in the 1990s, eleven MBA programs have sprouted across Hungary, a small country of ten million people, acting as "little princesses waiting for western suitors," as András Neményi, a former director of an international business school and a current professor and associate dean at a public business school, put it.[3] Western, mostly European, business schools interested in the emerging market in postsocialist East-Central Europe or wanting to catch up with world-class educational institutions that have already gone global have arrived and have engaged in various types of collaborations with the local private and public business schools.[4] Even though international collaborations most often entail fleeting relationships between Hungarian and Western schools and offer exchange programs for students, staff, and faculty, Hungarian business schools tend to advertise themselves via their foreign partner institutions. These institutional connections can be significant for nurturing a certain multicultural aura important in the globalized job market, as András emphasizes, but they do not necessarily open up additional flows of values, attitudes, and habits that are crucial for working in transnational corporations.

The focus of my research, however, was the East-Central European region's first private business school, the International Business Center (IBC), founded in 1988, a year before the state socialist regime collapsed. The three founding fathers—Sándor Demján, famous for establishing the Soviet Bloc's first cooperatively owned supermarket; George Soros, the Hungarian-born American financier and philanthropist; and Mark Palmer, Hungary's American ambassador at the time—agreed to establish a Western-style management school to provide training for an elite group of economic leaders who were riding market forces in Hungary at the time. When the state socialist regime fell a year later, the idea of "an American-style business education, [with] global perspectives and regional expertise," proved ever more relevant for the East European student body and the emerging market economies. Ever since, IBC, with the Soros branding, has been Hungary's only full-time English-language MBA program and has negotiated more successfully for international involvement than most other business schools in the country. In addition, while Hungarian business schools could usually develop European connections, mostly with England and France, IBC was able to establish prestigious North American collaborations. Transferring faculty, curricula, operation systems, students, deans, and the coveted American degree, the profile of the school has changed with the forging of each new institutional partnership.

Still, strong Western collaborations have eclipsed the Hungarian genealogy in IBC's history. The school first hired Hungarian professors and administrators who mostly came out of socialist leadership training programs (*szocialista vezetőképző szeminárium*) established and supported by liberal economic reforms first introduced at the end of the 1960s.[5] At that time, a couple of major universities in Budapest, one in eastern Hungary, and the National Leadership Training Center launched postgraduate management training programs and industry-specific training seminars. Each school had its particular character, defined by its director of organizational development, but they all focused on questions and problems relevant to the Hungarian context, developing theories and methods that provided solutions for socialist enterprises. These socialist seminars, however, also taught quality management, value analysis, organizational development, rationalizing methods, brainstorming, and budget analysis.

Coming of professional age in the 1970s, János Varga, one of the first professors hired at IBC, received the news about Hungary's newly established international business school on a study trip to the United States sponsored by a Soros fellowship in the late 1980s. He commented:

> I was on a presentation tour around the U.S., and one day I visited the Ford Corporation. At Ford I participated in some event, where they announced that a Hungarian was there visiting. Then someone came up to me, and gave me a current issue of *Wall Street Journal* or *Financial Times*, I don't remember exactly, where a short article announced the foundation of the first Hungarian business school. . . . When I returned to Budapest, I called the school's Hungarian CEO whose name was published in the newspaper, and told her I was interested in joining.

Accordingly, János and colleagues of similar pedigree became the newly established IBC's first core faculty and administrative body and started their so-called Young Management Program in 1988, referring to the young managers they targeted and following international MBA standards. János makes it clear that they wanted to prepare future generations (*jövő nemzedékét*) for business so they can "pass the torch on." Management consultants, trainers, and professors since the early 1970s, these first Hungarian professors and administrators performed well in both socialist enterprises and the academic world. Similarly, IBC's first chief executive ran the in-house management school in Demján's department store in the early 1980s. They were of a different generation than those young selects multinational corporations recruited around the same time when IBC was formed: they were already in their late thirties and early forties in the late 1980s and early 1990s, instead of their early twenties. The only American among them at the time was the first dean—a former assistant dean from Tulane's business school.

It was the University of Pittsburgh that first took interest in IBC and its Young Management Program. The Hungarians thus flew to Pittsburgh for six weeks in the summer to learn about the American MBA world and to receive mentorship on courses and administration. Although they could not observe how MBA classes were conducted over the summer months, they designed the first curriculum together with the Pittsburgh faculty and staff. Instead of a regular two-year American degree, the University of Pittsburgh agreed to launch an accelerated program in alignment with IBC's mission to (re)train young Eastern European managers for the changing regional marketplace. It thus offered Hungarian and Eastern European students twelve intensive months of study in Budapest, with an extra few months in Pittsburgh to finish their degrees.[6] Other universities, such as Tulane and Emory from the United States, and York from Canada, joined in to provide routes for the students to complete and "truly" internationalize their degrees.

American professors flew in from Pittsburgh and other North American business schools to co-teach courses with the Hungarian faculty. Co-teaching defined IBC's first few years, guaranteeing a certain quality of education, as well as providing a comparative perspective: Western professors discussed how things should be, while the easterners talked about how things actually were in the region. The irony of co-teaching was, as János admits, that Hungarian professors were only one or two classes ahead of the students, but still his American partner professor invited him to give a course on strategic management in a prestigious American business school the following year. In any case, co-teaching enabled this socialist cohort of Hungarian corporate educators to recognize the difference between their "old" and "new" styles of teaching and the shift toward ethics in business education: "For years, we tried to teach methods, techniques, models, and checklists in our seminars, and thought that if people learn to apply the methods, the country will flourish [*a haza fényre derül*]. But it didn't work—if the employees don't have the right values, they can't apply the methods to practice. Workers can't recognize why it is important to use these methods, so this is why they need to acquire the right values, attitudes, and habits."

As Pittsburgh started to foster new collaborations with other foreign universities, IBC needed to look after stronger international partners. In the mid-1990s, János, as director of the MBA program at the time, traveled to a business school conference in Barcelona and heard the dean of Case Western Reserve University give a lecture about their innovative MBA education. Based on research conducted with corporate executives and their expectations toward business schools, Case Western designed a new program that emphasized the development of skills and competences that managers and leaders needed in the corporate world. A year later at a similar conference in Athens, János met the same dean again, who mentioned that Case Western was looking into mobilizing their expertise across the globe. János invited the dean to Budapest, and IBC's new Hungarian-Canadian dean started a long process of negotiation about the details of their new partnership. Case Western imagined the relationship between the two business schools quite differently than Pittsburgh had earlier, and defined IBC as their branch overseas, to which they could recruit an additional hundred American students. Such a set-up entailed a very rigorous cooperation: IBC had to give the same courses and curriculum in Hungary as Case Western did in the United States. Students, faculty, and staff also had to meet the same requirements at both places, and therefore processes were very closely matched and monitored.

Many alumni acknowledge a course titled Management Assessment and Development (MAD) that Case Western University transferred to the Hungarian business school as its signature product. It conveyed a very particular training geared toward individual students. When young professionals entered the school, they had to go through tests and evaluations and then received a personal learning plan. Accordingly, students were assigned to specific classes and individual consultations that strengthened the skills and competences defined as weak or lacking in their evaluation. Case Western also sent a professor to IBC to co-teach the MAD course with Zsuzsa Czine, the Hungarian professor teaching Business English and Academic Skills at the time. Over three semesters they co-taught the course, as Zsuzsa learned the ins and outs of the complicated processes involved. Besides requiring too much administration, the course exposed the underlying tensions of such collaboration: Case Western was too rigid in its focus on the individual as a universal bundle of measurable qualities and thus did not support IBC in its attempt to adapt the course to its specific Eastern European cultural context and its particular student body.

The IBC–Case Western story had to come to an end. The deans on both sides left their particular schools, and the trust that is so crucial even at the institutional level, as András says, weakened. Incoming deans interpreted the collaboration differently, and no legal agreements existed that would have provided a framework for maintaining a partnership in the long run. The scandal that broke out was thus able to quickly erode and then terminate the relationship between the two schools. In 2000, the *Financial Times* published an article that Hungarian and Eastern European students were cheating in IBC's classrooms: they were giving information to one another during midterm and other tests. Although most Hungarian students and professors saw such behavior as a sign of cooperation and sharing, American students and professors interpreted it as a sign of ethical misconduct. In this instance, ideas about interpersonal connections and the socially embedded, socialist concept of person clashed with the capitalist idea of individualized and privatized personhood, exposing cracks in Case Western's cultural imposition.[7] And ironically, while Case Western had tried to ensure the inculcation of the right norms, attitudes, and habits by Eastern European students, young professionals nevertheless relied on their vernacular sense of self and sociality in order to gain those extra points to meet American expectations so they could travel to the United States to earn the coveted three letters. As a result of clashing disciplines, values, and personhoods, Case Western's new dean discontinued relations with IBC, only allowing the already admitted students to finish their degrees.

There were not many at IBC who really insisted on Case Western's staying. Including IBC's founders, CEOs and ambassadors, and deans and rectors of foreign-invested institutions from Hungary and the West, the board of trustees was very critical of Case Western's homogenizing attempts or, rather, its "take-over," as many put it. The English-language graduate school (EGS) closely linked to IBC through Soros funding and board membership used this moment to settle its own conflict with the business school. The university's rector and vice president, both members of IBC's board, voiced their critique about IBC faculty's lagging academic record. Even though Pittsburgh and Case Western had approved both the core and the visiting faculty at IBC, Hungary's EGS focused on the lack of a long list of PhD degrees and publications from the teaching staff's résumés. By pointing to the difference in the quality of their faculties, EGS expressed another of its frustrations—that around the (im)possibility of merging the two schools. George Soros founded and funded both institutions, but IBC received only partial funding and thus had to rely on its growing alumni network and executive programs to construct its budget, as business schools in the West often do. EGS imagined that IBC would become its "cash cow," once Soros put down its endowment for the graduate school. Since the alumni network and executive programs only brought in a limited amount of revenue, IBC could not meet this expectation. Hence, its budget allowed them to recruit only Hungary-based international visiting professors and business executives with various academic records.

When Case Western pulled out, IBC was renamed EGS Business School, realizing the American business school model for the third time in its short history. This time, in 2002, however, it didn't align itself with a U.S.-based business school. It aligned with EGS, which provides English-language graduate education for mostly Hungarian and Eastern European students and grants a degree that is most often licensed by the Regents of the State of New York.[8] Though an integral part of EGS, IBC still has a separate budget, faculty, and legal status. The newly re-fashioned institution receives greater Soros funding than ever before, but its new chief executive, a successful Hungarian entrepreneur, has pledged to make the school self-financing in the coming years. The Soros endowment has provided a hitherto unknown stable existence, as well as an inner and outer face-lift, marking fundamental changes in the business school's history.

The old Hungarian faculty and administration refer to the inner restructuring as "the massacre" (*vérfürdő*). The new institution did not rehire any of IBC's first Hungarian professors and administrators, except Zsuzsa Czine, who had to finish running the MAD course for the last Case Western cohort. The new dean, Paul Miller, recruited a larger, more academically oriented faculty, many of them with PhDs or ABDs, as well as with substantial publication records. The restructured business school has also enriched its academic offerings under separate but mostly standard business school department headings and established a Center for the Social Foundations of Business to mark a bridge between EGS's graduate and professional education and to contribute to new global trends in business ethics.

IBC presents these changes as a total relaunch, yet the institutional discontinuities obscure particular continuities. The school has appeared to remain faithful to its original mission of training Eastern European managers for the regional market while also opening its doors to students from more diverse backgrounds. The EGS Business School has also reintroduced the part-time MBA program, recast as a weekend MBA, in order to cater specifically to Hungarian professionals who cannot always afford to quit work for a year of schooling. And as before, the core international faculty consists of professors who have been living in Hungary for one reason or another, while other Western professors fly in on a visiting basis. Interestingly, most of the core Hungarian faculty comes from the same generation as the one fired, with roots in the liberalizing socialist past, but with an academic pedigree more recognizable in the West. Some of Case Western's program has also been kept with revisions. Most importantly, its MAD course has been broken up into various forms, such as a training session for incoming students, as well as courses titled Business Communication and Action Learning. In these events and courses the emphasis also falls onto infiltrating and transforming people's values, attitudes, and habits through the realignment of notions of "appropriateness" in the transnational business world.

IBC's story shows the institutional, methodological, and personal continuities and thus exposes a vernacular genealogy of business expertise, challenging the emphasis on newness and Western import solely. At the same time, the Western influx of business culture, as illustrated above, has greatly transformed Hungarian institutions, techniques, and actors of corporate education. This transformation, however, started before the fall of the state socialist regime, calling for a new periodization that exposes continuous processes of liberalization since the late 1960s. The next section on socialist entrepreneurship suggests, however, that emphasis on continuity alone is not sufficient.

Entrepreneurship in Hungary's Socialist Era

Like the business school professors and corporate trainers who trace their most crucial expertise to Western sources, my conversations with almost a hundred white-collar youth attest that the reasons young people seek employment at foreign-invested corporations are learning and self-development. Even professionals who plan to work in national firms admit that it is useful to put in a few years at a transnational corporation at the beginning of one's career in order to gain important professional experience. Talented young people from all over the country travel to Budapest and other urban centers, seeking employment with non-Hungarian companies. Their "strong technical knowledge alone," as many MBA professors and corporate trainers point out, is not quite enough for them to be considered "appropriate" corporate managers in the transnational business sphere. Accordingly, professors and trainers identify that Hungarian professionals lack confidence, assertiveness, and initiation and cannot present themselves, perform in teams, or exercise participatory management. Others complain about how hard it is for Hungarian corporate employees to work on projects for long hours and under intense time pressure.[9] Therefore, it takes a lot more work, claims Chris Davis, the IBC director and trainer, for Hungarian professionals to get a job or to be appreciated at work.

Multinational companies must therefore invest in retooling Hungarian corporate managers into entrepreneurial subjectivities, and human resource departments, international business schools, and local corporate training firms are particularly instrumental in affecting transformations of normative character, moral codes, and worldview. When asked, most professionals provide a long list about what it is they learned through corporate education. They emphasize teamwork, presentation, and working on projects, but some also mention communication with foreigners and exercising delegation in leadership. Many of IBC's alumni reflect on the complex perspective they have acquired in the schools. Mariann Lang, a first-generation student at IBC in 1989, also conveys that one of their professors listed on the board three qualities that in their minds they had to achieve: "you are the best," "aim high," and "you can do it." Indeed, confidence, career-mindedness, and self-activation appear to be recurring personality traits that other alumni also echo as crucial in their business education.

While business knowledge workers defined them missing, entrepreneurial values, skills, and habits were not new in postsocialist Hungary and East-Central and Eastern Europe. In fact, many scholars argue that various socialist, especially late socialist, institutions were critical in producing an entrepreneurial ethic and thus shaping socialist forms of entrepreneurial subjectivity (Lampland 1995;

Rona-Tas 1997; Szelenyi 1988). They thus point to the private, informal, second (or secondary) economy that developed under and coexisted with Hungary's state-socialist economy, especially in its later period, but they provide distinct explanations and genealogies.[10] Each conceptualizes the socialist second economy somewhat differently and traces its formation back to various historical periods.

By introducing conceptual shifts in economic policy, such as recognizing commodity markets, reinterpreting economic planning, and tying work to shifting monetary values, the liberal economic reforms of the late 1960s, called the New Economic Mechanism (NEM), intensified the prevalence of capitalist values, attitudes, and practices in late socialist Hungary (Lampland 1995; Rona-Tas 1997). The reforms encouraged productivity, profitability, and efficiency and justified the need for markets and the introduction of monetary incentives at the workplace according to a utilitarian understanding of action. While the concessions to the market led to the rise of a young technocracy, knowledgeable about markets and competition, and independent in thought and action, they also contributed to the strengthening of the second economy in which 50 percent of the population was engaged by the mid-1970s.[11] Second economy activities further increased autonomy, enhanced the economistic thinking and scheming of entrepreneurs, and fostered individual initiative and self-responsibility. In other words, a liberal ethical worldview accompanied the reforms, promulgating individualism, utilitarianism, and rational choice. Indeed, the emerging petit bourgeoisie was no longer considered greedy, selfish, and lacking in moral character, but positively valued for its rational calculation, optimizing behavior, and maximizing efforts (Rona-Tas 1997).

While to some degree Martha Lampland joined Akos Rona-Tas in tracing the formation of Hungarian entrepreneurial values, attitudes, and practices to the New Economic Mechanism and emphasizing their entrenchment in the liberalization process, she also develops another argument. She explores the collectivization of Hungarian agriculture and the thriving second economy and analyses how atomized, individualist, economistic, and utilitarian attitudes toward work, property, money, and morality, widely shared in Hungarian society, emerged under socialism, quite contrary to its ideals of collective property relations, community actions, and social accountability (Lampland 1995; Rev 1987). Collectivization and industrialization during the socialist period substantially altered the work experience of most adult Hungarians, who were regularly employed in formal, and often complex, enterprises. Lampland therefore locates emerging capitalist values even in early socialism, arguing that much of the villagers' experience was structured by practices resembling those in a capitalist political economy, accounting for the strange consequence of commodification of labor under socialism.

Such similarities include managerial hierarchies, wage packages, work shifts, and the limited influence of the rank and file over decision making, all of which contribute to the objectification, naturalization, and systematization of labor during state socialism. The difference between capitalist firms and socialist enterprises, however, lies in decision making, and Lampland brilliantly conveys how socialist planning particularly shapes economistic thinking. More specifically, the actual practice of fulfilling the plans revealed how the elites used calculus and politics for their own enhancement and therefore the ways in which the values of personal utility and individual interest permeated society. Such economism of planning, Lampland contends, contributed to the character of private economic activity and how citizens exploited, circumvented, and avoided socialist policies in late socialism.[12]

Socialist entrepreneurship presents an important set of practices, norms, and selves with which to problematize MBA professors' and corporate trainers' insistence that Hungarian professionals excelled only in technical knowledge and lacked entrepreneurial values, habits, and conducts. In contrast, an entrepreneurial ethic, as shown above, was fostered under socialism both by socialist politics and production and by the late socialist liberalization process. Tracing entrepreneurship back to only the late socialist liberalization process is therefore not sufficient. The argument about the continuity of liberalization between socialist and postsocialist times is problematic and overlaps with the dominant political discourse of the early 1990s, mentioned above, which hoped for the easy expansion and the development of the second economy into a capitalist market economy. Many thus considered the second economy as a relative training ground or laboratory for capitalism, for entrepreneurship, and for individual prosperity. Second economy entrepreneurs, however, did not quite meet the sociopolitical expectations of the so-called transition, marking the limits of such a political discourse. This tension points to processes of vernacularization and hybridization that question genealogical assumptions and thus problematize the neat and linear story of neoliberalization.

In other words, an emphasis on continuous processes of liberalization would suggest the general success of entrepreneurship, leading us to overlook the particularities of socialist second economy and the specificities of the new political economy. Socialist entrepreneurship, for example, was quite labor intensive, often based on the absence of tools and clever techniques on the one hand and the lack of financial investment on the other (Lampland 1995). The socialist private enterprise was insecure, since the legal and political environments were in constant flux, and lacked an insurance system, limited liability, or assurance about procuring supplies (Rona-Tas 1997). In addition, the socialist moderate entrepreneurialism, as Judit Bodnar (2001) puts it, developed in an economic context with low risk and low competition, as socialist social policies, such as full employment, protected the market sphere and infused it with a petit bourgeois spirit of security, characteristic of the Kadar regime. To paraphrase, the involvement in the second economy was a low-risk strategy of economic autonomization, with no real prospect for growth (Bodnar 2001). With the emergence of market risks and fierce competition, increasing unemployment and changing informality, dramatic shifts in the organization of work and technology, and the transformation of political and legal conditions of business, entrepreneurial values and activities have called for change.

Thinking about the discontinuity between or shift from socialist entrepreneurial to neoliberal entrepreneurial ethics, I rely on Alexei Yurchak's study of the late-Soviet Komsomol (2002) in order to elaborate the socialist characteristics of entrepreneurship.[13] By introducing the notion *socialist entrepreneurial governmentality*, Yurchak expands Lampland's argument about how socialism produces capitalistic norms, attitudes, and practices and cojoins it with Foucault's notion of governmentality (1979) and Rose's discussion about the enterprising, entrepreneurial self (1992, 1996). For Yurchak, Komsomol appears similar to business schools through teaching organizational skills, providing access to official resources, and allowing members to make money. The Communist Union of Youth thus spread a new pragmatic understanding of work, time, money, skills, and professional relations on the one hand and a particular hybrid understanding of the party-state's official plans, rules, laws, and institutions on the other. To spell it out, Komsomol workers learned to organize and manage public practice so they could achieve official goals in the context of state-imposed obstacles and forms of control, such as in times of shortage. Employing entrepreneurial technologies toward two, often coexisting, types of public sphere, the officialized and personalized, allowed late socialist Komsomol workers to separate meaningful and meaningless work and to juggle different meanings, produce different reports, and relate to state institutions, laws, and ideologies in different ways.

Individual agency, pragmatism, efficiency, utilitarianism, creativity, and flexibility thus characterize late-Soviet employees, that is, what I call here the socialist organizational man. Yurchak draws a direct link between the activities of Komsomol secretaries in the 1980s and how they reinvented themselves as businessmen in post-Soviet Russia (2002). It is not necessarily second-economy entrepreneurs, then, but the entrepreneurial qualities of the socialist organizational man that prove pivotal for tracing assemblages of global business knowledge. Challenging Yurchak's straightforward linkage, I want to draw attention to and emphasize a shift from socialist entrepreneurial governmentality to neoliberal entrepreneurial governmentality and argue how the same values and habits have been reinterpreted in terms of cosmopolitanism and presented in a systematic, professional, top-down manner to a new generation of professionals in the key nodes of transnational business knowledge. I show how business schools and corporate training firms harness and revise socialist entrepreneurship, especially its avatar in socialist enterprises and other organizations but, by relying on a generational shift, also burn the genealogical routes between the socialist and the postsocialist and neoliberal versions of entrepreneurship, purifying their figure of the "new" entrepreneurial subject.[14] In making corporate managers appropriate for the global economy, such processes of purification reconstitute and reconfigure the entrepreneurial subject as cosmopolitan and universal within the arena of transnational corporations and endow them with a new sense of privilege, aspiration, self-management, reflexivity, and professionalism. This reconfiguration of the Hungarian entrepreneur has implications for how we study ethnographic assemblages of new business knowledge and subjectivities—be they in postsocialist or postcolonial contexts.

Retooling the Entrepreneurial Subject in the Postsocialist Era

There are four salient and intersecting processes of corporate learning—selection, promotion, evaluation, and training—that are prominent technologies of governmentality for the circulation of neoliberal qualities and the reconfiguration of corporate subjects into entrepreneurial actors in Hungary's business world. Similarly to professionals who challenge earlier understandings of corporate learning tied only to business schools and corporate training events, I think of corporate learning in a wide sense, involving various processes that convey a turn to and in ethics.[15] Here I concentrate on evaluation and training promoting a shifting entrepreneurial ethic and show how particular attitudes and habits are internalized and negotiated by young Hungarian employees in transnational corporations.[16]

Performance appraisal is the third salient technology of subject formation in transnational corporations through which certain competences are measured, development needs are set, and further career aspirations are identified. While some companies, like Big Four consultancy firms, conduct these personal audits every three months, others, like Food&HomeCare, the main corporate site of my research project, only do them once a year. Both the direct boss and the employee in question fill out and discuss the elaborate forms of evaluations, matching qualities with concrete behavioral examples. In Food&HomeCare, four categories define white-collar professionals, depending on how well they do on these charts: foundation, developing, growth, and world class. The pompous language that wraps the competences in the transnational business world, such as "passion for growth," "seizing the future," and "breakthrough thinking," reveals an entrepreneurial character with a good understanding of business and organization and with the capability of envisaging opportunities. The world-class manager also has to foster development of self and others and build morale and cooperation within and across teams. Accordingly, these audit tools create motivated, self-reflexive, self-activating, self-developing, careerist persons who try to align themselves with the company's needs.

I was shadowing Gyöngyi Kelemen, a human resource consultant, at a multinational telecom company's factory in the countryside in spring 2004 as she tried to develop a management audit tool for the corporation, linking it to coaching and other development programs. Before brainstorming about relevant competences and levels of performance, she simply summed it up: "what people have to achieve for success." Gyöngyi presented the tool as an objective system that can set expectations, measure personal profiles, and provide routes for improvement and success. "If it really works," she says, "people cannot pretend to be anything but what they are." Hungarian professionals, however, have trouble accepting that such formal evaluations can really reflect the self and make a difference. Both corporate trainers and employees point to how quickly and exhaustively foreigners fill out the forms, while Hungarians sit on it for long and only do a superficial job. Besides the forms being a very time-consuming task in which one has to make sense of the obscure language and recall a range of concrete examples of the self and team members, Hungarian employees believe that other, intersubjective relations with higher managers figure more importantly than objective merit in one's career mobility.

While audit tools mask the social nature of power, as Dunn puts it (2004; see also Strathern 2000), many of my research participants emphasize that alternative models of evaluation co-exist, and point to the significance of social relations in determining one's performance. Rita Csanádi, for example, says, "I don't only have to meet expectations about skills and competences, but political ones too—to whom and how I relate." She thus argues that what it comes down to is "whether a person needs you, and then he or she will support your career." Zoltán Takács, a mid-level account manager who has been working for Food&HomeCare for ten years, contends that despite efforts to be objective and scientific, individualized evaluation results can be misinterpreted, so what influences one's success and career is "how you position yourself in small groups in the company, what kind of connections you can develop, and how you can show and shine [*fényezés*] your qualities in front of your bosses and colleagues." Professionals at Food&HomeCare thus voice "the catastrophic significance" of social or, as they put it, political relations that they interestingly interpret in two distinct ways. For example, Tamás Havas, a senior accountant in the company, understands such relations as a sign of socialist sociality, while others see them more as a mark of the new work ethics and allude to its connections to self-management.[17] Here I argue for recognizing the significance of social relations at the transnational corporate workplace as re-articulations of older ties under the neoliberal logic.

Closely tied to such practices as selection, promotion, and evaluation is corporate education, the fourth salient moment of subjectification in Hungary's transnational corporations. MBA professors and corporate trainers address a shift in how they convey appropriate business knowledge to young professionals, emphasizing a move away from formal lectures and toward a more informal and active participatory learning environment. When I conducted interviews at IBC and asked Hungarian part-time students why they chose IBC among the dozen other MBA schools in the country, they replied unanimously: they not only valued the international degree recognizable to multinational employers but they also pointed to the "quality" or "method of teaching." For example, Balázs Veres, a junior manager in a transnational telecommunication firm, explained to me that he selected IBC so he can work in groups, give presentations, and participate in discussions, which he would not be able to do in public and most other private business schools in the country. The slip between teaching quality and methodology is important to note, since it communicates how a particular teaching methodology, imported from the West through various channels and at different times, has become valorized in Hungary's transnational corporate arena.

The new Western methodology of corporate education also signals how internationally embedded business schools conceptualize MBA training as a simulation and transformation of work in the global economy. While IBC spread a range of knowledge from functional to organizational and strategic among its students, it has always put special emphasis on soft skills courses and immersion experiences that are particularly concerned with subjectification (see also Olds and Thrift 2005 and Ong 2006b). These soft skills classes dramatize how particular character traits and practices are internalized, clearly evoking the new terms of Hungary's market economy.[18] IBC's Business Communication class is a case in point. The class is structured as follows: First, Chris surveys how much experience people in the class have in, let's say, public speaking. Second, he tells students that every successful senior manager is good at giving presentations, even though "most managers fear public speaking more than death." Third, Chris invites students to give a one-minute speech about a random topic. After the performances, he provides useful practical advice, addressing how to hold the attention of the audience, how to respond to hostile questions, and how to deal with stress. The key, he says, is to be in control. Then, he asks the students to prepare a five-minute presentation on the same topic that builds on and improves their recent performance, includes no props or visual aids, and relates the theme to the groups from a particular business angle. Lastly, he lists the rules of presenting, ranging from its structure and body positioning to its mechanics. For the next class, students are dressed smartly, ready to give their prepared presentations. Chris analyzes these public speech events and then restates the right set of attitudes and behaviors that managers have to display in presentations.

Chris's normative statement about "every successful senior manager" frames these classes and presents students with two options: one through which they fulfill the demands of transformation and reposition themselves as successful senior managers and another where they remain part of a larger crowd of managers who can't, let's say, perform in public. The incapability of presentation is portrayed as the death of success. In one of the classes, however, an Eastern European woman voiced her concerns about the particular attitudes and habits Chris listed as necessary in networking, saying that in her country women can't act in such a fashion. By reinforcing the abstract category of "every successful manager," however, Chris encouraged this female student to eclipse her gender difference. As feminist scholarship has shown for decades, gender neutrality always refers to a masculine normative subject that excludes and subjugates femininity and female subjects.[19] Accordingly, "every successful manager" also implies masculine managerial subjects and thus either relegates female managers to the background or masculinizes them in their conduct and dispositions.

By juxtaposing the norms and rules of public speaking with personal performances, and oscillating between the two, students learn to constantly monitor and discipline themselves in order to ensure that they accommodate to Western models of conduct and disposition. From dark-suited American professors and world-class management gurus to the gold-coated and marble-covered business school building, concrete appearances of success everywhere in the business school reinforce the abstract reference to "every successful manager" in class, empowering Hungarian and Eastern European students to willingly become self-activating, self-realizing, and self-improving masculinized managers ready to maneuver in the fields of global business. Such neoliberal technologies of governmentality intersects with but also differs from socialist entrepreneurial governmentality and reengineers Hungarian corporate female and male subjects as cosmopolitan career-minded masculinized workers, capable of calculation, as Rose (1992) puts it, in order to better themselves.

The formation of corporate entrepreneurial subjects in the postsocialist era is thus not only the result of the new assemblages of transnational business knowledge with a vernacular genealogy but also the function of how corporate and political discourses and practices have hybridized, realigned, and reinterpreted socialist entrepreneurial norms and habits in neoliberal Hungary. Although most socialist entrepreneurs did not perform well in the new economy, the case of young and entrepreneurial corporate managers provides an example where entrepreneurial qualities live on, albeit in revised and reconfigured form. Enterprising employees also admit that their motivation, self-activation, and self-management reach their limits at the boundaries of the corporate world. Although they express their ambivalence toward corporate work, most of them cannot imagine themselves as entrepreneurs on their own. Such limits to entrepreneurialism not only produce loyalty to corporate work but also evoke both the socialist entrepreneur and the socialist organizational man once again, whose enterprising practices were confined within the state socialist economy.

Conclusion

In order to understand and describe in detail how assemblages are formed and work to shape the transnational business world, I have used ethnography to examine international business schools and transnational firms that form concrete connections and disconnections for the spread of business experts and expertise that reach back to the socialist past. Such an inquiry not only reflects the current mobility of middle managers and other knowledge workers in the corporate sphere, cross-cutting company and industry boundaries, but also draws attention to the widespread change in transnational corporate forms. Reconsidering corporate ethnography as an assemblage that highlights a complex web of concrete linkages and ruptures, multivalent effects, and transformations in this age of new transnational arrangements, we can think more closely about what John Van Maanen (2001) calls the *slippery and amorphous organizational borders* that alter today's corporations. As organizational studies mostly in the UK and business anthropology in the United States turn to anthropology's signature practice, corporate anthropologists in academia also need to be more attentive to how they present these shifting corporate boundaries and alliances and thus how they design their ethnography at the time of new global restructurings and regulations.

NOTES

I am grateful to all who shared their ideas and experiences of the emergent transnational corporate world with me. Earlier versions of this chapter were presented at the Canadian Anthropology Society (CASCA) conference in Toronto in spring 2007 and at the American

Anthropological Association (AAA) conference in Washington, D.C., in fall 2007. I would like to thank both audiences for their engaging comments and questions, and especially Carla Freeman and the two discussants, Kamari Clarke and Hirokazu Miyazaki. Finally, I am indebted to my two advisers, Kamari Clarke and Ivan Szelenyi, for their critical reading of various drafts of this essay, and to Mary Taylor, Éva Fodor, Rebecca Hardin, and Gwen Walker for their input during the writing of this text.

1. Elsewhere I also examine local corporate training firms, which provide the most widespread form of business expertise in Hungary's transnational world of corporate work. Although they mark a different node in the global circuit of business culture, their stories demonstrate a similar pattern of hybridization of forms, techniques, and actors of corporate education (Kalocsai 2010).

2. For discussing various cosmopolitan projects and methodologies see Charles Briggs (2005), David Harvey (2001), and Sheldon Pollock et al. (2000).

3. Between August 2002 and July 2004 I interviewed more than one hundred corporate professionals working at three types of corporate institutions in Budapest, Hungary: foreign-invested firms, international business schools, and corporate training firms. Most of the corporate white-collar workers I talked to had managerial jobs at transnational telecommunications, IT, electronic, pharmaceutical, and fast moving consumer goods (FMCG) industries. Twenty of my interviews, however, were conducted in one multinational FMCG corporation that I call Food&HomeCare in my study. In the international business schools and corporate training firms I interviewed both business school professors and trainers on the one hand and students on the other. Data collection also employed a combination of other methods, such as auditing courses at business schools, attending training sessions, shadowing consultants in company plants, and following the Hungarian- and English-language business media. All names of research participants and of business institutions are pseudonyms. The names of public figures, however, are kept unchanged. While some of the interviews were conducted in English, most were held in Hungarian. All interview translations are mine.

4. On how Western, mostly North American, business schools go global, see Aihwa Ong (2006b) and Kris Olds and Nigel Thrift (2005).

5. These economic reforms are discussed in detail in the third section of this chapter.

6. Shortly after the establishment of IBC, international business schools appeared in the Czech Republic, Poland, and Slovenia, recruiting most of the East-Central European student body. Thus, IBC has been mostly recruiting Hungarian and east European students, such as Romanians, Bulgarians, and students from the former Soviet Union.

7. See Elizabeth Dunn's ethnography (2004) on these two types of personhood in postsocialist Poland. In contrast to Dunn, I argue later that the socially embedded personhood presents only one form of Hungarian subjectivity that comes out of socialism. Individualistic, entrepreneurial personhood also emerged at the time (Lampland 1995).

8. Ever since the establishment of EGS Business School, there are new international authorities on postgraduate business education that accredit the school's MBA degree.

Since 2004, the Middle States Commission on Higher Education in the United States provides institutional accreditation, and since 2007, the international impartial authority, the Association of MBAs, recognizes the degree.

9. One of my dissertation chapters discusses the significant shifts in time that take place under the neoliberal logic in the transnational corporate arena (Kalocsai 2010).

10. The Hungarian Communist Party called the second economy *secondary economy* to mark its subordination.

11. As Akos Rona-Tas (1997) points out, estimates of the size of second economy varied, depending on definitions and estimators. The party used the widest interpretation and claimed that three-quarters of Hungarian society was involved in some sort of informal economy.

12. A third important theory of socialist entrepreneurship was developed by Ivan Szelenyi, who argued that socialist entrepreneurial activities show a biographical pattern, by individuals reaching back to family dispositions that were interrupted by the advent of state socialism in the 1940s (Szelenyi 1988). Since I am looking at the historical connections between socialist liberalization and postsocialist neoliberalization, I do not discuss his work in the main body of my text.

13. Komsomol was the Communist Union of Youth in the Soviet Union, closely linked to its Communist Party. It combined economic, cultural, and ideological production, managed by Komsomol committees (Yurchak 2002).

14. See Charles L. Briggs's work on hybridizing and purifying practices in modern cosmopolitan projects and thus linking these practices with processes of vernacularization (2005).

15. In an interview, Rita Harmath, manager for management recruitment and learning for Food&HomeCare, a corporation I studied, nicely charted how her position has changed as corporate education was reconfigured from training to learning in her firm.

16. Elsewhere I also explore the other processes of corporate learning in detail (Kalocsai 2010).

17. While Hungarians emphasize the significance of politics at the corporate workplace, Polish workers talk about *znajomosci* or connections based on gift exchange (Dunn 2004). For the discussion of the shifting meanings and practices of *quanxi* see Ong (2006a).

18. Krisztina Fehervary (2007) explores horoscopes as a particularly powerful genre transforming subjectivity in accord with the demands of a global, neoliberal capitalist order. She identifies similar personal qualities and values that I do through a very different medium popular among middle-class professionals in Dunaújváros, Hungary.

19. Elsewhere I analyze Hungary's new breed of glass ceiling in the transnational corporate arena (Kalocsai 2010).

Collaborative Conservation Science

An Anthropological Approach

REBECCA HARDIN and

MELISSA REMIS

Over the last two decades, there have been calls to action and arguments against irreconcilable differences between anthropological subfields (see, for instance, Cartmill 1994). In practice, however, few contemporary physical anthropologists or ecologists have joined forces with ethnographers to create biocultural research programs. Physical and cultural anthropologists often share research sites but only rarely share research "cites." They may meet in forest camps, work with the same local experts or informants, and work within the same institutional contexts, but they are rarely immersed in the same scientific literatures and intellectual or technical debates (Rodman 1999).

We designed a small-scale study in 1997 to enhance our respective ongoing research projects and to illustrate the potential of collaborative, place-based work for improved understandings of social and ecological dynamics within complex systems (we have published the results of that ongoing study in Hardin and Remis 2006 and Remis and Hardin 2009). This chapter describes challenges we have encountered in our collaboration as well as in our work as anthropologists among conservation biologists and environmental policy makers. In particular this essay addresses gender issues and the challenges of keeping our work inclusive of and relevant to both academic and nonacademic experts, while keeping it attuned to the needs and concerns of the field site's longest-term residents.

In writing together we seek to respect different fieldwork practices and also to recognize forest residents who have facilitated our work and understanding of wildlife/human interactions over the years. Anthropology for us is a profession but also a process that suffuses and enriches our lives, linking us to Central Africans whom we teach, from whom we learn, and with whom we have become friends and fictive kin. This essay explores the connections between our subfields of socio-cultural and physical anthropology and their respective links to changing human-wildlife relations in an equatorial African logging town. Bayanga, in southwestern Central African Republic (CAR), is not only our field site but is also a forest conservation site, suffused with both the colonial past and the complicated current politics of gender, group identity, national belonging, and economic change. Our respective approaches to studying such issues reveal multiple fault lines among expert communities, but also between them and the communities of practice and knowledge who reside in such forest sites and make research there possible for us. Finally, within those residents' lives gender relations and everyday work is changing dramatically in ways that our research processes have shaped.

Coming to Cross-Subfield Collaboration

It was in fact in a forest camp that we authors met; Remis was trained in physical anthropology at Yale University (PhD 1994). During fieldwork in southwestern CAR, she met Hardin, who was a Peace Corps volunteer in the same area. Hardin subsequently also trained at Yale in social and cultural anthropology (PhD 2000), under the mentorship of the same adviser, Alison Richard. During and after our graduate training we have worked from an analytical perspective that integrates distinct physical and cultural anthropology literatures that share increasing emphasis on complexity and change.

The political and intellectual stakes involved in human relationships to nature are increasingly complex, both in species-rich areas of the globe and in the sites of formal expertise such as international nongovernmental organizations (NGOs) and universities. As George Marcus suggests in his chapter (this volume), peda-gogical challenges abound, as the students we train may work in several different sorts of settings. Like previous generations of students, today's graduates have strong interests in evolutionary biology and zoology, but they also seek training in forensic anthropology and cultural perspectives on courses in life sciences, genetics, and bioethics. In other words, our field is confronted with its own roles in an era some now call the "anthropocene" (Crutzen and Stoermer 2000; Crutzen 2002). Anxieties abound about human abilities to influence, destroy, or even create non-human life forms.

Historically, the entanglements of anthropological subfields have been crucial to understandings of both biological and cultural diversity as they have evolved.

They underpin individual contributions toward emerging domains such as that of ethnoprimatology (Sponsel 1997; Wheatley 1999; Fuentes and Wolfe 2002; Cormier 2003). But for each example of such integrative anthropological work one can also find examples of increasingly pronounced methodological and intellectual differences. To participate in, observe, and interpret events—as Bateson describes in her chapter (this volume)—is a very different endeavor than to collect samples of plant or genetic materials or to record languages.

Remis did not always welcome Hardin's invitation to think reflexively about how ecological data collection and analysis, regardless of the sex of the researcher, is socially understood in these contexts as a male-gendered activity not unlike others such as logging or commercial hunting (that is to say, active, transformative, generative of cash and therefore dominant relative to subsistence activities). Hardin was often reluctant to link theories about social power and narratives about historical memory to the materiality of wildlife and human movements through the forests, as Remis insisted that she do. We both see value in these struggles to communicate and collaborate, both for our own intellectual growth and for the institutional and cultural challenges implicit in processes of forest conservation.

Over the course of our careers, conservation science has become increasingly polarized. Ethnographers chronicle and critique conservation interventions by states, NGOs, and communities as physical anthropologists convey information about nonhuman primates and their responses to increasing human pressures on their resource bases and social structures. If the former sometimes seem at least partially prone to advocacy of rural residents against the powerful interests of emerging international environmental NGOs, the latter often chronicle the partial and incomplete power of such NGOs to effectively protect wildlife populations, including endangered apes, from the relentless expansion of humans into wildlife habitat and the intensifying pressures faced by wildlife species that become commodities in increasingly transnational trade networks for live animals and animal parts or products. Few disaggregate local communities and ecosystems as we do, to convey the role of nonlocals in shaping details of their interactions with wildlife, as those interactions are in turn shaped by changing factors such as gender roles (see Martin Shaw 1980), ethnic identities, and economic or subsistence niches at subnational levels in developing areas.

Ecologies and Economies of Social Difference

Our research is based in the Dzanga-Ndoki Park and Dzanga-Sangha Dense Forest Reserve (RDS) in CAR. This protected area is situated in a region most often portrayed in international news as a crisis zone, for some of the very political and economic reasons sketched in Kamari Maxine Clarke's essay (this volume). Social and ecological factors that interact in today's RDS, creating a wide array of human/animal encounters, include extensions in territorial range and intensifications in hunting technology by BaAka hunters and gatherers, more broadly known as "Pygmy" peoples of the reserve area. These changing practices reflect, reveal, and drive changes in abundance and density of wildlife over time in a region where most people rely on wild meat as their primary protein source; increasingly, they also sell surplus meat for cash income.

BaAka as an internally varied group are among the most dependent on the hunting economy. Historically excluded from formal education, loans, and other options for their economic development, BaAka still hold the most specialized knowledge base about the forest. They have historically rooted exchange relations with horticulturalist and fishing groups, agriculturalists, and traders. In focusing on BaAka in our work, we strive to situate their communities with respect to other human actors, suggesting further research agendas well beyond the scope of our study. We have documented a range of behavioral and spatial change patterns within human and animal communities throughout the reserve area. Our results extend analysis of interactions from snapshot views used in forest assessment for exploitation or protection to a panorama of regional processes unfolding within competing resource-use regimes, such as logging and conservation.

Many scholars have noted the role of the human/animal opposition in structuring social relations of forest use and group identity interdependence in the Congo Basin. For Jacqueline Thomas and Simha Arom (1974) the half-human/half-animal figure of the Miimbo or hunting spirit among the Gbaaka is a cipher for the power and alterity, or "otherness," of Pygmies upon whom the Gbaaka were dependent for survival upon their migration into the forest hundreds of years ago. Michelle Kisliuk (1998) catalogues the ambiguous role of Sumbu the chimpanzee in Pygmy repertoires of song and dance in communities in southern CAR, noting its similarity to Western mythological "Pan" as well as its incompatibility with Christian missionary teachings.

Changing relationships between forest peoples, as well as more recent incursions by other groups from savannahs further north, and all these peoples' interactions with nonhuman forest neighbors are creating new pressures on that ecosystem. But they are also fostering new forms of upward mobility within the highly fluid and mobile societies of this equatorial African region. These new forms of power and affluence are far from evenly distributed, and despite the senses in which these forests are frontiers of economic opportunity, there remains much social asymmetry and injustice, especially for BaAka.

For Roy Richard Grinker (1994), the pair "human/animal" serves with other oppositions (including male/female and insider/outsider) in socially unequal but economically and ecologically complementary relationships between foragers and farmers in the Ituri forest. His work complements a very narrow tradition of French ethnography (see also Thomas and Arom 1987) that links this set of symbolic relations of difference and derision to material interdependence and to contacts between colonizers and colonized in the forests of the Congo. At whatever scale, animality seems to be embedded in the construction of human social difference (Wolch and Emel 1998). Human encounters with animals are not always literal encounters; yet we maintain that the physical presence of animals has profound effects on how humans experience forest worlds, as well as how they construct their social ones. In our work we thus center some significant part of our analysis on what we can know about their populations in response to recent economic and ecological changes. We also consider animals as crucial symbolic and material resources for those humans we study (see Giles-Vernick and Rupp 2006).

Most BaAka in Bayanga are still highly dependent upon animal populations for their livelihoods and thus function within nested systems of symbolic inequalities and material interdependence. In describing how the nature of their dependency on animals is shifting, we also chronicle the professionalization and commoditization of forest work within the hunting, logging, and conservation sectors. Changes in their skills, knowledge, and activities are occurring against a backdrop of overall intensification of forest use and increase of population in the study area, and also development of infrastructure in each of these rival yet interdependent economic domains. As a result of the area's position along international borders, and due to its wealth of resources including timber, fish, and diamonds, state infrastructure and civil servants have also constituted a steadily expanding feature of the Bayanga landscape since we each began research in the area. Now flanked by both an active logging and conservation complexes, Bayanga is filled with people who may for generations have mixed hunting, gathering, fishing, and farming but now also work in one or more of these major local industries, at least part-time.

Forest Encounters: Social Contradictions and Cross-Species Interaction

Dzanga-Sangha's principal tourist attraction is a saline clearing of approximately one by three kilometers called Dzanga, where natural minerals in the soil deposits attract up to one hundred forest elephants at a time. The forest surrounding Dzanga is laced with clearings of various sizes, "maintained" by the activity of elephants that fell trees and use the clearings and streams running through them for mud baths, minerals, and socializing. Other herbivores such as western gorilla (*Gorilla gorilla gorilla*), forest buffalo (*Caffir nanus*), sitatunga (*Tragelaphus spekei*), several species of duiker (*Cephalophus*), giant forest hogs (*Hylocherus meinertzhageni*), and bush pigs (*Potamochoerus porcus*) also use the clearings.

Initially intending to replace a logging economy, which began in the 1970s in the area, conservation professionals have instead had to contend with competition from loggers since the late 1980s. The combination of economic activities has lured further immigrants to the area and altered conditions under which humans and animals interact. During our fieldwork in Bayanga in the early 1990s, elephants and hippos presented obstacles to those on foot at night and were often encountered even within the limits of the town. Some mornings saw groups of angry farmers, mostly women, marching to the front door of conservation offices with the crushed remnants of their corn or manioc plants, complaining about the nightly ravages of elephants in their fields. Young men harvesting palm wine often found DeBrazza's monkeys (*Cercopethicus neglectus*) rummaging in the jugs they had left overnight in the treetops; groups of children and their parents washing at the town's riverbanks regularly gazed across at a lone blackback gorilla that frequented the opposite bank, washing himself and splashing.

Such banal yet entertaining encounters with animals in the lives of towns-people are now almost entirely a thing of the past. Surprisingly, a small population of hippos remained in the stretch of the Sangha River that runs along the shores of Bayanga. Seeking refuge perhaps from hunting pressures up and down river, this group of hippos persisted throughout the logging booms and busts of the 1980s and 1990s, with their attendant waves of in-migration and attendant fluctuations in consumption of wildlife. We used to see their tracks along the river's edge each morning, and even children knew to be silent as dugout canoes approached the town at evening time, for fear of disturbing them nearby. However, a relative of a local resident visiting the area from another region of CAR killed the last cow of that small group in fall 2008. In the days that followed the death, as the cow's nursing calf slowly starved in the river and Bayangans divided up the meat from the mother's carcass, they waited ambivalently for the trial of the hunter. Some expressed a sense of loss over these dangerous and fascinating creatures with whom they had cohabited for so long; others felt that the value of such a group was precisely as a reserve of protein to be exploited from time to time.

The fact that the small group of only four or five hippos had remained for over a decade near so large a town testifies to the effectiveness of formal and informal conservation efforts there. Now unable to reproduce, that hippo population is even more quickly doomed, cut off from other remaining populations in the broader region. This signals the pressures for wildlife conservation efforts in this area, where the viability of some populations is no longer a given.

Forest Communities: From Fictive Kin to Formal Experts

While wildlife viewing is increasingly rare in town, encounters with charismatic wildlife species continue to occur (if less and less frequently) in the lives of hunters and gatherers and those who visit them in forest camps. Conservation practices as currently implemented contain no easy solution to this decline in the variation and frequency of human/wildlife interactions. While the professionalization of conservation and research transforms forest life for local inhabitants, it also relegates certain ritual forms, knowledge forms, and family-related practices to the margins of the protected area, where they must compete with other uses. Employment experiences in the still fledgling tourism and research sectors foster new values among young BaAka men. These include aspirations to literacy, numeracy, and competence in technical fields beyond the specialized domains of hunting and gathering.

Perhaps as an expansion of their traditional roles as large game hunters, or perhaps in relation to their histories of labor in the timber industry, a male-centered professionalism is emerging around research- and tourism-related encounters with wildlife in this part of the core protected area. These BaAka trackers, often middle-aged men, impart information and advice to less experienced (and often female) expatriates and primarily male Bilo researchers and younger BaAka during forest research. They thus also expand their knowledge bases while increasing their skills in management of information, logistics, and new technologies. These roles contrast markedly with their temporary employment as porters and trackers for Bilo park guards during anti-poaching patrols, about which many BaAka complain bitterly due to the lack of respect they are accorded in that context.

Their changing roles within research camps are illustrated by Remis's experiences learning Sango and as the lone expatriate and only woman in charge of male research assistants at the Bai Hokou Gorilla Research station within RDS for a total of twenty months in the early 1990s. As a result of the loneliness and isolation during early days of dissertation fieldwork on gorilla ecology (Remis 1994, 1997), she began to invite the wives and children of her hired wildlife trackers to join their husbands at the camp. This was also an effort to reduce absenteeism by male employees longing for town and for their families. Their defections were taking a toll on gorilla tracking—an activity that relies on daily presence and cumulative knowledge about the movements of the animals.

This early period at Bai Hokou represented the beginning of long years during which Remis negotiated her roles as patron/researcher and woman/community member, simultaneously engaging BaAka trackers as employees, teachers, and friends. Over the course of residence and work together in the camp, these actors did not reconcile these contradictory images of each other but resorted to them at different times during day and evening camp life. Having the women and children in camp increased Remis's social connectedness to her research team and also enriched her development as an anthropologist, instilling an appreciation of the very real conservation dilemmas facing both the human and animal communities at RDS.

Upon reflection and discussion with other expatriate research colleagues, Remis's experiences and relationship to the field and the community seemed to differ from those of more ecologically oriented and trained colleagues at neighboring research camps—some of whom were also women but who relied solely on rotating male teams of trackers to maximize data collection and minimize human impact on the areas around the research camps, without concern for the sense of ownership, entitlement, or collaborative engagement by wider communities of human inhabitants of the area.

Of course, in developing an alternative and more residential or kinship-related approach to field research, we cannot estimate the relative impact of Remis's anthropological training versus personal qualities and local circumstances that led to her research design. Certainly, these logistical and social arrangements did not always enhance research progress; often Hardin found herself listening to Remis complain incredulously of the gall of her campmates, leaving their children unsupervised in camp without mentioning that they would be gone for a day of gathering leaves and medicines in the forest. Especially on Sundays, Remis would emerge from long hours of data transcription and analysis in her hut to find several young children who had been left on the porch for the day. Tired of patiently waiting, they would demand to be fed rice and hot cocoa.

Upon their return, the mothers were perplexed that Remis did not share their perception that any camp-based task would be more compatible with childcare than long-distance walking with the mothers. Describing data-analysis and its incompatibility with supervising small children proved a frustrating exercise in cross-cultural communication.[1] It also pointed to the significant distinctions between the socially complex, holistic, and ecologically nuanced ways of knowing the forest that BaAka women held versus the species-specific tracking skills held by BaAka men and valued by the research and tourism economy. Further, the use of that specialized knowledge was to forge solitary and ecologically specific careers as individual researchers, which we have subsequently attempted to craft into collaborative work with one another and with Central African colleagues in what we might call a gendered female ecology of knowledge.

This is not to deny the specificity and economic value of some women's forest knowledge. One woman, Masende, made numerous contributions to the camp. She freely dispensed medicinal herbs and made a strong example of how to negotiate with grace and humor the occasional heated dramas that emerged in the intimacy of forest camp life. Overall, the informal residential and research process recognizes the varied relationships between expatriate researchers and local collaborators/assistants and employees; it can be seen as making room for multiple roles to flourish. Further, it addressed intergenerational issues. It permitted the BaAka to blend the benefits of forest camp life and ritual with employment, inasmuch as the situation emulated some aspects of the traditional gathering honey and hunting camp life. Thus young children would have an opportunity to learn forest skills from their fathers (Hewlett 1991), who would otherwise be away much of the time due to research employment.

The experiment in residential research camp community structure was so successful that it became common research practice at RDS in the 1980s and early 1990s. The blend of research and traditional BaAka forest camp provided for musical and ideational as well as ecological and economic sharing of resources and knowledge. There was a section of camp with circles of huts where BaAka personnel would nightly sing and dance for the benefit of the children, thereby continuing some form of *gano*, which Jerome Lewis (2002) and Kisliuk (1998) both describe as an essential practice of knowledge transmission through songs and stories about human encounters with animals. Often singers would improvise, inserting research-related tales into traditional narratives.

In their shared life over the years with the BaAka families at the Bai Hokou Camp, non-Aka research assistants such as Marc, a Central African, and his family from a savanna farming community also learned forest lore and skills (Thomas and Arom 1987). Further, a doctoral student mentored by Remis and Hardin brought her young children to live with her in Bayanga during her course of research on market women sellers of bushmeat. Her young son's first words were "Sango," and his three-year-old sister learned to cook over an open fire in the style of the other neighborhood children. Their presence rendered our student's relationship to key female informants more dimensional and facilitated her work by dissipating tensions surrounding talk about bushmeat as an increasingly criminalized commodity.

Subsequent reserve policy, however, has discouraged the practice of a BaAka camp within the research camp, largely in order to reduce human resource use in the core park zone. Now, men who work as guides and trackers for ongoing research initiatives reluctantly leave their wives and children back at the roadside settlement when they embark on two-week-long stints of forest-based research work. Researchers are also cut off from the intimacy of family camp life and opportunities for cross-cultural exchange. Such tricky policy choices at the micro level are not unique to this site; Hardin noted during field research and teaching in the Mpala Research Center in Laikipia, Kenya, in summer 2010 that similar debates were being held about the danger to women and children from large animals such as buffalo, with some proponents arguing that only research personnel and not their broader families should be allowed to reside on and move about the research center's property. Others felt that the fabric of family life was important to the well-being of employees and to relations among varied groups on the center's land (Hardin 2011).

Perhaps, however, that fabric also allows particular social hierarchies along ethnolinguistic lines to persist within research camps. Back in Bayana, some research initiatives now integrate BaAka tracker housing into the central camp space. A standard infrastructure of research and tourism is emerging, modeled on the development of park structures in the United States and Europe (Osaki and Abbaté 1995). It reflects the shifting exchanges of knowledge and power across distinct social categories. Ironically, this infrastructural and interpersonal change is occurring around an activity that is less and less likely to occur outside of such wildlife-rich cores of the reserve: face-to-face encounters between humans and gorillas.

At a regional level, this professionalization informs salary levels, working conditions, and camp structures throughout the reserve. Experienced trackers have been able to travel to different parts of the RDS, extending their abilities described above to train younger, less experienced trackers as a kind of "consultant." While such labor arrangements empower some BaAka men in terms of earning ability and relative status within these complex regional communities, it has weakened the status of women within the BaAka community and their capacity to spend time in the forest. Now that families are no longer permitted to accompany their husbands and fathers to research camps in the park, women are increasingly focused on agricultural labor in roadside settlements, with less meat to feed their children (Noss and Hewlett 2001). Culturally, they find fewer opportunities to use and transfer their forest skills and the social interactions of lucid play and lore about men, women, and nonhuman primates. Perhaps because of the tensions that this balancing act between forest and town produces, when asked about the new conservation-based economy, women tended to emphasize their relative cultural and nutritional impoverishment over the potential benefits of greater faunal abundance within the park sector.

During her dissertation fieldwork on tourism, Hardin taught young BaAka men literacy skills so that they could be formally employed within the RDS. Taking time out from her research on encounters between tourists, trackers, guides, and various wildlife species, she offered afternoon classes at a central location in the village. Her students, many of whom had attended school intermittently in younger years, and most of whom had abandoned schooling due to social intolerance from villagers or serious economic hardship, were assiduous. Copying letters on crumpled bits of paper from project waste, students would often arrive unannounced at Hardin's small house on the banks of the Sangha River to demonstrate their skill and request corrections of their writing and spelling.

Further, in Hardin's research group, her university-trained collaborator in a four-person data collection team, archaeologist Henri Zana, began to set aside time each day to enforce the literacy skills of his BaAka collaborators, a kind of reciprocity for their enforcement of his forest skills and access to their communities. He selected an interesting passage from the novelist laureate of the CAR, Étienne Goyémidé, for the daily writing exercises of Aka collaborators Depaki and Singalo, former literacy students from Hardin's classes who had expressed avid interest in improving their writing and reading skills through work with us. They sat in the evenings, after conducting interviews, copying the passage again and again according to Zana's careful corrections.

The passage Zana chose from Goyémidé's 1984 novel *Le Silence de la Foret* (The Silence of the Forest) satirizes CAR's civil servants and chronicles the journey of one such overeducated "bowtie" functionary back into the forests of the Dzanga region, toward the roots of his national and African cultural patrimony. About this journey, he writes (translation ours):

> I am not an ethnologist. I did not come here with the fixed intent to expose "the Lives and Customs of the Babingas of the Equatorial Forest" to the civilized world. . . . If I find myself here in this clearing, in this hut made of bark and built by the hands of pygmies, it is not to violate their personality, nor is it to steal their cultural, sociological, ethnographic or other patrimony, but it is simply to live with them, within their daily life, their joys, their pain, in their natural context, considering them as they deserve, as a mature and respectable people, and not as a sort of laboratory specimen. (97)

The paragraph reveals as much about forest residents in a postcolonial context as it does about the disturbing legacies of science as cultural power in broader colonial encounters. Alive to such issues, Goyémidé was himself an exceptional figure in CAR. He was one of the few writers who maintained productive work even as he became minister of arts and culture and worked to reform and strengthen CAR's educational system before his untimely death from HIV/AIDS (Hardin 2011). His legacy, in turn, shaped the ideals and actions of our collaborator, Zana, whose comments as a voice-over to his own film footage in 2003 displays proud sentiments about these "pygmies who can write, speak French, and wear shoes."

Such paternalistic, if reciprocally useful, relationships cannot easily be "managed" in the interest of conservation and research but must be respected for the intimacies they produce among RDS residents, who play multiple and sometimes contradictory roles for one another. Zana's Aka colleagues had often assisted him (and Hardin) in the difficult physical work of forest walking, instructing him in forest ecology and basic navigation through forest paths and playing the role of teacher to us, too. At times when our encounters with wildlife stressed or frightened large animals such as gorillas or buffalo, Aka trackers literally physically restrained us from flight as we could have endangered our own lives.

These reversals of power relations were real and frequent for each of us. We relied upon them as we struggled, in our different ways, to find footing on career paths that would enable continued engagements on favorable terms with forest sites. The Aka who were thus "educated" through and for their work on Hardin's research project have gone on to become educators and interpreters in the increasingly interpenetrating health, conservation, and tourism sectors in Bayanga. Depaki, for his part, has become the only Aka hired as a tourism guide in the area and is now responsible for translating and guiding forest activities for tourists, as previously only villagers with formal schooling were hired to do. He also does basic bookkeeping tasks for the project, an unprecedented role for Aka staff, who in the past were hired primarily to guide and carry equipment for tourists or to cut the long grasses growing around the project's buildings outside of town.

Engagement in Education and/as Research

The inequities and contradictions described above along gender and ethnic lines are nested within others at national and international scales. The CAR, like many other species-rich habitat countries, currently has an ambitious conservation-management program but little infrastructure to support the spectrum of social and biological biodiversity science necessary for appropriate management. It is essential that those Central Africans who will carry out conservation and economic development programs and direct biodiversity policies have the tools necessary for assessing and analyzing biological diversity and human-wildlife interactions (e.g., Saterson 1990; Cracraft 1995).

To date, expatriates rather than national scientists have carried out much of the biodiversity assessment and research on wildlife in the CAR, in some ways strengthening but in other ways impeding that country's capacity to carry out their conservation and wildlife management programs independently. Further, the abilities of expatriate scientists to provide the expertise for current research, development, and conservation projects are limited by competing commitments to their home academic institutions. Research and educational institutions within equatorial Africa have been challenged by tumultuous political and economic transitions in recent years, and in the CAR the school system closed altogether for a total of two years in the early 1990s. As a result of such complex circumstances in many African contexts, contributions of expatriate researchers to fledgling local research communities may foster dependency, rather than independence (Diawara 1997).

On the other hand, even during times of political and civil crisis when expatriate development or foreign service professionals have elected to leave or have been evacuated from CAR, ongoing research projects have maintained operations in rural areas. Particularly in border regions such as the upper Sangha River, easy access among research sites in different countries creates the possibility for continued data collection and development of African research capacities over time. Such contributions merit monitoring and reinforcement, given upheaval in urban areas across the equatorial African forests at present.

Further, the research process can provide development of human resources and economic systems without entailing uncontrolled growth of population centers and attendant ecological and political dilemmas associated with urbanization and migration. Enhancement of scientific capacity and knowledge of host country researchers can thus promote use of natural resources to benefit a range of national and regional communities while providing a sustainable foundation for growth in the private sector (Rudran, Wemmer, and Singh 1990).

In 1997, with Dr. Justina Ray, now of Wildlife Conservation Society Canada, we initiated more formal training in anthropological and ecological methods of inquiry for Central African master's students. As women, we were sometimes forced to confront the historical fact of a male-dominated academic system in the region. Our sole female student, Claudine, had sociological rather than ecological training. However, she was eager to have an opportunity to obtain field training in primatological methods. She had read Diane Fossey's book in French translation and was as taken with the idea of a life in the forest with gorillas as Remis herself had been as a young student. Both were responding, albeit in different cultural contexts, to the powerful roles of animals as emblems of alternative interactive worlds whereby those people who feel stuck with less social status (for instance, women) can explore and redefine social limits.

Certainly, Claudine did not feel stuck with less social status during life in the Bai Hoku research camp. As had we, she took to the pleasures of a cool shower under the gentle waterfall of a forest stream. She embraced (and frequently photographed herself in) roles of discovery and exploration, in ways that Hardin (2010) has described elsewhere as ambivalent tropes in Central African literature, both emulating and rejecting colonial travel literatures. Indeed, Claudine would laugh good-naturedly as she described her fellow trainee's disenchantment with the dirt, physical labor, and lack of creature comforts involved in conducting forest-based fieldwork. Her derision and apparent embrace of the clean outdoor life of the forest angered him. He became further agitated when Claudine was persistently uninterested in any romantic liaison to help pass the time they were to spend together learning basic transect-based field methods from Remis.

The last straw was when Remis prohibited him from requiring his BaAka tracker to haul his supplies and wash his clothing for him. He opted to leave the forest training behind and return to a more urban university setting, which he found less exploitative and disrespectful of his notions of social order and personal pride. In the end, Claudine was better able to negotiate the urban-forest transition and adopt a more egalitarian role with the BaAka trackers although, like Zana, some of her attitudes seemed to us patronizing or naive. This is something we also perceive in one another, and in ourselves; it is perhaps even something that has been transmitted to us by some of our own teachers and trainers, including professors and senior conversation colleagues. There is, after all, some element of naive or romantic fascination that makes the daily slog through muddy settings seem exciting and worthwhile.

Alain can be seen in some respects as representative of the many experts, Central Africans and Americans such as ourselves, who have found more value and prestige in analytical writing and social networking associated with high-paid consulting work than in independent research and fieldwork (Garland 2008). More specifically, his case illustrates the extent to which French policies made academicians into politicians, mining the universities to fill rapidly shifting ministries and making the condition of what Mahmood Mamdani (1996) has termed "citizenship" in francophone cultural and political networks highly contingent upon literacy and an embrace of particular French-language concepts and expressive registers.

It is this legacy that has left Steven Feierman's (1990) "Peasant Intellectuals" constrained to particular rural powerbases, outside of the growing transnational circuits of expertise and economic development. Even more ironically, in our interactions with French field scientists, business people, and policy experts we have heard the phrase "noeud de pap" (short for *noeud de papillon*, or bow tie) used as skeptical shorthand for politically successful and sartorially professorial Central Africans. They are seen as dandies, often absent for meetings and shopping trips in Paris. Yet they can be gatekeepers in the very research processes we describe, signing permits for work or the allocation of concessions.

This is not to neglect the significant role of literacy and education in catalyzing new forms of critical engagement and activism in African political contexts (Hanna 1975; Miller 1993). It is simply to show how many forces conspire to denigrate Central Africans closest to the informal end of the educational spectrum, rather than integrating their perspectives in the construction of knowledge or in policy debates. Depaki, who trained in Hardin's research team described above, was a key presenter and one of the only BaAka to publish in proceedings from our July 1997 collaborative work sessions for researchers, both local and expatriate, in Bayanga. These work sessions brought together members of biological and social science research teams working in the trinational region with civic leaders, NGO staff, and logging personnel to analyze the economic and educational roles of research in these forests.

Using the Dzanga-Sangha Reserve as a case study in the context of the wider Sangha region, indigenous experts, community research agents, university-trained scholars, and nongovernmental and ministry representatives analyzed perceptions of research projects by various residents of the protected area. We also tried to characterize existing educational exchanges within and among research teams and describe research as a part of economic development, tracing trends in wages, health benefits, and skill acquisition and comparing such trends to other forms of employment available in forest conservation zones. Based on these results, we made recommendations for improved communication between researchers and the communities within which they work.[2]

Disappointment and frustration with the elitist academic and research structures in the CAR meant that one of our long-term research assistants, whom we will call Paul, was initially reluctant to participate in conferences or seminars. He had relatively little formal education but was widely respected for his non-academic expertise in direct confrontations with wildlife, his skill at supervising and training research teams, and his persistence in solving the relentless logistical challenges of access to and maintenance of field sites in these dense forests. His work had been indispensable to the creation of RDS and to the success of at least four dissertation projects, two of them at Yale University. Nevertheless, he felt undervalued—even by Remis, who served as godmother to his children and considered him an essential ally and partner in her research process.

His grudging participation in the workshop resulted in a professional and highly successful presentation. However, it placed him under strain and caused friction between him and Remis for quite some time afterward. In our troubled discussions of his reactions, we were forced to confront our own assumptions that he wanted or needed our advocacy, rather than resenting its intrusions and limitations. In 2000, Paul's contributions to conservation science and practice in RDS were formally recognized when he received the Getty Award. This major environmental prize is intended to reward informal and often undervalued forms of expertise and action toward conservation ends. Paul subsequently traveled widely within CAR and also consulted in Gabon to further inter-African and transnational training and research experience.

Our relations with him once again normalized, and he felt valued by the international conservation community that he had served without being able to acquire much formal status within its structures. He is proud of his rural roots, despite his sensitivity about being an autodidact in a country where national educational systems frequently flounder and fail to provide basic education. Indeed, he has in recent years welcomed young students from Bayanga to a home he built in the Bangui area, where they would attend high school and attempt university-level studies. He conveyed our remittances to young students from Bayanga by regular Western Union, recognizing as we did the importance of even small contributions from our academic salaries back in the midwestern United States to help those who had hauled water, copied maps, counted samples, and otherwise supported our research processes over the years. In this way we became, again, a team with Paul: helping to support a next generation through the trials of formal education and advancement toward that scarcest of resources in CAR: a regular salary.

Conclusion

Our various research outputs describe sites of spatially and socially distinct forest use practices, as people rely on a combination of subsistence sources, from sporadic wage labor in conservation or logging industries to farming or "traditional" hunting practices (such as hunting with nets made from local plant fibers). Many increasingly use modified traditions requiring new technology (such as nylon nets or wire snares) and new methods (such as firearms or night hunting with flashlights). All these activities are facilitated by the grids of easily traveled trails that are laid down for the purposes of logging, prospecting, and timber harvesting. But the proliferation of wage labor activities corresponds to ever-shrinking access to the forest as a social and subsistence resource.

Many older BaAka compensate for constrained forest access through the time-tested arsenal of intermarriage, kinship, and mobility (Kretsinger and Hardin 2003). They do so differently depending upon their labor histories, marriage practices, and migration patterns. While some, more mobile (and almost always male) BaAka are branching out into more entrepreneurial hunting or professional tracking practices, commercial hunting of elephants and other hard-to-capture species is largely the domain of a different network of hunters, mostly villagers and many of them political elites who have larger hunting radii, greater access to motorized transport, large rifles, and ammunition.

In the midst of this activity, the nature of encounters with animals has shifted; yet the importance of the encounter with animals remains powerful for BaAka at RDS. Hunting prowess still matters immensely to politics, courtship, and economic viability in Aka communities and households. A few individuals still practice skillful spear hunting of large prey. Indeed, the more influential men within the political economy of hunting camps may represent a range of skills from ancestral knowledge to the ability to operate a chain saw, drive a truck, or speak in French with foreign visitors. Rather than simply supplanting older forms of knowledge or practice, new ones may supplement or complement the old, depending on local economic and ecological cycles and individual mobility given the kinds of pro-liferating labor streams we have described here.

Our research also suggests that this diversity of forest uses by a range of BaAka and other forest residents is not sustainable. In combination with the uses made of the forest by loggers, farmers, researchers, tourists, traders, commercial hunters, and others, diversity of use may contribute to depletion of the very biological diversity upon which it depends. For the moment, the different activities of logging, trophy hunting, and conservation hang in balance in a "two-company town." Logging activities create intensified, uncontrolled forest-based subsistence for commercial hunting in combination with wage labor and also create the grid of roads used by trophy hunters and political elites whose guns are carried by locals who use the area for trade in valued game meat and animal products. At the same time, and in part in response to these pressures, conservation activities are creating alienation from richer forest access, saved for specialized tourism and research. Both economies together risk the depletion of wildlife populations, and in the end of a variety of ways of being in the forest—ways that the BaAka and their horticulturalist and hunter/fisher neighbors have created and maintained through hundreds, if not thousands, of years.

The particular challenges and legacies of that life have been brought home to us through long-term fieldwork. They have led us to a cross-subfield approach that takes human and animal communities in relation to one another, not in isolation, also recognizing the multiple and sometimes contradictory roles played by individuals within those communities. We have had to educate one another, for we have each internalized powerful stylistic and substantive concerns from our respective subfields.

For us, anthropology remains one of the few long-term intellectual "homes" for widely divergent ways to study both human and nonhuman life. It is thus well positioned for innovation in the changing worlds of critical and scientific inquiry at present, despite its multiple internal fault lines. Such innovation will come not only from individual work but also from collaboration; not only from the theoretical and institutional imperatives of scholarship but also from the unpredictable intimacies of fieldwork, such as those we have experienced with wildlife, local experts on the forests of the Congo basin, and indeed with one another. Had Hardin not met Remis during her Peace Corps service there, she might not have considered studying anthropology; had Remis not met Hardin there, she might not have ventured to place her work on lowland gorillas in dialogue with the study of human uses of those forests, from subsistence hunting to scientific research.

Beyond our published research results, our research is a complex social process that bridges our own distinct training and thinking habits. Each set of methods brings important information to bear offering enhanced understanding of human use patterns in relation to those of animals; of spatial trends in relation to temporal ones; and of the dynamics of social difference and status that persist despite awareness that they may be unjust or anathema to sustainability in the long term. We advocate a research program that combines these multiple modes of analysis and shares a commitment to the sort of long-term field research and detailed descriptive analysis that remains a unifying characteristic of increasingly divergent anthropological practices. Further, we feel that directions for anthropological pedagogy and practice must increasingly reflect the needs and concerns of our many partners in the messy yet powerfully generative process of fieldwork. Many of them are indispensable to our own constructions of expertise, and yet they are increasingly marginalized from the expert knowledge economies currently taking transnational shape.

NOTES

1. At the time of initial revisions to this manuscript, Hardin was in Kolkata, India, reluctantly supervising groups of small children at play during a family visit. All the male relatives were either reading newspapers or working on cell phones and laptops. Knowing not to disturb the men in the household, children continuously interrupted this revision, to

ask "Auntie" how to play a certain game, or find hair oil, or pull the seeds out of a pomegranate. Sticky fingered and frustrated after each response to their requests, Hardin smiled at the irony of revising these paragraphs in such circumstances. They echo the challenges outlined by Mary Catherine Bateson and others in this volume about how gender and social identity matter in finding a balance between participation and observation in effective cultural immersion.

2. For versions of those proceedings in English, French, and Sango, see http://www.yale.edu/sangha/confer/CNF_SET.html.

Conclusion

REBECCA HARDIN and

KAMARI MAXINE CLARKE

Initially offered as talks at Yale University, the essays included here were originally prompted (and, at times, challenged) by questions from students who were curious about ethnographic practices and faculty engaged in the development of a range of new field projects involving transnational, multisited, or new institutional projects. Their concerns came from both within and beyond the field of anthropology and were not only intellectual but also professional and experiential in nature. Many were seeking anthropological knowledge for projects beyond the confines of academic anthropology. They prompted us, however, to rethink what is understood by ethnographic knowledge. Ethnography, as a major component of "what anthropologists do," still evokes what Michel-Rolph Trouillot (1991) has called the "savage slot" that distinguishes the topic of study for sociocultural anthropologists from those topics studied by other social scientists. This is surprising, given the new directions sketched in the essays in this volume. The persistence of practices including ethnographic fieldwork and production of monographs within the field of anthropology seems almost anachronistic, yet these are still crucial criteria for membership in the "tribe of anthropology."

At the same time that such traditional ethnographic studies and products persist, anthropology has undergone unprecedented change in recent decades. Those transformations have been summarized in this volume in terms of ethnography's topics, techniques, and increasing tendencies to interrogate its own objectivity or advocacy. As we have argued in our introduction and demonstrated in our chapters, ethnography is now used more widely and in more ways than before, beyond the confines of academic scholarship. This is true despite its recent infusion with reflexive, critical energies. These encourage its practitioners to consider its far-reaching consequences, even as they surrender to its embrace of intimacy and immediacy in research design.

Sidney Mintz challenged us with humor and an ingenious use of that most delicate of practices, caricature, to distinguish between the travels and writing of an ethnographer, a TV reporter, a tourist, and a novelist. What, in this day and age, distinguishes ethnography from other intercultural expressions and encounters? Most academic ethnographers are acutely conscious of the fact that their field places them outside of the emerging political economies of large grant-driven research and writing in social and natural science. Nor, however, are we generating theory as we used to; debates rage about whether theory emerges at all from our activities, and from where. One such debate, catalyzed by arguments in the recent book *Theory from the South: How Euro-America is Evolving Toward Africa* (Comaroff and Comaroff 2011), was published in the *Cultural Anthropology* online forum.[1] Its "bloggy" immediacy reminds us of how often anthropologists these days contribute to journalistic and popular modes of knowledge production, writing opinion pieces or fragments from their broader ethnographic projects.[2] Mintz's answers to such proliferating knowledge production, both during his talk and in later correspondence with us about this book, distinguish ethnography from other social scientific and descriptive endeavors through its sustained, intimate engagement with contexts and communities, rather than temporary or superficial sharing of lives and ideas.

Mintz also advanced the idea of the ethnographer's own vulnerability; his or her willingness to impose uncomfortably upon others in the interest of building new forms of intimacy; his or her self-doubt, when faced with cultural incompetence despite aspirations to communicate effectively; his or her uncertainty about the "right" things to do with data and knowledge in complicated political scenarios. Many anthropologists cherish their place along the margins of more reproducible, scalable, saleable forms of knowledge production. Mintz would remind us that simply because we refuse to fully embrace new political economies of expert knowledge we cannot be content with irrelevance to policy and popular debate about major questions of justice, social difference, or inequality.

These are the challenges at the very heart of the discipline, but it is increasingly exposed to challenges arising at its edges, through its interfaces with other sectors. The chapters in this volume present a series of views on anthropology's past and on its position and prevalence in contemporary life. This book is anchored by authors whom we chose to invite to campus, for discussion of such challenges in accessible terms. Further, they were willing to put that "thinking out loud" in print for the benefit of future students who may become enthralled, as did Jennifer Staple, by the history of transformations in ethnography and in anthropology, whether they become academic anthropologists or not. What is important for most of us included here is a set of impulses in ethnography—those toward intimacy and those toward analysis. These impulses, apparently contradictory, complement one another in our lives and experiences and continually prompt us to work across various social divides. They help create our continued commitment to the various crafts—and increasingly varied careers—of doing ethnography.

Perhaps as much as in the corporate sectors Csilla Kalocsai describes, global health sectors—represented by the essay by Marcia Inhorn and brought to life by Jennifer Staple's work on eye-health educators—also demand attention to the management of learning relationships, managerial dynamics, and interpersonal communication within and across institutional settings. Through the Internet and telecommunication, Staple, for example, listens, discusses, and communicates with volunteers in local communities throughout the world. The volunteers, trained as eye health educators, disseminate their knowledge to thousands in their own village, town, or city. This participant observation, experienced by both Staple and the eye health educator volunteers, is exactly the type of anthropological practice discussed by Mary Catherine Bateson in this volume.

For Bateson, participant observation is "not just something that happens in the field, but something that is potentially pervasive in life and that is hugely helpful." To liberate such a core ethnographic method from a specific bounded field encounter, to consider it as a perspective on everyday life beyond the challenge of monographic production, is challenging if we are also to attend to its continuing core characteristics and specific intellectual merits for a narrow community of specialists. To have such concomitant discussions among anthropologists and between them and other practitioners of ethnography requires dialogue across hierarchies such as undergraduate/doctoral/faculty roles within academic institutions and between the academy and other sectors. It is this remarkable ability of anthropology to expand and to adapt to changes in human life that makes it so relevant even to those who do not necessarily define themselves as (or only as) anthropologists.

The proliferating power of ethnography (that anachronistically named endeavor) beyond the anthropological field, however, is more of a puzzle. How is it that the primary and most portable toolkit of anthropology has come to be called so widely "ethnographic methods?" How is it that such a moniker can often be seen in other disciplines, or even in entirely nonacademic domains? The contradictory impulses described in the previous paragraph, and indeed throughout this book, are not easily compatible with a simple "toolkit" that can be lifted and applied to social problems. They can, however, foster commitments to and careful planning for necessary interventions in some cases, such as those outlined by Kamari Clarke, and those taken up by Jennifer Staple in Unite For Sight. What does such extension of the meanings and uses of ethnography mean for those of us who self-identify—sometimes not only professionally but deeply personally—as ethnographers?

Are we, as George Marcus suggests in his contribution to this volume, moving from an anthropological crisis of the power relations embedded in the acts of representation toward crises regarding the reception and use of our work? Have "we" assimilated much of what the 1980s attentiveness to anthropological analysis as narrative power offered? Are we thus more and more instinctively adjusting what Marcus terms study "design," becoming increasingly aware of and accountable to the varied constituencies to whom we must speak? Others beg to differ, and have used Mintz's work to suggest that the postmodern deconstruction of authority disabled anthropology's ability to effectively advance more nuanced views of culture, power, and practice within popular culture and knowledge (Fox 1991, 3; Roseberry 1989, 33).

Or, as Sidney Mintz suggested in one of the heated discussions among students and faculty that appear here as transcribed questions and answers, should we be more willing to assume the awkward imposition that is ethnographic incursion into others' lives, and more fully shoulder the responsibilities for communicating the knowledge thus acquired? Wherever one sits on the battlefields of the culture wars that characterized the last decades of academic life, many of us cherish both the marginality of our subjectivity and the centrality of knowledge production in the larger spheres at play. Our identities as ethnographers have been nourished and affirmed by belonging to a community of peers who have also dedicated substantial amounts of their time, their minds, their tastes, their travels, in short, their *selves* to living otherwise than what might have been easy or normal for them to do.

Then, not content to rest in the shelter such intimacies can afford from the confrontation of one's own culture, comes the work of analyzing what it means to move thus among social worlds and to reflect critically on the assumptions and enactments of privilege entailed by such mobility and interpretive ability. We have struggled to become smarter than to assume patronizing or imperialistic stances of advocacy that foreground our heroic adventures and academic prowess at the expense of the intricacies of social action in actual worlds. At the same time, we are now struggling to define and redefine our ethics of fieldwork in a rapidly changing and integrating world and to position our work intelligently so as to make it widely accessible to both expected and unexpected audiences. We are struggling to redefine "we" without losing the intellectual autonomy and space for descriptive and analytical risks that "disciplines," rather than problem-driven research, can provide.

Those of us who have worked together to make the conversations in this book happen see the challenges and contributions of ethnography not only with respect to cultures, and countries, and colonial conflicts, but also with respect to sectors, and the social work of increasingly integrated, if still all too often imperialist, worlds. It is our hope that other ethnographers—be they academic anthropologists or those, like Jennifer Staple, who draw from anthropology to enrich and critically engage other endeavors—will take up these questions as a challenge for both analysis and action, thereby showing many of us new directions forward.

NOTES

1. See http://www.culanth.org/?q=node/500, last accessed March 25, 2012.

2. For example, see a medical and legal anthropology opinion column, http://www.huffingtonpost.com/s-lochlann-jain/, last accessed March 25, 2012.

Works Cited

Abbasi-Shavazi, Mohammad Jalal, Marcia C. Inhorn, Hajiieh Bibi Razeghi-Nasrabad, and
Ghasem Toloo. 2008. "The Iranian ART Revolution": Infertility, Assisted Reproductive
Technology, and Third-party Donation in the Islamic Republic of Iran. *Journal of
Middle East Women's Studies* 4 (2): 1–28.

Abimbọla, Wande. 1976. Yoruba Religion in Brazil: Problems and Prospects. In *Actes du
42e Congrès International des Américanistes*, vol. 6, 619–39. Paris: Société des Américanistes Musée de l'Homme.

Abraham, Nabeel, and Andrew Shryock, eds. 2000. *Arab Detroit: From Margin to Mainstream*. Detroit: Wayne State University Press.

Agamben, Giorgio. 1998. *Homo Sacer: Sovereign Power and Bare Life*. Stanford, CA: Stanford
University Press.

Aguilera, Francisco E. 1996. Is Anthropology Good for the Company? *American Anthropologist* 98 (4): 735–42.

Allen, Barbara L. 2003. *Uneasy Alchemy: Citizens and Experts in Louisiana's Chemical Corridor
Disputes*. Boston: MIT Press.

Allison, Anne. 1994. *Nightwork: Sexuality, Pleasure, and Corporate Masculinity in a Tokyo
Hostess Club*. Chicago: University of Chicago Press.

American Anthropological Association (AAA). 1986. Statements on Ethics: Principles of
Professional Responsibility. Adopted by the Council of the American Anthropological
Association May 1971 (as amended through November 1986). http://www.aaanet.org/
stmts/ethstmnt.htm (accessed December 19, 2007).

———. 1998. Code of Ethics of the American Anthropological Association (approved June
1998). http://www.aaanet.org/committees/ethics/ethcode.htm (accessed December 26,
2007).

Appadurai, Arjun. 1990. Disjuncture and Difference in the Global Cultural Economy.
Public Culture 2 (2): 1–24.

———. 2002. Deep Democracy: Urban Governmentality and the Horizon of Politics.
Public Culture 14 (1): 21–47.

———. 2006. *Fear of Small Numbers: An Essay on the Geography of Anger*. Durham, NC:
Duke University Press.

Asad, Talal, ed. 1973. *Anthropology and the Colonial Encounter*. London: Ithaca Press.

Ashforth, Blake E., and Fred Mael. 1989. Social Identity Theory and the Organization. *Academy of Management Review* 14 (1): 20–39.

Atran, Scott. 2003. Genesis of Suicide Terrorism. *Science* 299 (5612): 1534–39.

Augé, Marc, and Jean-Paul Colleyn. 2006. *The World of the Anthropologist.* Translated by John Howe. Oxford, UK: Berg.

Axel, Brian Keith. 2001. *The Nation's Tortured Body: Violence, Representation, and the Formation of a Sikh "Diaspora."* Durham, NC: Duke University Press.

Baer, Hans A. 2008. Toward a Critical Anthropology on the Impact of Global Warming on Health and Human Societies. *Medical Anthropology* 27 (1): 2–8.

Baer, Hans A., and Merrill Singer. 2009. *Global Warming and the Political Ecology of Health: Emerging Crises and Systemic Solutions.* Walnut Creek, CA: Left Coast Press.

Bakan, Joel. 2004. *The Corporation: The Pathological Pursuit of Profit and Power.* New York: Free Press.

Bandag CEO Promotes Sustainability Model for Organizations. 2004. Ross School of Business, University of Michigan. http://www.bus.umich.edu/NewsRoom/Article Display.asp?news_id=2627 (accessed November 23, 2008).

Bascom, William R. 1972. *Shango in the New World.* Austin: African and Afro-American Research Institute, University of Texas at Austin.

Bastide, Roger. (1960) 1978. *The African Religions of Brazil.* Translated by Helen Sebba. Baltimore: Johns Hopkins University Press.

Bateson, Gregory. 1958. *Naven, a Survey of the Problems Suggested by a Composite Picture of the Culture of a New Guinea Tribe Drawn from Three Points of View.* Stanford, CA: Stanford University Press.

Bateson, Mary Catherine. 1989. *Composing a Life.* New York: Penguin.

———. 1994. *Peripheral Visions: Learning Along the Way.* New York: HarperCollins.

———. 2004. *Willing to Learn: Passages of Personal Discovery.* Hanover, NH: Steerforth Press.

Behar, Ruth. 1993. *Translated Woman: Crossing the Border with Esperanza's Story.* Boston: Beacon Press.

Bell, Diane. 1983. *Daughters of the Dreaming.* Melbourne, AU: McPhee & Gribble/Allen & Unwin.

Benedict, Ruth. 1934. *Patterns of Culture.* New York: Houghton Mifflin.

———. 1946. *The Chrysanthemum and the Sword.* Boston: Houghton Mifflin.

Benedict, Ruth, and Gene Weltfish. 1943. *The Races of Mankind.* Public Affairs Pamphlet no. 85. New York: Public Affairs Committee.

Bennett, John William. 1976. *The Ecological Transition: Cultural Anthropology and Human Adaptation.* New York: Pergamon Press.

Berman, Jonathan E., and Tobias Webb. 2003. *Race to the Top: Attracting and Enabling Global Sustainable Business.* Washington, DC: World Bank.

Birenbaum-Carmeli, Daphna, and Marcia C. Inhorn. 2009. *Assisting Reproduction, Testing Genes: Global Encounters with the New Biotechnologies.* New York: Berghahn Press.

Bodnar, Judit. 2001. *Fin de Millenaire Budapest: Metamorphoses of Urban Life*. Minneapolis: University of Minnesota Press.

Boellstorff, Thomas. 2008. *Coming of Age in Second Life: An Anthropologist Explores the Virtually Human*. Princeton, NJ: Princeton University Press.

Borges, Jorge Luis. (1969) 1974. *In Praise of Darkness*. New York: Dutton.

Boslough, Mark B., James A. Sprigg Jr., George A. Backus, Mark A. Taylor, Laura A. McNamara, Joy Fujii, Kathryn M. Murphy, Leonard A. Malczynski, Leonard A. Malczynski, and Rhonda K. Reinert. 2004. Climate Change Effects on International Stability: A White Paper. SAND Report, Sandia National Laboratories, December. http://archives.sprigg.net/reports/ClimateStability.pdf (accessed March 9, 2010).

Bourdieu, Pierre. 1990. The Scholastic Point of View. *Cultural Anthropology* 5 (4): 380–91.

———. 1991. *Language and Symbolic Power*. Edited by John Thompson. Translated by Gino Raymond and Matthew Adamson. Cambridge, MA: Harvard University Press.

Brenneis, Don. 2004. Presidential Address: A Partial View of Contemporary Anthropology. *American Anthropologist* 106 (3): 580–88.

Briggs, Charles L. 2005. Genealogies of Race and Culture and the Failure of Vernacular Cosmopolitanism: Rereading Franz Boas and W. E. B. Du Bois. *Public Culture* 17 (1): 75–100.

Brosius, J. Peter. 1997. Prior Transcripts, Divergent Paths: Resistance and Acquiescence to Logging in Sarawak, East Malaysia. *Comparative Studies in Society and History* 39 (3): 468–510.

———. 1999. Analyses and Interventions—Anthropological Engagements with Environmentalism. *Current Anthropology* 40 (3): 277–309.

Brown, Wendy. 2003. Neoliberalism and the End of Liberal Democracy. *Theory & Event* 7:1. http://muse.jhu.edu/journals/theory_and_event/v007/7.1brown.html (accessed March 25, 2012).

Burawoy, Michael. 2000. Introduction: Reaching for the Global. In *Global Ethnography: Forces, Connections, and Imaginations in a Postmodern World*, by Michael Burawoy, Joseph A. Blum, Sheba George, Zsuzsa Gille, Theresa Gowan, Lynne Haney, Maren Klawiter, Steven H. Lopez, Seán Riain, and Millie Thayer, 1–40. Berkeley: University of California Press.

Burawoy, Michael, Joseph A. Blum, Sheba George, Zsuzsa Gille, Theresa Gowan, Lynne Haney, Maren Klawiter, Steven H. Lopez, Seán Riain, and Millie Thayer. 1991. *Ethnography Unbound: Power and Resistance in the Modern Metropolis*. Berkeley: University of California Press.

Button, Gregory. 2010. *Disaster Culture: Knowledge and Uncertainty in the Wake of Human and Environmental Catastrophe*. Walnut Creek, CA: Left Coast Press.

Calhoun, Craig. 2004. A World of Emergencies: Fear, Intervention, and the Limits of Cosmopolitan Order. *Canadian Review of Sociology and Anthropology* 41 (4): 373–95.

Canter, Richard S. 1978. Dispute Settlement and Dispute Processing in Zambia: Individual Choice versus Societal Constraints. In *The Disputing Process: Law in Ten Societies*, edited by Laura Nader and Harry F. Todd Jr., 247–80. New York: Columbia University Press.

Cartmill, Matt. 1994. Reinventing Anthropology: American Association of Physical Anthropologists Luncheon Address, April 1, 1994. *Yearbook of Physical Anthropology* 37:1–9.

Cattelino, Jessica. 2005. Tribal Gaming and Indigenous Sovereignty, with Notes from Seminole Country. Special issue, Indigenous People of the United States. *American Studies* 46 (3/4): 187–204; co-published in *Indigenous Studies Today* 1 (Fall 2005/Spring 2006).

Checker, Melissa. 2005. *Polluted Promises: Environmental Racism and the Search for Justice in a Southern Town.* New York: New York University Press.

Clarke, Kamari Maxine. 2004. *Mapping Transnational Networks: Power and Agency in the Making of Yoruba Transnational Communities.* Durham, NC: Duke University Press.

———. 2007a. Neoliberal Reorderings: Training Centers and the Crafting of Cosmopolitan Subjects. Discussion for CASCA-AES Conference on Indigeneities and Cosmopolitanisms, University of Toronto, May 8–12.

———. 2007b. Transnational Yorùbá Revivalism and the Diasporic Politics of Heritage. *American Ethnologist* 34 (4): 721–34.

———. 2009. *Fictions of Justice: The International Criminal Court and the Challenge of Legal Pluralism in Sub-Saharan Africa.* Cambridge: Cambridge University Press.

Clarke, Kamari, and Deborah Thomas. 2006. *Globalization and Race: Transformations in the Cultural Production of Blackness.* Durham, NC: Duke University Press.

Clarke, Morgan. 2009. *Islam and New Kinship: Reproductive Technology and the Shariah in Lebanon.* New York: Berghahn Books.

Clarke, Morgan, and Marcia C. Inhorn. 2011. Mutuality and Immediacy between *Marja'* and *Muqallid*: Evidence from Male In Vitro Fertilization Patients in Shi'i Lebanon. *International Journal of Middle East Studies* 43 (3): 409–27.

Clifford, James. 1988. *The Predicament of Culture: Twentieth-Century Ethnography, Literature, and Art.* Cambridge, MA: Harvard University Press.

Clifford, James, and George E. Marcus. 1986. *Writing Culture: The Poetics and Politics of Ethnography.* Berkeley: University of California Press.

Cohn, Bernard S. 1987. *An Anthropologist among the Historians and Other Essays.* New York: Oxford University Press.

Cole, Jonathan R. 2003. The Patriot Act on Campus: Defending the University post 9/11. *Boston Review: A Political and Literary Forum* 28 (3–5): 16–18.

Collier, Jane Fishburne. 1988. *Marriage and Inequality in Classless Societies.* Stanford: Stanford University Press.

Collier, Stephen J., and Aihwa Ong. 2005. Global Assemblages, Anthropological Problems. In *Global Assemblages: Technology, Politics, and Ethics as Anthropological Problems*, edited by Aihwa Ong and Stephen J. Collier, 3–22. Malden, MA: Blackwell.

Collins, Jim. 2001. *Good to Great: Why Some Companies Make the Leap . . . and Others Don't.* New York: HarperCollins.

Comaroff, Jean, and John L. Comaroff. 2006. *Law and Disorder in the Postcolony*. Chicago: University of Chicago Press.

———. 2011. *Theory from the South: How Euro-America is Evolving Toward Africa*. Boulder: Paradigm Publishers.

Conklin, Harold C. 1968. Ethnography. In *International Encyclopedia of the Social Sciences*, edited by David L. Sills, 172–78. New York: Macmillan.

Cormier, Loretta A. 2003. *Kinship with Monkeys: The Guajá Foragers of Eastern Amazonia*. New York: Columbia University Press.

Cracraft, J. 1995. The Urgency of Building Global Capacity for Biodiversity Science. *Biodiversity and Conservation* 4:463–75.

Cramer, Janet M., and Michael McDevitt. 2004. Ethnographic Journalism. In *Qualitative Research in Journalism: Taking It to the Streets*, edited by Sharon Hartin Iorio, 127–44. Mahwah, NJ: Lawrence Erlbaum.

Crate, Susan A., and Mark Nuttall. 2009. *Anthropology and Climate Change: From Encounters to Actions*. Walnut Creek, CA: Left Coast Press.

Crutzen, Paul J. 2002. Geology of Mankind. *Nature* 415 (6867): 23.

Crutzen, Paul J., and Eugene F. Stoermer. 2000. *IGBP Newsletter* 41. Royal Swedish Academy of Sciences.

Das, Veena. 1985. Anthropological Knowledge and Collective Violence: The Riots in Delhi, November 1984. *Anthropology Today* 1 (3): 4–6.

———, ed. 1990. *Mirrors of Violence: Communities, Riots and Survivors in South Asia*. Delhi: Oxford University Press.

Davenport, Tom. 2007. The Rise of Corporate Anthology. *The Next Big Thing* (blog), November 28. http://blogs.hbr.org/davenport/2007/11/the_rise_of_corporate _anthropo_1.html (accessed August 12, 2008).

Deacon, Terrence W. 1997. *The Symbolic Species: The Co-evolution of Language and the Brain*. New York: W. W. Norton.

Deleuze, Gilles, and Félix Guattari. (1980) 1987. *A Thousand Plateaus: Capitalism and Schizophrenia*. Translated by Brian Massumi. Minneapolis: University of Minnesota Press.

De Lorenzo, Mauro, Terence McNamee, and Greg Mills. 2007. U.S. Sweet Talk Fails to Seduce Africa. *Sunday Independent* (Johannesburg), July 22, 2007. Article posted by American Enterprise for Public Policy Research, http://www.aei.org/article/foreign-and-defense-policy/regional/subsaharan-africa/us-sweet-talk-fails-to-seduce-africa/ (accessed December 28, 2007).

Demerath, Peter. 2009. *Producing Success: The Culture of Personal Advancement in an American High School*. Chicago: University of Chicago Press.

DeVore, I., ed. 1965. *Primate Behavior: Field Studies of Monkeys and Apes*. New York: Holt, Rinehart and Winston.

Dezalay, Yves, and Bryant G. Garth. 1996. *Dealing in Virtue: International Commercial Arbitration and the Construction of a Transnational Legal Order*. Chicago: University of Chicago Press.

———. 2002. *The Internationalization of Palace Wars: Lawyers, Economists, and the Contest to Transform Latin American States.* Chicago Series in Law and Society. Chicago: University of Chicago Press.

Diamond, Stanley. 1974. *In Search of the Primitive: A Critique of Civilization.* New Brunswick, NJ: Transaction.

Diawara, Mamadou. 1997. You Know Everything. Why Do You Ask Us? Paper presented for the Words and Voices: Critical Studies in African Oral Historiography Conference, Ann Arbor, Michigan, March 20–23.

Di Leonardo, Michaela. 1991. *Gender at the Crossroads of Knowledge: Feminist Anthropology in the Postmodern Era.* Berkeley: University of California Press.

Doh, Jonathan P., and Hildy Teegen. 2003. *Globalization and NGOs: Transforming Business, Government, and Society.* Westport, CT: Praeger.

Downey, Gary Lee, and Joseph Dumit, eds. 1997. *Cyborgs and Citadels: Anthropological Interventions in Emerging Sciences and Technologies.* Santa Fe, NM: School of American Research Press.

Downey, Greg, and Melissa S. Fisher. 2006. Introduction: The Anthropology of Capital and the Frontiers of Ethnography. In *Frontiers of Capita: Ethnographic Reflections on the New Economy,* edited by Melissa S. Fisher and Greg Downey, 1–33. Durham, NC: Duke University Press.

Dufoix, Stephane, 2008. *Diasporas.* Translated by William Rodarmor. Berkeley: University of California Press.

Dunn, Elizabeth C. 2004. *Privatizing Poland: Baby Food, Big Business, and the Remaking of Labor.* Ithaca, NY: Cornell University Press.

———. 2005. Standards and Person-Making in East Central Europe. In *Global Assemblages: Technology, Politics, and Ethics as Anthropological Problems,* edited by Aihwa Ong and Stephen J. Collier, 337–54. Malden, MA: Blackwell.

Ehrenreich, Barbara. 2001. *Nickel and Dimed: On (Not) Getting By in America.* New York: Metropolitan Books.

Evans-Pritchard, E. E. 1946. Applied Anthropology. *Africa* 16 (2): 92–98.

Fabian, Johannes. 1983. *Time and the Other: How Anthropology Makes Its Object.* New York: Columbia University Press.

Farmer, Paul. 2003. *Pathologies of Power: Health, Human Rights, and the New War on the Poor.* Berkeley: University of California Press.

Farmer, Paul, and Jim Yong Kim. 1998. Community Based Approaches to the Control of Multidrug Resistant Tuberculosis: Introducing "DOTS-Plus." *British Medical Journal* 317:671–74.

Fehervary, Krisztina. 2007. Hungarian Horoscopes as a Genre of Postsocialist Transformation. *Social Identities* 13 (5): 561–76.

Feierman, Steven. 1990. *Peasant Intellectuals: Anthropology and History in Tanzania.* Madison: University of Wisconsin Press.

Felstiner, William L. F., Richard L. Abel, and Austin Sarat. 1980–81. The Emergence and Transformation of Disputes: Naming, Blaming, Claiming . . . *Law & Society Review* 15 (3/4): 631–54.

Feuchtwang, Stephan. 1973. The Colonial Formation of British Social Anthropology. In *Anthropology and the Colonial Encounter*, edited by Talal Asad, 71–100. New York: Humanities Press.

Firth, Raymond. 1981. Engagement and Detachment: Reflections on Applying Social Anthropology to Social Affairs. *Human Organization* 40 (3): 193–99.

Fisher, Melissa S. 2004. Corporate Ethnography in the New Economy. *Anthropology News*, April 15.

———. 2006. Navigating Wall Street Women's Gendered Networks in the New Economy. In *Frontiers of Capital: Ethnographic Reflections on the New Economy*, edited by Melissa S. Fisher and Greg Downey, 209–37. Durham, NC: Duke University Press.

Fortun, Kim. 2001. *Advocacy after Bhopal: Environmentalism, Disaster, New Global Orders*. Chicago: University of Chicago Press.

Foucault, Michele. 1979. On Governmentality. *Ideology and Consciousness* 6:5–21.

Fox, Richard G., ed. 1991. *Recapturing Anthropology: Working in the Present*. Santa Fe, NM: School of American Research Press.

Frake, Charles O. 1964. Notes on Queries in Ethnography. *American Anthropologist* 66 (3), pt. 2:132–45.

———. 1980. *Language and Cultural Description: Essays*. Stanford, CA: Stanford University Press.

Freedman, Diane, and Olivia Frey, eds. 2003. *Autobiographical Writing across the Disciplines: A Reader*. Durham, NC: Duke University Press.

Freeman, Carla. 2000. *High Tech and High Heels in the Global Economy: Women, Work, and Pink-Collar Identities in the Caribbean*. Durham, NC: Duke University Press.

Fuentes, Agustin, and Linda D. Wolfe, eds. 2002. *Primates Face to Face: Conservation Implications of Human and Nonhuman Primate Interconnections*. New York: Cambridge University Press.

Fullwiley, Duana. 2006. Biosocial Suffering: Order and Illness in Urban West Africa. *Bio-Societies* 1 (4): 421–38.

Garland, Elizabeth. 2008. The Elephant in the Room: Confronting the Colonial Nature of African Conservation. *African Studies Review* 51 (3): 51–74.

Geertz, Clifford. 2000. *Available Light: Anthropological Reflections on Philosophical Topics*. Princeton, NJ: Princeton University Press.

Gelvin, James L. 2005. *The Modern Middle East: A History*. New York: Oxford University Press.

Giles-Vernick, Tamara, and Stephanie Rupp. 2006. Visions of Apes, Reflections on Change: Telling Tales of Great Apes in Equatorial Africa. *African Studies Review* 49 (1): 51–73.

Gill, Lesley. 2004. *The School of the Americas: Military Training and Political Violence*. Durham, NC: Duke University Press.

Gilroy, Paul. 1993. *The Black Atlantic: Modernity and Double Consciousness*. Cambridge, MA: Harvard University Press.

———. 2004. *Between Camps: Nations, Cultures and the Allure of Race*. London: Routledge.

Gingrich, Andre, and Richard G. Fox, eds. 2002. *Anthropology by Comparison*. London: Routledge.

Ginsburg, Faye D., and Rayna Rapp, eds. 1995. *Conceiving the New World Order: The Global Politics of Reproduction*. Berkeley: University of California Press.

Ginsburg, Faye D., Lila Abu-Lughod, and Brian Larkin, eds. 2002. *Media Worlds: Anthropology on New Terrain*. Berkeley: University of California Press.

Gluckman, Max. 1955. *The Judicial Process among the Barotse of Northern Rhodesia*. Manchester: Manchester University Press.

Good, Byron J. 1994. *Medicine, Rationality, and Experience: An Anthropological Perspective*. Lewis Henry Morgan Lectures. Cambridge: Cambridge University Press.

Goodale, Mark. 2009. *Surrendering to Utopia: An Anthropology of Human Rights*. Stanford: Stanford University Press.

Gordon, Colin. 1991. Governmental Rationality: An Introduction. In *The Foucault Effect: Studies in Governmentality*, edited by Graham Burchell, Colin Gordon, and P. Miller, 1–51. London: Harvester Wheatsheaf.

Gordon, George G. 1991. Industry Determinants of Organizational Culture. *Academy of Management Review* 16 (2): 396–415.

Goyémidé, Étienne. 1984. *Le Silence de la Foret*. Paris: Hatier.

Grinker, Roy Richard. 1994. *Houses in the Rain Forest: Ethnicity and Inequality among Farmers and Foragers in Central Africa*. Berkeley: University of California Press.

Gulliver, P. H. 1963. *Social Control in an African Society: A Study of the Arusha: Agricultural Masai of Northern Tanganyika*. New York: New York University Press.

Gupta, Akhil, and James Ferguson. 1997. *Anthropological Locations: Boundaries and Grounds of a Field Science*. Berkeley: University of California Press.

Gürtin, Zeynep B., and Marcia C. Inhorn. 2011. Introduction—Travelling for Conception and the Assisted Reproduction Market. *Reproductive BioMedicine Online* 23 (5): 535–37.

Gusterson, Hugh. 2003. Comment: Defending the Nation? Ethics and Anthropology after 9/11: Wartime Dilemmas of an Ethical Anthropology. *Anthropology Today* 19 (3): 25–26.

———. 2004. *People of the Bomb: Portraits of America's Nuclear Complex*. Minneapolis: University of Minnesota Press.

Gusterson, Hugh, and David Price. 2005. Spies in Our Midst. *Anthropology News* 46 (6): 39–40.

Handler, Richard, ed. 2006. *Central Sites, Peripheral Visions: Cultural and Institutional Crossings in the History of Anthropology*. History of Anthropology 11. Madison: University of Wisconsin Press.

Hanna, William John, ed. 1975. *University Students and African Politics*. New York: Holmes and Meier.

Hansen, Thomas Blom, and Finn Stepputat, eds. 2005. *Sovereign Bodies: Citizens, Migrants, and States in the Postcolonial World*. Princeton, NJ: Princeton University Press.

Haraway, Donna. 1991. *Simians, Cyborgs, and Women: The Reinvention of Nature*. New York: Routledge.

———. 2003. *A Companion Species Manifesto: Dogs, People, and Significant Otherness*. Chicago: Prickly Paradigm Press.

Hardin, Rebecca. 2010. Narrative, Humanity, and Patrimony in an Equatorial African Rainforest. In *In the Name of Humanity: The Government of Threat and Care*, edited by Ilana Feldman and Miriam Ticktin, 86–114. Durham, NC: Duke University Press.

———. 2011. Collective Contradictions of "Corporate" Environmental Conservation. *FOCAAL: European Journal of Global and Historical Anthropology* 60:47–60.

Hardin, Rebecca, and Melissa Remis. 1997. Conference Proceedings from the Seminar on Scientific Research and Rural Development, Dzanga-Sangha Reserve, Central African Republic, July 31–August 2. http://www.yale.edu/sangha/confer/CNF_SET.html (accessed March 25, 2012).

———. 2006. Biological and Cultural Anthropology of a Changing Tropical Forest: A Fruitful Collaboration across Subfields. *American Anthropologist* 108 (2): 273–85.

Harvey, David. 1990. *The Condition of Postmodernity: An Enquiry into the Origins of Cultural Change*. Cambridge, MA: Blackwell.

———. 2001. Cosmopolitanism and the Banality of Geographical Evils. In *Millennial Capitalism and the Culture of Neoliberalism*, edited by Jean Comaroff and John L. Comaroff, 271–311. Durham, NC: Duke University Press.

Hayden, Cori. 2003. *When Nature Goes Public: The Making and Unmaking of Bioprospecting in Mexico*. Princeton, NJ: Princeton University Press.

Herbert, Christopher. 1991. *Culture and Anomie: Ethnographic Imagination in the Nineteenth Century*. Chicago: University of Chicago Press.

Herskovits, Melville J. (1941) 1958. *The Myth of the Negro Past*. Boston: Beacon Press.

Hewlett, Barry. 1991. *Intimate Fathers: The Nature and Context of Aka Pygmy Paternal Infant Care*. Ann Arbor: University of Michigan Press.

Hirsch, Susan. 2006. *In the Moment of Greatest Calamity: Terrorism, Grief, and a Victim's Quest for Justice*. Princeton, NJ: Princeton University Press.

Hoebel, E. Adamson. 1954. *The Law of Primitive Man: A Study in Comparative Legal Dynamics*. New York: Atheneum.

Hoffman, Lisa. 2006. Autonomous Choices and Patriotic Professionalism: On Governmentality in Late-Socialist China. *Economy and Society* 35 (4): 550–70.

Holmes, Douglas. 2000. *Integral Europe: Fast Capitalism, Multiculturalism, Neofascism*. Princeton, NJ: Princeton University Press.

Hooker, James. 1963. The Anthropologist's Frontier: The Last Phase of African Exploitation. *Journal of Modern African Studies* 1.4:455–59.

Horkheimer, Max, and Theodor W. Adorno. 1972. *Dialectic of Enlightenment*. Translated by John Cumming. New York: Herder and Herder. Originally published in 1947 as *Philosophische Fragmente*.

Hyde, Sandra Teresa. 2009. *Eating Spring Rice: The Cultural Politics of AIDS in Southwest China*. Berkeley: University of California Press.

IGNCA at the 14th ICAES, Williamsburg 1998. 1998. *IGNCA News* 6. http://ignca.nic.in/ nl_01209.htm (accessed December 14, 2008).

Inhorn, Marcia C. 1994. *Quest for Conception: Gender, Infertility, and Egyptian Medical Traditions*. Philadelphia: University of Pennsylvania Press.

———. 1996. *Infertility and Patriarchy: The Cultural Politics of Gender and Family Life in Egypt*. Philadelphia: University of Pennsylvania Press.

———. 2003. *Local Babies, Global Science: Gender, Religion, and In Vitro Fertilization in Egypt*. New York: Routledge.

———. 2006. Making Muslim Babies: IVF and Gamete Donation in Sunni versus Shi'a Islam. *Culture, Medicine and Psychiatry* 30 (4): 427–50.

———. 2008. Medical Anthropology Against War. *Medical Anthropology Quarterly* 22 (4): 416–24.

———. 2012. *The New Arab Man: Emergent Masculinities, Technologies, and Islam in the Middle East*. Princeton, NJ: Princeton University Press.

Inhorn, Marcia C., and Daphna Birenbaum-Carmeli. 2008. Assisted Reproductive Technologies and Culture Change. *Annual Review of Anthropology* 37:177–96.

Inhorn, Marcia C., and Michael Hassan Fakih. 2006. Arab Americans, African Americans, and Infertility: Barriers to Reproduction and Medical Care. *Fertility and Sterility* 85 (4): 844–52.

Inhorn, Marcia C., and Loulou Kobeissi. 2006. The Public Health Costs of War in Iraq: Lessons from Post-war Lebanon. *Journal of Social Affairs* 23:13–47.

Inhorn, Marcia C., and Pasquale Patrizio. 2009. Rethinking Reproductive "Tourism" as Reproductive "Exile." *Fertility and Sterility* 92 (3): 904–6.

Inhorn, Marcia C., Pasquale Patrizio, and Gamal I. Serour. 2010. Third-party Reproductive Assistance around the Mediterranean: Comparing Sunni Egypt, Catholic Italy, and Multisectarian Lebanon. *Reproductive BioMedicine Online* 21 (7): 848–53.

Inhorn, Marcia C., and Gamal I. Serour. 2011. Islam, Medicine, and Arab-Muslim Refugee Health in America after 9/11. *The Lancet* 378:935–41.

Inhorn, Marcia C., and Pankaj Shrivastav. 2010. Globalization and Reproductive Tourism in the UAE. *Asia-Pacific Journal of Public Health* 22:68–74.

Inhorn, Marcia C., and Soraya Tremayne, eds. 2012. *Islam and Assisted Reproductive Technologies: Sunni and Shia Perspectives*. New York: Berghahn Books.

Inhorn, Marcia C., and Frank van Balen, eds. 2002. *Infertility around the Globe: New Thinking on Childlessness, Gender, and Reproductive Technologies*. Berkeley: University of California Press.

Kalocsai, Csilla. 2010. Corporate Hungary: Recrafting Youth, Work, and Class in Global Capitalism. PhD dissertation, Yale University.

Keane, Webb. 2003. Self-Interpretation, Agency, and the Objects of Anthropology: Reflections on a Genealogy. *Comparative Study of Society and History* 45 (2): 222–48.

Kelly, Tobias. 2006. *Law, Violence and Sovereignty among West Bank Palestinians*. Cambridge: Cambridge University Press.

Kent, Susan. 1996. *Cultural Diversity among Twentieth-Century Foragers: An African Perspective*. New York: Cambridge University Press.

Kisliuk, Michelle. 1998. *Seize the Dance! BaAka Musical Life and the Ethnography of Performance*. Oxford: Oxford University Press.

Kleinman, Arthur. 1997. *Writing at the Margins: Discourse between Anthropology and Medicine*. Berkeley: University of California Press.

Klinenburg, Eric. 2002. *Heat Wave: A Social Autopsy of Disaster in Chicago*. Chicago: University of Chicago Press.

———. 2007. *Fighting for Air: The Battle to Control America's Media*. New York: Metropolitan Books.

Kondo, Dorinne K. 1990. *Crafting Selves: Power, Gender, and Discourses of Identity in a Japanese Workplace*. Chicago: University of Chicago Press.

Kottak, Conrad. 1999. The New Ecological Anthropology. *American Anthropologist* 101 (1): 23–35.

Kretsinger, Anna, and Rebecca Hardin. 2003. Watershed, Weddings, and Workforces: Migration, Sedentarization, and Social Change among the BaAka of Southwestern Central African Republic. *African Studies Monographs* 28:123–41.

Kroeber, A. L. 1953. *Anthropology Today: An Encyclopedic Inventory*. Chicago: University of Chicago Press.

Kubik, Gerhard. 1979. *Angolan Traits in Black Music, Games and Dances of Brazil: A Study of African Cultural Extensions Overseas*. Lisbon: Junta de Investigações Científicas do Ultramar/Centro de Estudos de Antropologia Cultural.

Lakoff, George, and Mark Johnson. 1980. *Metaphors We Live By*. Chicago: University of Chicago Press.

Lampland, Martha. 1995. *The Object of Labor: Commodification in Socialist Hungary*. Chicago: University of Chicago Press.

Leacock, Eleanor B., and Richard B. Lee, eds. 1982. *Politics and History in Band Societies*. Cambridge: Cambridge University Press.

Lee, Benjamin, and Edward LiPuma. 2001. Democracy and Derivatives. Unpublished manuscript.

Lewis, Jerome. 2002. Chimpanzees and Gorillas: Ethnic Stereotyping in the Ndoki Forest, Northern Congo-Brazzaville. Paper presented at the Ninth International Conference on Hunting and Gathering Societies, Edinburgh, September 9–13.

Li, Tania Murray. 2002. Engaging Simplifications: Community-Based Resource Management, Market Processes and State Agendas in Upland Southeast Asia. *World Development* 30 (2): 265–83.

Lindenbaum, Shirley. 2001. Kuru, Prions, and Human Affairs: Thinking about Epidemics. *Annual Review of Anthropology* 30:363–85.

Llewellyn, K. N., and E. Adamson Hoebel. 1941. *The Cheyenne Way: Conflict and Case Law in Primitive Jurisprudence*. Norman: University of Oklahoma Press.

Lock, Margaret. 2002. *Twice Dead: Organ Transplants and the Reinvention of Death*. Berkeley: University of California Press.

MacGaffey, Janet, and Rémy Bazenguissa-Ganga. 2000. *Congo-Paris: Transnational Traders on the Margins of the Law*. Oxford: James Curry.

Mamdani, Mahmood. 1996. *Citizen and Subject: Contemporary Africa and the Legacy of Late Colonialism*. Princeton, NJ: Princeton University Press.

———. 2001. *When Victims Become Killers: Colonialism, Nativism, and the Genocide in Rwanda*. Princeton, NJ: Princeton University Press.

Marcus, George E. 1995. Ethnography in/of the World System: The Emergence of Multi-Sited Ethnography. *Annual Review of Anthropology* 24:95–117.

———, ed. 1999. *Critical Anthropology Now: Unexpected Contexts, Shifting Constituencies, Changing Agendas*. Santa Fe, NM: School of American Research Press.

Marcus, George E., and Michael J. Fischer. 1986. *Anthropology as Cultural Critique: An Experimental Moment in the Human Sciences*. Chicago: University of Chicago Press.

Mariniello, Silvestra, and Paul Bové. 1998. *Gendered Agents: Women and Institutional Knowledge*. Durham, NC: Duke University Press.

Martin Shaw, Carolyn. 1980. Land and Food, Women and Power, in Nineteenth Century Kikuyu. *Africa* 50 (4): 357–70.

Mather, Lynn, and Barbara Yngvesson. 1980–81. Language, Audience, and the Transformation of Disputes. *Law & Society Review* 15 (3/4): 775–822.

Matory, J. Lorand. (1994) 2005. *Sex and the Empire That Is No More: Gender and the Politics of Metaphor in Oyo Yorùbá Religion*. 2nd ed. New York: Berghahn Books.

———. 1999. The English Professors of Brazil: On the Diasporic Roots of the Yorùbá Nation. *Comparative Studies in Society and History* 41 (1): 72–103.

———. 2005. *Black Atlantic Religion: Tradition, Transnationalism, and Matriarchy in the Afro-Brazilian Candomblé*. Princeton, NJ: Princeton University.

Mattingly, Cheryl, and Linda C. Garro, eds. 2000. *Narrative and the Cultural Construction of Illness and Healing*. Berkeley: University of California Press.

Mbembe, Achille. 2003. Necropolitics. *Public Culture* 15 (1): 11–40.

McFate, Montgomery. 2005a. Anthropology and Counterinsurgency: The Strange Story of Their Curious Relationship. *Military Review* 85 (2): 24.

———. 2005b. The Military Utility of Understanding Adversary Culture. *Joint Forces Quarterly* 38:42–48.

Meneley, Anne, and Donna J. Young. 2005. *Auto-Ethnographies: The Anthropology of Academic Practices*. Toronto: Broadview Press.

Merry, Sally Engle. 1992. Anthropology, Law and Transnational Processes. *Annual Review of Anthropology* 21:357–79.

———. 2006. *Human Rights and Gender Violence: Translating International Law into Local Justice*. Chicago: Chicago University Press.

Milicevic, Aleksandra. 2006. Off to War: Secret Agents, Paramilitaries, and Patriots in the Balkans War of Secession, 1991–1995. Paper presented at the annual meeting of the American Sociological Association, Montreal Convention Center, Montreal, August 11. http://www.allacademic.com/meta/p105311_index.html (accessed October 2006).

Millen, David R. 2000. Rapid Ethnography: Time Deepening Strategies for HCI Field Research. In *Proceedings of the 3rd Conference on Designing Interactive Systems: Processes, Practices, Methods, and Techniques*, 280-86. New York: ACM (Association for Computing Machinery).

Miller, C. L. 1993. Nationalism as Resistance and Resistance to Nationalism in the Literature of Francophone Africa. *Yale French Studies* 82:62-100.

Mintz, Sidney W. 1960. *Worker in the Cane: A Puerto Rican Life History*. New Haven, CT: Yale University Press.

Mintz, Sidney W., and Richard Price. (1976) 1992. *The Birth of African-American Culture: An Anthropological Perspective*. Boston: Beacon.

Moore, Henrietta L. 1988. *Feminism and Anthropology*. Cambridge: Polity Press.

Moore, Sally Falk. 1978. *Law as Process*. London: Routledge & Kegan Paul.

Mowafi, Hani. 2011. Conflict, Displacement and Health in the Middle East. *Global Public Health* 6 (5): 472-87.

Murphy, Thomas F. 1990. *The Body Silent*. New York: W. W. Norton.

Nachtigall, Robert D. 2006. International Disparities in Access to Infertility Services. *Fertility and Sterility* 85 (4): 871-75.

Nader, Laura. 1972. Up the Anthropologist: Perspectives Gained from Studying Up. In *Reinventing Anthropology*, edited by Dell H. Hymes, 284-311. New York: Pantheon Books.

———. 2002. *The Life of the Law*. Anthropological Projects. Berkeley: University of California Press.

Nader, Laura, and Harry F. Todd Jr., eds. 1978. *The Disputing Process: Law in Ten Societies*. New York: Columbia University Press.

Network of Concerned Anthropologists. 2007a. The Network of Concerned Anthropologists Pledges to Boycott Counterinsurgency. *Anthropology News* 48 (9): 4-5.

———. 2007b. Pledge of Non-participation in Counter-insurgency. Unpublished manuscript. http://sites.google.com/site/concernedanthropologists/home (accessed February 28, 2012).

Nguyen, Vinh-Kim. 2004. Antiretroviral Globalism, Biopolitics, and Therapeutic Citizenship. In *Global Assemblages: Technology, Politics, and Ethics as Anthropological Problems*, edited by Aihwa Ong and Stephen J. Collier, 124-44. Malden, MA: Blackwell.

Nordstrom, Carolyn. 1997. *A Different Kind of War Story: Ethnography of Political Violence*. Philadelphia: University of Pennsylvania Press.

Noss, Andrew, and Barry Hewlett. 2001. Contexts of Female Hunting in Central Africa. *American Anthropologist* 103 (4): 1024-40.

Okonofua, Friday E. 1996. The Case Against New Reproductive Technologies in Developing Countries. *British Journal of Obstetrics and Gynaecology* 103 (10): 957-62.

Olds, Kris, and Nigel Thrift. 2005. Cultures on the Brink: Reengineering the Soul of Capitalism—On a Global Scale. In *Global Assemblages: Technology, Politics, and Ethics as Anthropological Problems*, edited by Aihwa Ong and Stephen J. Collier, 270-91. Malden, MA: Blackwell.

Ong, Aihwa. 1987. *Spirits of Resistance and Capitalist Discipline: Factory Women in Malaysia*. Albany: State University of New York Press.

———. 2005. Ecologies of Expertise: Assembling Flows, Managing Citizenship. In *Global Assemblages: Technology, Politics, and Ethics as Anthropological Problems*, edited by Aihwa Ong and Stephen J. Collier, 337–534. Malden, MA: Blackwell.

———. 2006a. Corporate Players, New Cosmopolitans, and Guanxi in Shanghai. In *Frontiers of Capital: Ethnographic Reflections on the New Economy*, edited by Melissa S. Fisher and Greg Downey, 163–91. Durham, NC: Duke University Press.

———. 2006b. Higher Learning in Global Space. In *Neoliberalism as Exception: Mutations in Citizenship and Sovereignty*, 139–56. Durham, NC: Duke University Press.

———. 2008. Self-Fashioning Shanghainese: Dancing across Spheres of Value. In *Privatizing China: Socialism from Afar*, edited by Li Zhang and Aihwa Ong, 182–97. Ithaca, NY: Cornell University Press.

Ong, Aihwa, and Stephen J. Collier, eds. 2005. *Global Assemblages: Technology, Politics, and Ethics as Anthropological Problems*. Malden, MA: Blackwell.

Orlove, Ben. 1980. Ecological Anthropology. *Annual Review of Anthropology* 9:235–73.

O'Rourke, Bill. 2004. Leadership and Sustainability in Alcoa Aluminum's Health and Safety Audits. Presentation to the Corporate Environmental Management Program (CEMP) and the School of Natural Resources and Environment's Center for Sustainable Systems, University of Michigan, Ann Arbor.

Osaki, John, and Mike Abbaté. 1995. *Tourism in Dzanga Sangha: An Interpretation and Visitor Services Plan*. Washington, DC: World Wildlife Fund.

Osseo-Assare, Abena Dove. 2005. Poisoned Arrows, Strophanthus Hispidus, and the Rise of Pharmaceutical Chemistry in Britain and the Gold Coast (1880–1922). Paper presented at the conference for the History of Science Society, Minneapolis, MN, November 3–6.

Paine, Robert. 1996. In Chief Justice McEachern's Shoes: Anthropology's Ineffectiveness in Court. *PoLAR: Political and Legal Anthropology Review* 19 (2): 59–70.

Peet, Richard, and Michael Watts. 1996. *Liberation Ecologies: Environment, Development, Social Movements*. London: Routledge.

Peterson, J. T. 1978. *The Ecology of Social Boundaries: Agta Foragers of the Philippines*. Urbana: University of Illinois Press.

Petryna, Adriana, Andrew Lakoff, and Arthur Kleinman, eds. 2006. *Global Pharmaceuticals: Ethics, Markets, Practices*. Durham, NC: Duke University Press.

Pierpont, Claudia R. 2004. The Measure of America: How a Rebel Anthropologist Waged War on Racism. *New Yorker*, March 8, 48–63.

Pierson, Donald. 1942. *Negroes in Brazil: A Study of Race Contact at Bahia*. Chicago: University of Chicago Press.

Pollock, Sheldon, Homi K. Bhabha, Carol A. Breckenridge, and Dipesh Chakrabarty. 2000. Cosmopolitanisms. *Public Culture* 12 (3): 577–89.

Price, David. 2002. Interlopers and Invited Guests: On Anthropology's Witting and Unwitting Links to Intelligence Agencies. *Anthropology Today* 18 (6): 16–21.

———. 2004. *Threatening Anthropology: McCarthyism and the FBI's investigation of American Anthropologists*. Durham, NC: Duke University Press.

Rabinow, Paul. 1999. *French DNA: Trouble in Purgatory*. Chicago: University of Chicago Press.

Raffles, Hugh. 2002. *In Amazonia: A Natural History*. Princeton, NJ: Princeton University Press.

———. 2011. *Insectopedia*. New York: Vintage.

Rappaport, Roy A. (1984) 2000. *Pigs for the Ancestors: Ritual in the Ecology of a New Guinea People*. 2nd ed. Long Grove, IL: Waveland Press.

Reiter, Rayna R., ed. 1975. *Toward an Anthropology of Women*. New York: Monthly Review Press.

Remis, Melissa J. 1994. Feeding Ecology and Positional Behavior of Western Lowland Gorillas at Dzanga-Sangha Reserve, Central African Republic. PhD diss., Yale University.

———. 1997. Western Lowland Gorillas as Seasonal Frugivores: Use of Variable Resources. *American Journal of Primatology* 43:87–109.

Remis, Melissa J., and Rebecca Hardin. 2007. Anthropological Contributions to Protected Area Management. In *Transforming Parks and Protected Areas: Policy and Governance in a Changing World*, edited by Kevin Hanna, Doug Clark, and Scott Slocombe, 85–109. Oxon, UK: Routledge.

———. 2009. Transvalued Species in an African Forest. *Conservation Biology* 23 (6): 1588–96.

Rev, Istvan. 1987. The Advantages of Being Atomized: How Hungarian Peasants Coped with Collectivization. *Dissent* 34:335–50.

Rhode, David. 2007. Army Enlists Anthropology in War Zones. *New York Times*, October 5.

Ribiero, Gustavo Lins, and Arturo Escobar. 2006. *World Anthropologies: Disciplinary Transformations within Systems of Power*. Oxford: Berg.

Richard, A. F., and S. R. Schulman. 1982. Sociobiology: Primate Field Studies. *Annual Review of Anthropology* 11:231–55.

Ridgeway, James, Daniel Schulman, and David Corn. 2008. There's Something about Mary: Unmasking a Gun Lobby Mole. *Mother Jones*, July 30. http://motherjones.com/politics/2008/07/theres-something-about-mary-unmasking-gun-lobby-mole (accessed August 14, 2008).

Riles, Annelise. 2001a. *The Network Inside Out*. Ann Arbor: University of Michigan Press.

———. 2001b. Real Time: Governing the Market after the Failure of Knowledge. Unpublished manuscript.

Roberts, Simon. 1979. *Order and Dispute: An Introduction to Legal Anthropology*. New York: St. Martin's Press.

Rodman, Peter S. 1999. Whither Primatology? The Place of Primates in Contemporary Anthropology. *Annual Review of Anthropology* 28:311–39.

Roitman, Janet. 2005. *Fiscal Disobedience: An Anthropology of Economic Regulation in Central Africa*. Princeton, NJ: Princeton University Press.

Rona-Tas, Akos. 1997. *The Great Surprise of the Small Transformation: The Demise of Communism and the Rise of the Private Sector in Hungary*. Ann Arbor: University of Michigan Press.

Rose, Nikolas. 1992. Governing the Enterprising Self. In *Values of the Enterprise Culture: The Moral Debate*, edited by Paul Heelas and Paul Morris, 141–65. London: Routledge.

———. 1996. *Inventing Ourselves: Psychology, Power, and Personhood*. Cambridge: Cambridge University Press.

Roseberry, William. 1989. *Anthropologies and Histories: Essays in Culture, History, and Political Economy*. New Brunswick, NJ: Rutgers University Press.

Rosengarten, Dale. 1986. *Row upon Row: Sea Grass Baskets of the South Carolina Low Country*. Columbia: McKissick Museum, University of South Carolina.

———. 1997. Social Origins of the African-American Low Country Basket. PhD diss., Harvard University.

Rubin, Gayle S. 1984. Thinking Sex: Notes for a Radical Theory of the Politics of Sexuality. In *Pleasure and Danger: Exploring Female Sexuality*, edited by Carole S. Vance, 3–44. London: Routledge.

———. 2011. *Deviations: A Gayle Rubin Reader*. Durham, NC: Duke University Press.

Rudran, A., C. M. Wemmer, and M. Singh. 1990. Teaching Applied Ecology to Nationals of Developing Countries. In *Race to Save the Tropics*, edited by R. Goodland, 125–40. Washington, DC: Island Press.

Sahlins, Marshall. 1976. *The Use and Abuse of Biology: An Anthropological Critique of Sociobiology*. Ann Arbor: University of Michigan Press.

Sassen, Saskia. 1996. Whose City Is It? Globalization and the Formation of New Claims. *Public Culture* 8:205–23.

Saterson, K. 1990. Integration of Biological Conservation with Development Policy: The Role of Ecological Analysis. In *Race to Save the Tropics*, edited by Robert Goodland, 1141–59. Washington, DC: Island Press.

Scales, Major General Robert H. Jr. U.S. Army (retired). 2004. Culture-Centric Warfare. *US Naval Institute Proceedings* 130 (October): 32–33. http://www.military.com/NewContent/0,13190,NI_1004_Culture-P1,00.html.

Scheper-Hughes, Nancy, and Loïc Wacquant, eds. 2002. *Commodifying Bodies*. London: Sage.

Schneider, David M. 1968. *American Kinship: A Cultural Account*. Chicago: University of Chicago Press.

———. 1984. *A Critique of the Study of Kinship*. Ann Arbor: University of Michigan Press.

Schneider, David M., and Kathleen Gough, eds. 1961. *Matrilineal Kinship*. Berkeley: University of California Press.

Segal, Daniel A., and Sylvia J. Yanagisako. 2005. *Unwrapping the Sacred Bundle: Reflections on the Disciplining of Anthropology*. Durham, NC: Duke University Press.

Serour, Gamal I. 2008. Islamic Perspectives in Human Reproduction. *Reproductive BioMedicine Online* 17 (suppl. 3): 34–38.

Shaheen, Jack G. 2008. *Guilty: Hollywood's Verdict on Arabs After 9/11*. New York: Olive Branch Press.

Shamir, Ronen. 2004. Between Self-Regulation and the Alien Tort Claims Act: On the Contested Concept of Corporate Social Responsibility. *Law & Society Review* 38 (4): 635–64.

Shostak, Marjorie. 1981. *Nisa: The Life and Words of a !Kung Woman*. Cambridge, MA: Harvard University Press.

Shryock, Andrew, ed. 2004. *Off Stage on Display: Intimacy and Ethnography in the Age of Public Culture*. Stanford, CA: Stanford University Press.

Sik, Endre. 1994. Traktátus a vállalkozó szerepének demisztifikálásáról [Tract on demystifying the role of entrepreneurs]. *Replika* 15-16:7–13.

Sluka, Jeffrey A. 2010. Curiouser and Curiouser: Montgomery McFate's Strange Interpretation of the Relationship between Anthropology and Counterinsurgency. *PoLAR: Political and Legal Anthropology Review* 33 (suppl. 1): 99–115.

Solway, Jacqueline S., and Richard B. Lee. 1990. Foragers, Genuine or Spurious? Situating the Kalahari San in History. *Current Anthropology* 31 (2): 109–46.

Spar, Debora L. 2006. *The Baby Business: How Money, Science, and Politics Drive the Commerce of Conception*. Cambridge, MA: Harvard Business School Press.

Sponsel, Leslie E. 1997. The Human Niche in Amazonia: Explorations in Ethnoprimatology. In *New World Primates: Ecology, Evolution, and Behavior*, edited by Warren G. Kinzey, 143–65. New York: Aldine de Gruyter.

Staple, Jennifer. 2004. Forging Activist Identities from Epidemic Control: The Leprosy Patients of the Kalaupapa Settlement. Senior essay, Yale University.

Starr, June. 1978. *Dispute and Settlement in Rural Turkey: An Ethnography of law*. Leiden: Brill.

———. 1989. The "Invention" of Early Legal Ideas: Sir Henry Maine and the Perpetual Tutelage of Women. In *History and Power in the Study of Law: New Directions in Legal Anthropology*, edited by June Starr and Jane Collier, 345–68. Ithaca, NY: Cornell University Press.

———. 1992. *Law as Metaphor: From Islamic Courts to the Palace of Justice*. Albany: State University of New York Press.

Stocking, George W. 1983. *Observers Observed: Essays on Ethnographic Fieldwork*. Madison: University of Wisconsin Press.

———. 1996. *Volksgeist as Method and Ethic: Essays on Boasian Ethnography and the German Anthropological Tradition*. Madison: University of Wisconsin Press.

Strathern, Marilyn. 2000. Introduction: New Accountabilities. In *Audit Cutures: Anthropological Studies in Accountability, Ethics, and the Academy*, edited by Marilyn Strathern, 1–19. New York: Routledge.

Sunderland, Patricia, and Rita M. Denny. 2007. *Doing Anthropology in Consumer Research*. Walnut Creek, CA: Left Coast Press.

Sutton, Felix. 1959. *The Illustrated Book about Africa*. Illustrated by H. B. Vestal. New York: Grosset & Dunlap.

Szelenyi, Ivan. 1988. *Socialist Entrepreneurs: Embourgeoisement in Rural Hungary*. Cambridge, MA: Polity Press.

Taussig, Michael. 1986. *Shamanism, Colonialism, and the Wild Man: A Study in Terror and Healing*. Chicago: University of Chicago Press.

———. 2003. Flexible Eugenics: Technologies of the Self in the Age of Genetics. In *Genetic Nature/Culture: Anthropology and Science beyond the Two-Culture Divide*, edited by Alan H. Goodman, Deborah Heath, and M. Susan Lindee, 58–75. Berkeley: University of California Press.

Taylor, Julie. 1998. *Paper Tangos*. Durham, NC: Duke University Press.

Thomas, Jacqueline, and Simha Arom. 1974. *Les Mimbo, Genies de la piegage rurale et le monde surnaturel des Ngbaka de la Lobaye, Republique Centrafricaine*. Paris: SELAF.

———. 1987. *Relations sociales et projections idéologiques: Exemple des Ngbaka-ma'bo et des Pygmées Aka de l'Afrique Centrale*. Paris: Cahiers du LACITO.

Thompson, Charis. 2005. *Making Parents: The Ontological Choreography of Reproductive Technologies*. Cambridge, MA: MIT Press.

Ticktin, M. 2006. Medical Humanitarianism in and beyond France: Breaking Down or Patrolling Borders? In *Medicine at the Border: Disease, Globalization and Security, 1950 to the Present*, edited by Alison Bashford, 116–35. New York: Palgrave Macmillan.

Trouillot, Michel-Rolph. 1991. Anthropology and the Savage Slot: The Poetics and Politics of Otherness. In *Recapturing Anthropology: Working in the Present*, edited by Richard G. Fox, 17–44. Santa Fe, NM: School of American Research Press.

———. 1995. *Silencing the Past: Power and the Production of History*. Boston: Beacon.

———. 2003. *Global Transformations: Anthropology and the Modern World*. New York: Palgrave Macmillan.

Tsing, Anna. 2009. Supply Chains and the Human Condition. *Rethinking Marxism* 21 (2): 148–76.

Turner, Lorenzo D. 1949. *Africanisms in the Gullah Dialect*. Chicago: University of Chicago Press.

Tylor, Edward Burnett. 1873. *Primitive Culture*. London: Bradbury, Agnew, and Company.

United States. Office of the White House. 2007. President Bush Creates a Department of Defense Unified Combatant Command for Africa. Press release. http://georgewbush-whitehouse.archives.gov/news/releases/2007/02/20070206-3.html (accessed February 28, 2012).

Van Maanen, John. 2001. Natives 'R' Us: Some Notes on the Ethnography of Organizations. In *Inside Organizations: Anthropologists at Work*, edited by David N. Gellner and Eric Hirsch, 231–63. Oxford: Berg.

Varhola, Christopher. 2004. Commentary: The U.S. Military in Iraq: Are We Our Own Worst Enemy? *Practicing Anthropology* 26 (4): 39–42.

Washburn, Sherwood. L. 1951. The New Physical Anthropology. *Transactions of the New York Academy of Sciences*, Series 2, 13 (7): 298–304.

Wax, Murray. 2003. Comment: Defending the Nation? Ethics and Anthropology after 9/11: Wartime Dilemmas of an Ethical Anthropology. *Anthropology Today* 19 (3): 23–24.

Wheatley, Bruce Panton. 1999. *The Sacred Monkeys of Bali*. Prospect Heights, IL: Waveland Press.

Williams, Brackette. 1991. *Stains on My Name, War in My Veins: Guyana and the Politics of Cultural Struggle*. Durham, NC: Duke University Press.

Williams, Raymond 1978. *Marxism and Literature*. Oxford: Oxford University Press.

Wilson, Edward Osborne. 1975. *Sociobiology: The New Synthesis*. Cambridge, MA: Belknap Press.

Wilson, Richard. 2005. *The Politics of Truth and Reconciliation in South Africa: Legitimizing the Post-Apartheid State*. New York: Cambridge University Press.

———. 2008. *Humanitarianism and Suffering: The Mobilization of Empathy*. Cambridge: Cambridge University Press.

Wolch, Jennifer R., and Jody Emel. 1998. *Animal Geographies: Place, Politics, and Identity in the Nature-Culture Borderlands*. New York: Verso.

Yelvington, Kevin A., ed. 2006. *Afro-Atlantic Dialogues: Anthropology in the Diaspora*. Santa Fe, NM: School of American Research.

Yngvesson, Barbara. 1985. Dispute Processing: Re-examining Continuing Relations and the Law. *Wisconsin Law Review* 3:623–46.

———. 1988. Making Law at the Doorway: The Clerk, the Court and the Construction of Community in a New England Town. *Law & Society Review* 22 (3): 409–48.

Young, Allan. 1995. *The Harmony of Illusions: Inventing Post-Traumatic Stress Disorder*. Princeton, NJ: Princeton University Press.

Yurchak, Alexei. 2002. Entrepreneurial Governmentality in Postsocialist Russia: A Cultural Investigation of Business Practices. In *The New Entrepreneurs of Europe and Asia*, edited by Victoria Bonnell and Thomas Gold, 278–325. New York: Armonk.

Zihlman, Adrienne L. 2000. A Skeletal Survey of Physical Anthropology in the US. *Rivista di Antropologia* 78:57–66.

Contributors

MARY CATHERINE BATESON is a writer and cultural anthropologist who divides her time between New Hampshire and Cambridge, Massachusetts, where she completed three years as a visiting professor at the Harvard Graduate School of Education. She has written and coauthored many books and articles, lectures across the country and abroad, and for thirty years was president of the Institute for Intercultural Studies in New York City. Until 2004 she was the Clarence J. Robinson Professor in Anthropology and English at George Mason University, and is now professor emerita. Recent projects include celebrating the 2004 Gregory Bateson Centennial; organizing Granny Voters for the 2004 electoral season; and finishing her books *Willing to Learn: Passages of Personal Discovery* (2004) and *Composing a Further Life: The Age of Active Wisdom* (2010).

KAMARI MAXINE CLARKE was trained in political science and international relations at Concordia University, anthropology at the New School for Social Research and at the University of California–Santa Cruz, and law at the Yale Law School. She is a professor of anthropology and international and area studies at Yale University and a senior research scientist at the Yale Law School. She works on issues related to religious nationalist movements and human rights/rule of law legal movements. Her areas of research have included Northern and Southern Nigeria, Yoruba communities in the United States, international forums in the United Nations, and international criminal tribunals. Her books *Mapping Yoruba Networks: Power and Agency in the Making of Transnational Communities* (2004) and *Globalization and Race: Toward a Cultural Politics of Blackness* (2006) both explore issues related to particular global transformations in the ethnographic sphere. Her book *Fictions of Justice: The International Criminal Court and the Challenge of Legal Pluralism in Sub-Saharan Africa* (2009) explores the complexities of lawmaking as it is related to local legal institutions and international legal spheres. She is the chair of the Council on African Studies and the former director of the Yale University Center for Transnational Cultural Analysis.

REBECCA HARDIN is an associate professor in the School for Natural Resources and Environment at the University of Michigan. Her work on the western Congo basin region links the ethnography of interdependent foraging and horticulturalist groups with oral, historical, and archival sources on colonial practices to reconsider contemporary debates among local, national, and international actors about environmental management. Publications in *Current Anthropology, Science*, and *FOCAAL: Journal of Global and Historical Anthropology* focus on actors such as logging and mining interests as they interact with conservation organizations and complex communities in rural Africa to shape forest tenure and management. Recent work examines comparative sites in Cameroon and Congo Brazzaville (in protected areas and timber concessions), South Africa (in the platinum mining zones of the North West province), and Kenya (in the ranches and conservancies of the Laikipia region), connecting analysis of ecosystem and human health to changes in the economies and ecologies of African landscapes. She has published widely in both French and English, and is currently completing a book about ecotourism and hunting in equatorial Africa, as they relate to international surveillance and monitoring of disease emergence and wildlife trades.

MARCIA C. INHORN is the William K. Lanman Jr. Professor of Anthropology and International Affairs at Yale University, where she served as chair of the Council on Middle East Studies (CMES) in the MacMillan Center for International and Area Studies (2008–11). As past president of the Society for Medical Anthropology (SMA) of the American Anthropological Association, she was the program chair of the SMA conference "Medical Anthropology at the Intersections: Celebrating 50 Years of Interdisciplinarity," held at Yale on September 24–27, 2009. Her research revolves around science and technology studies (STS), gender and feminist theory (including masculinity studies), religion and bioethics, globalization and global health, cultures of biomedicine and ethnomedicine, and stigma and human suffering. Over the past twenty-five years, she has conducted multisited research on the social impact of infertility and assisted reproductive technologies (ARTs) in Egypt, Lebanon, the United Arab Emirates, and Arab America. She is the author of four books on the subject, *The New Arab Man: Emergent Masculinities, Technologies, and Islam in the Middle East* (2012); *Local Babies, Global Science: Gender, Religion, and In Vitro Fertilization in Egypt* (2003); *Infertility and Patriarchy: The Cultural Politics of Gender and Family Life in Egypt* (1996); and *Quest for Conception: Gender, Infertility, and Egyptian Medical Traditions* (1994), which have won the American Anthropological Association's Eileen Basker Prize and Diana Forsythe Prize for outstanding feminist anthropological research in the areas of gender, health, science, technology, and biomedicine.

CSILLA KALOCSAI received her PhD at Yale University, where she studied cultural anthropology, and is currently a visiting scholar at the Centre for Women's Studies in Education at the University of Toronto's Ontario Institute for Studies in Education. She is working on a book manuscript that explores how transnational business institutions participate in a neoliberal project, transforming formally socialist corporate environments, populations, knowledges, and practices in Hungary. She is the recipient of the Association for Feminist Anthropology's Sylvia Forman Prize and the Society for European Anthropology's Graduate Paper Prize.

Contributors

GEORGE E. MARCUS is on the faculty at the University of California, Irvine. He studies collaborations at the core of the contemporary practice of diverse ethnographic research. He is interested in participating with others in the systematic rearticulation, and in some sense reinvention, of the norms and forms of the classic modality of research in social/cultural anthropology: fieldwork with the writing of ethnography as outcome. He has been a pioneer in the marginal, incomplete, and belated specialty of the cultural/ethnographic study of elites in anthropology (subsuming the early projects of his career, in Tonga, on capitalist dynasties, for instance). For him, this has become the means of pursuing an anthropology of contemporary change. It is the necessity of working with experts and counterparts of various kinds as an orientation to fieldwork, along with an abiding interest in the conditions of ordinary—often subaltern—life that generates the complexities of multisited research, about which he has written. In recent collaborations, he has pursued this interest in inquiries involving Portuguese nobles, European politicians, Latin American artists, U.S. bankers, and Brazilian intellectuals. Well-known titles include *Lives in Trust: The Fortunes of Dynastic Families in Late Twentieth-Century America* (1992) with Peter Dobkin Hall; *Anthropology as Cultural Critique: An Experimental Movement in the Human Sciences* (1986) with M. Fischer; *Writing Culture* (1986) with J. Clifford; and *Elites: Ethnographic Issues* (1983).

J. LORAND MATORY is a professor of anthropology and of Afro-American studies at Harvard University. He researches the diversity of African, African American, and Latin American cultures, with an emphasis on how various peoples understand gender, sexuality, class, race, and national identity. He began his anthropological career studying gender and the politics of metaphor in the Yoruba civilization of West Africa, which are the subject of his book *Sex and the Empire That Is No More* (1994, 2005), which was chosen by *Choice* magazine as one of the outstanding scholarly books of the year. His book *Black Atlantic Religion* (2005) concerns the role of free black travelers, merchants, and writers in the making of such Yoruba-inspired religions as Candomblé and Santería, which have typically been regarded as mere "survivals" of African culture in the Americas. His further recent publications address the rapid penetration of such Afro-Latin religions into the U.S. urban landscape. Matory's latest and most controversial project concerns the tension-fraught ethnic diversity of black North America: *The Other African Americans* concerns dark immigrants from Jamaica, Nigeria, Cuba, and other nations, as well as Americans of African descent who have not always considered themselves black—such as mulattoes and biracials, Louisiana Creoles, New Jersey's Ramapo Mountain people, and numerous Native American tribes east of the Mississippi. Their experience is taken to illustrate how the most naturalized of U.S. social categories, "blackness," has been subject to continual negotiation, reinterpretation, and internationally inspired cultural elaboration over the past two centuries. This book is also intended to challenge the unexamined premises of the "identity" concept articulated in both the academy and U.S. popular culture since the 1960s.

SIDNEY MINTZ has studied Caribbean rural life, social history, and the Afro-Caribbean tradition, from his first fieldwork in Puerto Rico (1948) through the publication of *Three Ancient Colonies* (2010). He currently works as well on the anthropology of food and eating. Mintz's aim throughout has been to wed the anthropological concept of culture to materialist interpretations of history. In 1956, his study of a sugarcane village became part of *The People of Puerto Rico*, a work that helped to change anthropology's subject matter. His *Worker in the Cane* (1960) and *Caribbean Transformations* (1974) followed. In 1985, *Sweetness and Power* appeared. It dealt with sugar both as food and, as it turned out, much else. This book is now available in most European languages, as well as in Arabic, Chinese, Japanese, Korean, and Turkish. Mintz is currently at work on what he calls "a tormenting subject."

MELISSA REMIS is a professor of anthropology at Purdue University. Her field-based research in the Central African Republic focuses on the behavioral ecology of western gorillas, which were poorly known before she initiated her field research in the late 1980s. She also maintains an experimentally based research program on the evolution of feeding strategies among the African apes, which employs research on captive apes in zoological facilities. She has authored or coauthored more than fourteen scientific articles in peer-reviewed journals such as the *American Journal of Primatology*, *American Journal of Physical Anthropology*, *International Journal of Primatology*, and *Primates*. She has presented papers at national and international conferences and has been invited to participate at special conferences on gorilla ecology and primate locomotion, including being the only woman among twelve senior international scholars of African apes invited to Japan in honor of retiring primatologist Dr. Toshida Nishida. Her current work considers the effectiveness of ape conservation in relation to other species at Dzanga-Sangha, through collaborative longitudinal studies that increasingly include analysis of human health under changing patterns of hunting and conservation practices.

Index

The letter *t* following a page number denotes a table.

AAA (American Anthropological Association), 14, 29, 85, 146, 147–54

Abimbọla, 110–11

academic anthropologists, 85, 86, 201–5

accessibility, and anthropology, 72

action and inaction paradoxes, 140–41. *See also* engaged ethnography

activism, 85–86

African-diaspora cultural history, 95, 112; Africa and, 93–94, 96–100, 103–4, 107–10; Afro-Brazilian religions and, 101–5, 110–11; Brazil and, 94, 98, 101–5, 109–11; Candomblé and, 101, 103, 105, 110–12; Catholicism and, 97–98, 104, 110; Christianity and, 94, 97–98, 110–11; collective memory metaphor and, 102–5, 107–8, 111–12; commemoration and, 103; creolization model and, 100–102; Cuba and, 93–94, 95, 97–98, 101, 103–5, 111; dialogue metaphor and, 108–10, 111–12; diaspora metaphor and, 96, 102, 106–7, 109; Euro-American culture and, 97–98, 110–11, 112; Gullah/Geechee people and, 99–100, 108–9; Lagosian Cultural Renaissance and, 103–5; litotes metaphor and, 98–99; maps in context of metaphors and, 93–95; memory as term of use and, 103; metaphors and, 93–96, 105–6; orisạ worship and, 110–12; power relations and, 103, 108–9, 112; remembering and, 102, 107–9, 111; rhizomes metaphor and, 106–7; roots metaphor and, 100, 106–7, 109–12; Santería/Ocha religion and, 93–94, 110–12; ships and vehicles metaphor and, 107; survival metaphor and, 96–100,

109–10, 111; Yoruba and, 94, 101, 102, 103–4, 108–9, 110–11

Africans and Africa: African-diaspora cultural history and, 93–94, 96–100, 103–4, 107–10; colonialism and, 100, 105, 119, 143, 151; political economy of Northern interests in, 146–47; postcolonialism and, 143–44; power relations and, 141, 143–44, 147; violence in histories of, 143–45. *See also* collaborative conservation science in CAR

AFRICOM (U. S. Africa Command), 144–46; engaged ethnography and, 140; ethics and, 137; political economy of Northern interests in Africa and, 146–47; professional responsibilities and, 151–53. *See also* engaged ethnography; U.S. military

Afro-Brazilian religions, 101–5, 110–11. *See also* African-diaspora cultural history

Agamben, Giorgio, 25

Allen, Barbara L., 22

American Anthropological Association (AAA), 14, 29, 85, 146, 147–54

animal populations, and collaborative conservation science in CAR, 183–87

anthropology, 4, 51; AAA and, 14, 29, 85, 146, 147–54; accessibility and, 72; as applicable to contemporary life, 38–40, 47, 50, 67–68, 203; British, 7, 9, 10, 52, 153; changes in contemporary, 63–66, 68, 86–87, 201, 203; colonialism and, 73–74, 151–53, 159n6; cross-subfield collaboration and, 182–83; ethics and, 29, 68, 71, 147–51; ethnography and, 52–53, 58–60, 61, 70, 202; fieldwork

Clarke, Kamari Maxine: on cultural diversity, 11; engaged ethnography and, 28, 137–59; internal and international asymmetries in ethnography and, 11–12; on journalism, literature, and ethnographic writings, 72; reception and, 86; transnational ethnography and, 96; on universal personhood assumptions, 162

Clifford, James, 10

Code of Ethics of AAA, 147–51

Cole, Jonathan R., 32

collaborative conservation science in CAR, 22, 23, 32, 181–82, 196–98; animal populations and, 183, 185–86; BaAka peoples and, 184–85, 187–91, 194–95, 197; Bayanga and, 182, 185–86, 189, 192, 195–96; colonialism and, 182, 191, 194; cross-species interactions and, 185–87; cross-subfield collaboration and, 182–83; ecology and, 181, 183–85, 188–89, 193, 197; education and/as research and, 191, 192–96, 193–94; fictive kin relationships and, 187–90, 195; gender and, 181–83, 188–89, 192, 193–94; human/animal pair and, 184–85, 187; knowledge across social categories and, 190–92, 194–96; local communities and animal communities' interactions, 184–85, 186; local communities as experts and, 188–92, 195–96; participant observation and, 188, 198n1; postcolonialism and, 191; power of fieldwork and, 198; power relations between researchers and local communities and, 191–92; power relations in context of human subjects and, 183, 184, 190, 193–95, 197; RDS and, 183–84; social contradictions and, 186; social difference in context of ecologies and economies and, 183–85

collective memory metaphor, and African diaspora, 102–5, 107–8, 111–12. *See also* African-diaspora cultural history; remembering

Collier, Stephen J., 161–62

Collins, Jim, 18, 34n7

colonialism: Africa and, 100, 105, 119, 143, 151; anthropology and, 73–74, 151–53, 159n6; collaborative conservation science in CAR and, 182, 191, 194; engaged ethnography and,

146, 151–53, 155–57, 158; ethnography and, 5–6, 10–13, 137–38; political economies and, 30–31. *See also* postcolonialism

Comaroff, Jean, 139–40, 202

Comaroff, John, 139–40, 202

commemoration, 103. *See also* African-diaspora cultural history

commonality of humanity, 52–53. *See also* anthropology

contemporary ethnography. *See* ethnography and ethnographers

contemporary life: anthropology as applicable to, 38–40, 47, 50, 67–68, 203; complexity of, 12–16

co-religion, and ARTs, 127–29

corporate ethnography: elite subjects and, 78, 87n1, 88n3; female subjects and, 161, 177. *See also* ethnography and ethnographers

corporate ethnography in Hungary, 19, 160–63, 178–79; corporate firms and, 179n1; corporate learning in socialist era and, 161, 163–69, 174, 179n6, 179n8, 180n15; corporate subjects and, 161–63, 170–71, 174, 176–77, 179n7, 180n18; entrepreneurial shift in postsocialist era and, 163, 174–78, 180n15, 180nn17–18; entrepreneurship during socialist era and, 163, 170–74, 179n7, 180nn10–13; ethics and, 161–63, 166–67, 169–76, 180n17; gendered subjects and, 177; global assemblages and, 19, 161–63, 173, 177–78; governmentality and, 161, 173–74, 177; neoliberal policies and, 161–63, 170, 172–74, 176–78, 180n9, 180n18; power relations and, 162, 175, 177; second economy/secondary economy and, 170–71, 180nn10–13; socially embedded personhood and, 167, 179n7; time shifts and, 170, 180n9; transnational business and, 160–61, 169, 170, 173–75, 177–78; Western business culture and, 160, 163, 164–69, 176–77. *See also* corporate ethnography

corporate firms, and Hungary, 179n1. *See also* corporate ethnography in Hungary

corporate learning, in Hungary, 161, 163–69, 174, 179n6, 179n8, 180n15. *See also* corporate ethnography in Hungary

emerging sector ethnographies, xii, 113–16, 132. *See also* return reproductive tourism in the Middle East

emotions, and ethnographers, 41–43, 62–63, 202

engaged ethnography, 28, 137–40, 157–58; action and inaction paradoxes and, 140–41; AFRICOM and, 140; anthropological approach to, 153–57; applied anthropology and, 142; colonialism and, 146, 151–53, 155–57, 158, 159n6; definition of, 142–43; ethics and, 137–38, 141; ethnography as technology of knowledge and power and, 142–43, 203–4; genealogies of ethnography and, 138; global South and, 138, 156, 157; governmentality and, 142, 148; human rights and, 150, 151, 154, 155; legal anthropology and, 138–40; multiple field pedagogy and, 142; neoliberal policies and, 142, 144; politics and, 138, 139, 140, 149–51, 156–58; postcolonialism and, 140–42, 154, 155–57, 159n6; praxis and, 140–42, 146, 156n2; professional ethnography and, 140. *See also* AFRICOM

entrepreneurship in Hungary: postsocialist era shift and, 163, 174–78, 180n15, 180nn17–18; during socialist era, 163, 170–74, 179n7, 180nn10–13. *See also* corporate ethnography in Hungary

environmental areas, and ethnography, 7, 19–23, 25. *See also* collaborative conservation science in CAR; ecology/ies

epigenetics, 25. *See also* genetics

Escobar, Arturo, 4, 32

ethics: anthropology and, 29, 68, 71, 147–51; corporate ethnography in Hungary and, 161–63, 166–67, 169–76, 180n17; engaged ethnography and, 137–38, 141, 147–51; participant observation and, 44

ethnographic knowledge, 3–5, 201; anthropology schools and, 4; applications for, 4, 5–7, 33nn2–3; applied anthropology and, 4, 5–7, 16, 17, 29, 85–86, 142; challenges in contemporary ethnography and, 29–31; complexity of contemporary life and, 12–16; ethics and, 29; ethnography defined and, 8–11; etymology of ethnography and, 3–4; gender and,

15, 22, 25, 34n6; global anthropologies and, 6, 33n2, 65–67; local anthropologies and, 5–6, 33n2; power relations and, 10, 12, 142–43, 148–49, 191–92, 203–4; self-identification and, 3, 4, 5, 10, 27, 30, 34n11, 203, 204. *See also* descriptive or prescriptive ethnography; ethnography and ethnographers; ethnography's implications for anthropology; knowledge and knowledge production

ethnographic writings: journalism and, 49, 55, 56–57, 59–60, 67–68, 72, 202; literature and, 55, 57–58, 60, 67–68, 70, 72; tourism and, 55–56, 59–60, 67–68, 70. *See also* anthropology

ethnography and ethnographers: anthropology and, 52–53, 58–60, 61, 70, 202; challenges in contemporary, 29–31, 202–3; colonialism and, 5–6, 10–13, 137–38; complexity of contemporary life and, 12–16; definition of, 8–11; desire for, 75–76; ecology and, 20–23, 25; of emerging global technology, 113–16, 132; emotions of, 41–43, 62–63, 202; ethnographic authority critique and, 12, 54, 57, 73–74, 83–84, 204; etymology of, 3–4; genealogies of, 138; internal and international asymmetries in, 8, 11–12, 31; multisited, 68; political economies and, 202; power relations in context of human subjects and, 14–15, 21, 30, 32–33, 73–76, 82, 139, 151–53, 155–58; professional responsibilities of, 151–53, 204; reflexivity and, 43–44, 48, 50, 67, 201–2. *See also* corporate ethnography; engaged ethnography; ethnographic writings; reflexivity

ethnography's implications for anthropology, 32, 83–84; academic anthropologists and, 85, 86, 201–5; activism and, 85–86; applied anthropology and, 85–86; being-there-ness and, 83, 84; changes in anthropology and, 86–87; cultural anthropology defined and, 73; design for multisited fieldwork and, 76–78, 79–84, 87n1, 88n3, 204; desire for ethnography and, 75–76; elite subjects and, 78, 87n1, 88n3; ethnographic authority critique and, 12, 54, 57, 73–74, 83–84, 204; financial

observation. *See* participant observation

Ocha (Santería) religion, 93–94, 110–12. *See also* African-diaspora cultural history

Ong, Aihwa, 96, 161–62

Opala, Joseph, 100

oriṣa worship, 110–12. *See also* African-diaspora cultural history

Orlove, Ben, 21

Ortiz, Fernando, 104

Osseo-Assare, Abena Dove, 25

Palestinians, and ARTs, 114, 118, 120t, 121–22, 129

para-ethnography, 77–78, 87n1, 88n3

participant observation, x, 32, 203; as applicable to contemporary life, 38–40, 47, 50, 203; and balance between observation and participation, 46, 48–49, 199n1; child rearing and, 40–41; collaborative conservation science and, 188, 198n1; death and dying and, 42; disciplined subjectivity and, 43–44, 48; education and, 37–38, 44–45; ethics and, 44; gender and, 40–41, 188, 198n1; global health and, 203; journalism and, 49; objectivity and, 42–43, 47–48; observation during fieldwork and, 62, 183; participation and observation balance and, 46, 48–49, 199n1; participation during fieldwork and, 62, 183; reflexivity and, 43–44, 48, 50; similarity in context of compatibility and, 39; thought and emotion connection and, 41–43. *See also* Bateson, Mary Catherine

Partridge, Damani, 18–19

pedagogy (education). *See* education (pedagogy)

Peet, Richard, 21

personhood, socially embedded, 167, 179n7

Peterson, J. T., 21

phenotype, and ARTs, 129–30

physical anthropology (biological anthropology), 4, 20–22, 25, 51. *See also* collaborative conservation science in CAR

Pierson, Donald, 103

politics and political economies: anthropology and, 68, 69; colonial/postcolonial, 30–31; ecology and, 22; engaged ethnography and, 138, 139, 140, 149–51, 156–58; ethnographers and, 202; Northern interests in Africa

and, 146–47; of science, 3, 202. *See also* economies

postcolonialism: Africa and, 143–44; anthropology and, 20, 23, 140–42; collaborative conservation science in CAR and, 191; engaged ethnography and, 140–42, 154, 155–57, 159n6; political economies and, 30–31. *See also* colonialism

Powdermaker, Hortense, 97

power relations: African-diaspora cultural history and, 103, 108–9, 112; Africans and, 141, 143–44, 147; collaborative conservation science in context of human subjects and, 183, 184, 190, 193–95, 197; corporate ethnography in Hungary and, 162, 175, 177; ethnographic knowledge and, 10, 12, 142–43, 148–49, 203–4; ethnography in context of human subjects and, 14–15, 21, 30, 32–33, 73–76, 82, 139, 151–53, 155–58; race/racism and, 27, 103, 131–32, 137–38; between researchers and local communities in CAR, 191–92

praxis, 140–42, 146, 156n2

Price, David, 26, 28, 100–102

professional anthropology (professional ethnography), 78, 84–85, 86, 87n1, 88n3, 140, 151–53

professional responsibilities, of ethnographers, 151–53, 204

psychological comforts, and ARTs, 130–31

"Pygmy" peoples (BaAka peoples), 184–85, 187–91, 194–95, 197. *See also* collaborative conservation science in CAR

Rabinow, Paul, 25–26

race/racism, and power relations, 27, 103, 131–32, 137–38

Radcliffe-Brown, Alfred, 9–10

Ramos, Arthur, 97–98

Rapp, Rayna, 25

RDS (Dzanga-Ndoki Park and Dzanga-Sangha Dense Forest Reserve), 183–84. *See also* collaborative conservation science in CAR

the real, 10, 30

reception, and ethnography, 74, 78–80, 85–87

reflexivity, 43–44, 48, 50, 67, 201–2. *See also* self-identification, and ethnographic knowledge